Political Communication in the Republic of Ireland

Edited by

Mark O'Brien and Donnacha Ó Beacháin

LIVERPOOL UNIVERSITY PRESS

First published 2014 by
Liverpool University Press
4 Cambridge Street
Liverpool
L69 7ZU

British Library Cataloguing-in-Publication data
A British Library CIP record is available

ISBN 978-1-78138-027-7 (cased)
ISBN 978-1-78138-148-9 (paperback)

Typeset by Carnegie Book Production, Lancaster
Printed and bound by Booksfactory.co.uk

POLITICAL COMMUNICATION
IN THE REPUBLIC OF IRELAND

Contents

List of Illustrations   vii

Glossary   viii

Notes on Contributors   ix

Acknowledgements   xii

Introduction   1

Part One: Political Communication and Politicians

1 Political communication: an overview   7
Farrel Corcoran

2 Elections and political communication   25
Donnacha Ó Beacháin

3 A pragmatic partnership: politicians and local media   45
Sarah Kavanagh

4 Political communication and the 'loony left'   63
Bryce Evans

Part Two: Political Communication and Journalism

5 'Sources say ...': political journalism since 1921   79
Mark O'Brien

6 In sickness and in health: politics, spin, and the media   97
Mark Byrne

7 Media advisers and programme managers   115
  Tom Clonan

8 A limited focus? Journalism, politics, and the Celtic Tiger   129
  Declan Fahy

Part Three: Political Communication and the Public

9 A private affair? Lobbying and transparency in modern Ireland   149
  Gary Murphy

10 Equal time for Judas Iscariot? Broadcast treatment of political
   contests in the Republic of Ireland   167
   Colum Kenny

11 'There now follows ...': The role of the party political broadcast
   and the 2007 'peace broadcast'   185
   Kevin Rafter

12 Social media and political communication   201
   Martin Molony

13 Mediating elections in Ireland: evidence from the 2011 general
   election   217
   Eoin O'Malley, Roddy Flynn, Iain McMenamin, Kevin Rafter

Conclusion   237

Index   245

Illustrations

1   *Put Him In to Get Him Out. Vote for McGuinness: The Man In Jail For Ireland* [1918]   62

2   *The Shadow of the Gunman: Keep It from Your Home. Vote for Cumann na nGaedheal* [1932]   62

3   *Wives! Get Your Husbands Off to Work. Vote Fianna Fáil* [1948]   114

4   *Straight Vote* [1959]   114

5   *President of the Nation. Vote De Valera* [1966]   114

6   *Fianna Fáil: The Way Forward* [1982]   128

7   *Fine Gael: Now Let's Build the Nation* [1987]   128

8   *H-Block. Vote 1 Doherty, K.* [1981]   166

9   *Mary Robinson: A President with a Purpose* [1990]   166

10 *A Young Leader for a Young Country. Fianna Fáil* [1997]   166

11 *Seán Gallagher: For an Independent President* [2011]   216

12 *Lynn Boylan: Sinn Féin* [2014]   216

13 *Seanad Referendum: Socialist Party* [2013]   216

Glossary

Áras an Uachtaráin	official residence of the President of Ireland
Ard fheis(eanna)	Party conference(s)
Ceann Comhairle	Speaker of parliament
CIÉ	Córas Iompair Éireann – the statutory body responsible for most public transport in the Republic of Ireland
Cumann	Party branch (used by Fianna Fáil and Sinn Féin)
Dáil Éireann	Lower house of parliament
GAA	Gaelic Athletic Association
Garda(í) Síochána	Irish police
Leaving Certificate	Final examination in the Irish secondary school system
MEP	Member of the European Parliament
Oireachtas	Collective term for both houses of parliament
PR-STV	Proportional Representation – Single Transferable Vote (electoral system)
RTÉ	Raidió Telefís Éireann (national broadcaster)
Seanad	Upper house of parliament
Sipo	Standards in Public Office Commission
Tánaiste	Deputy Prime Minister
Taoiseach	Prime Minister
TD	Teachta Dála (member of parliament)

Notes on Contributors

Mark Byrne is communications manager of the school of medicine and medical science at University College Dublin. He previously held communications positions at a number of NGOs in the mental health and social policy sectors, including the European Anti-Poverty Network and the Higher Education Authority. He has worked on several local and national election campaigns in Ireland.

Tom Clonan is a retired army officer (Captain) with experience in the Middle East and former Yugoslavia. He is now a lecturer at the school of media at Dublin Institute of Technology. He is the *Irish Times* security analyst and the author of *Blood, Sweat and Tears* (2012) and *Whistleblower, Soldier, Spy: A Journey into the Dark Heart of the Global War on Terror* (2013).

Farrel Corcoran is former professor of communications, Dublin City University, where he served as head of the school of communications and dean of the faculty of humanities. From 1995 to 2000 he served as chairman of the RTÉ Authority. He is the author of *RTÉ and the Globalisation of Irish Television* (2004) and co-editor of *Democracy and Communication in the New Europe* (1995).

Bryce Evans is a lecturer in modern history at the department of politics, history, media and communication, Liverpool Hope University. He is the author of *Ireland during the Second World War: Farewell to Plato's Cave* (2014) and *The Other Lemass* (2011). He was campaign manager for a United Left Alliance candidate in election 2011.

Declan Fahy is assistant professor at the school of communication, American University, Washington, DC. His research examines the role of journalism in communicating knowledge, expertise, and complexity, focusing in particular on science and financial news. He previously worked as a reporter for the *Irish Times* while his recent journalism has appeared in *The Scientist* and online at the *Columbia Journalism Review*.

Roddy Flynn is a lecturer at the school of communications, Dublin City University. He is co-editor of *John Huston: Essays on a Restless Director* (2010) and *Historical Dictionary of Irish Cinema* (2007).

Sarah Kavanagh is a senior research officer for Fine Gael in Dáil Éireann, having previously worked as a parliamentary assistant for Fine Gael TDs between 2005 and 2011. She holds an MA degree in Politics (UCD, 2001), an MA degree in Political Communication (DCU, 2007), and a Barrister-at-Law degree (The Honorable Society of King's Inns, 2012).

Colum Kenny is professor of communications, Dublin City University and a member of the Broadcasting Authority of Ireland. A barrister and former reporter/presenter with RTÉ, he is the author of *The Power of Silence: Silent Communication in Daily Life* (2011) and *Moments That Changed Us* (2005). As an independent expert, he swore an affidavit for the applicant in the McCrystal case giving his opinion that the government's booklet and website supported the case for voting 'yes' in the 2012 children's rights referendum.

Iain McMenamin is a senior lecturer at the school of law and government, Dublin City University. His work on political communication has appeared in the *International Journal of Press/Politics* and the *European Political Science Review*. He is the author of *If Money Talks, What Does It Say? Corruption and Business Financing of Political Parties* (2013) and many articles on comparative politics in journals such as *World Politics*, *European Journal of Political Research*, and *International Studies Quarterly*.

Martin Molony is a lecturer at the school of communications, Dublin City University. He teaches professional communications skills and public relations skills for the MA in Political Communication and the MSc in Science Communication. He is currently completing his PhD at Trinity College Dublin.

Gary Murphy is associate professor of politics and head of the school of law and government, Dublin City University. Recent publications include *In Search of the Promised Land: The Politics of Post-War Ireland* (2009), *Continuity, Change and Crisis in Contemporary Ireland* (2010) co-edited with Brian Girvin, and *Regulating Lobbying: A Global Comparison* (2010) with Raj Chari and John Hogan.

Mark O'Brien is a lecturer at the school of communications, Dublin City University. He is the author of *The Irish Times: A History* (2008) and *The Truth in the News? De Valera, Fianna Fáil and the Irish Press* (2001). He also co-edited *Political Censorship and the Democratic State: The Irish Broadcasting Ban* (2005) and *Independent Newspapers: A History* (2012). He is chairman of the advisory board of the Media History Collection, DCU Library & Archive.

Eoin O'Malley is a senior lecturer at the school of law and government, Dublin City University. His research is mainly on Irish politics and he is the author of over 40 peer-reviewed articles or scholarly chapters. He is author of *Contemporary Ireland* (2011) and co-editor of *Governing Ireland* (2012) and was co-editor of the journal *Irish Political Studies* between 2008 and 2011.

Donnacha Ó Beacháin is director of research in the school of law and government at Dublin City University and the author of *The Irish Government and the Northern Ireland Question since 1922: The Politics of Partition* (forthcoming), and *The Destiny of the Soldiers: Fianna Fáil, Irish Republicanism and the IRA* (2010). He also co-edited *Life in Post-Communist Europe After EU Membership: Happy Ever After?* (2012) and *The Colour Revolutions in the Former Soviet Republics: Successes and Failures* (2010).

Kevin Rafter is an associate professor in the school of communications at Dublin City University. Prior to 2008 he worked as a political journalist and held senior editorial positions with RTÉ and several Irish national newspapers. He is the author of several political biographies and histories of Democratic Left (2011), Fine Gael (2011) and Sinn Féin (2005). He is co-editor of *The Irish Presidency: Power, Ceremony and Politics* (2013) and *Independent Newspapers: A History* (2012) and editor of *Irish Journalism before Independence: More a Disease than a Profession* (2011).

Acknowledgements

This book arises from a symposium held at Dublin City University in April 2011, and represents the first attempt to map the contours of political communication in the Republic of Ireland. Our thanks are due to the Faculty of Humanities and Social Sciences which hosted the event, particularly to the Dean, Dr John Doyle. Our gratitude is also due to all those who participated in the symposium and informed the critical debate that occurred that day from a multitude of academic and practitioner perspectives. In moving from symposium to publication we were fortunate in having the support of Alison Welsby and her team at Liverpool University Press. The editors would also like to acknowledge the support of the Humanities and Social Sciences Publication Fund at Dublin City University. Donnacha Ó Beacháin would like to thank Karolina Ó Beacháin Stefańczak for her love and support, and to make a special dedication to Gaia Ní Bheacháin who was born in Tbilisi on 9 May 2013 while this book was in progress.

Mark O'Brien and Donnacha Ó Beacháin
May, 2014

Introduction

The field of political communication – where politicians, public relations professionals, journalists, and the public intersect and interact – has always been a highly contested one fuelled by suspicion and mutual dependence. To reach the public, politicians need the media, while to inform and serve the public, journalists need access to politicians. For most of the time what emerges is a relatively stable relationship of mutual dependence with the boundaries policed by public relations professionals. Access is negotiated, information is supplied, politicians fly kites about potential initiatives, and journalists analyse the possible outcomes.

However, every so often, in times of political crisis or upheaval, this closely regulated relationship gives way to a near free-for-all. Politicians, press secretaries, and sometimes even journalists, become fair game in the battle for public accountability and support. The determination of public relations professions to avoid this breakdown and keep the relationship based on mutual dependence has become a central component of modern statecraft and systems of governance. The need to keep politicians and journalists 'on message' and use the media to inform, shape and manage public discourse has become central to the workings of government, opposition and interest groups. On the other hand, the packaging of politics has potentially troublesome implications for the democratic process. What does it mean for journalists tasked with providing independent assessments of politicians and policies? Have politics and political communication become characterised by style over substance? With a near-instant news cycle, new communication technologies and constant opinion polling, where does information end and misinformation begin? And with millions of euros being spent annually on advisors, spin-doctors and lobbyists, is the system transparent or open to manipulation?

This book presents an overview of political communication in the Republic of Ireland from a multiplicity of academic and practitioner perspectives. It does not advance the view that political communication in the republic has become dominated by politicians, public relations practitioners or journalists – more so it seeks to explore critically the sometimes open, sometimes fraught relationship dynamics that are at the heart of political communication. It appears at a time of increased concern about the way in which politics and journalism interact within the public sphere. Against the backdrop of the rise and fall of a property-fuelled economic boom and a bailout by the EU and IMF, politics and political communication have come under sustained scrutiny by a concerned public. In a phrase that is so often used as a shorthand device to discourage critical discussion, questions remain to be asked about why 'we are where we are' – economically and politically.

At the outset we can say that politics and political communication, as demonstrated by the landmark general election and the controversial presidential election of 2011, have become more far more sharply contested with established media and newer communication technologies playing increasingly central roles. At such a critical juncture, it is appropriate to examine how the relationship between politics, journalism, and the public is configured. What constitutes political communication? How does it operate during and between electoral contests? What form does it take at national and local level? What factors influence whether or not a party's message is effective? How has political journalism developed over the decades? What is the role played by government appointed press officers? How much do they cost and do they operate in a transparent manner? How do the media cover the relationship between big business and politics? Are political parties too close to vested interests who communicate through extensive and expensive lobbying? How do broadcasters handle coverage of elections and referenda? What is the role and impact of party political broadcasts? Have social media radically altered the political landscape? Do the media frame election contests as policy or personality contests? In different ways and from a multitude of critical perspectives, these are the questions that this book seeks answers to.

In part one we consider the relationship between politicians and political communication. Farrel Corcoran presents an overview of the field, maps the development of the discipline and outlines the issues that have arisen over the decades and, more latterly, in the internet age. Election campaigns are the most obvious and intense form of political communication, and in his chapter, Donnacha Ó Beacháin outlines how those seeking election have communicated with the electorate. The contours of those campaigns, from the 1920s onwards, illustrate that personal contact remains a crucial component. In the era of the 'permanent campaign', local media and particularly local radio play a crucial role in the political communication process. Sarah Kavanagh examines the relationship that exists between politicians and local media professionals and finds that politicians are highly attuned to their local media coverage. The difficulties in securing media coverage for a new political movement are examined by Bryce Evans, who outlines the media strategies employed by the United Left Alliance during the 2011 general election and compares the different levels of campaign spending by new and established parties during that campaign.

In part two we consider the relationship between journalism and political communication. Mark O'Brien traces the development of political journalism from 1921 onwards and identifies the factors that have influenced the relationship between governments and political correspondents over the decades. The other element in that often frosty relationship, the government press secretary, is examined by Mark Byrne. Having interviewed many previous post holders, he finds that the notion of spin as a pejorative function of the modern political environment is overstated. Whether spin-doctors or programme managers represent value for money or an attempt to obscure the workings of government is the issue considered by Tom Clonan, who concludes that more transparency and accountability is needed in such political appointments. Central to the political communication landscape of the Celtic Tiger era was auction politics, and in his chapter Declan Fahy examines the many constraints journalists faced in reporting the building boom and the odium they faced for questioning its soundness.

In part three we consider the relationship between political communication and the public. Gary Murphy considers the role that lobbyists play in the political communication process and argues that lobbying is central to our understanding of the building boom and the bank guarantee that followed. How broadcasters cover elections and referenda is the central concern of Colum Kenny's chapter. What constitutes fairness, objectivity and impartiality is often the subject of dispute but the right of all sides to have their views aired is, he concludes, central to any democratic system. The role and impact of party political broadcasts is considered by Kevin Rafter. He examines the regulatory regime, public attitudes towards such broadcasts and how the 'peace broadcast' of 2007 demonstrates that personalisation has become central to modern election strategies. The role of social media in political communication is examined by Martin Molony who finds that the effectiveness of such media in campaigns very much depends on how such technologies are utilised by political actors and the public alike. The final chapter, by Eoin O'Malley, Roddy Flynn, Iain McMenamin, and Kevin Rafter examines how the media covered the 2011 general election. Amid increased concerns that media coverage of elections concentrates on process over substance by treating politics as a game rather than a sphere of policy choices, they find that the media coverage of election 2011 was dominated not by personality politics but by policy discussions. The conclusion synthesises the findings of each chapter to determine how the contours of political communication are configured in modern Ireland.

PART ONE

Political Communication
and Politicians

CHAPTER ONE

Political communication:
an overview

Farrel Corcoran

It is not a trivial challenge to answer the question – what is political communication? – and this overview is an attempt to provide a number of perspectives on the answer. At its most obvious level, it refers to the role of communication in the political process, especially during the periodic enactment of the central ritual of all modern democracies – the election of new governments. It includes the speeches of politicians, televised debates between candidates, the reporting by political correspondents of candidates' behaviour, especially their public utterances, the use of billboards and posters on lamp-posts to show off party emblems and slogans, and new uses of the internet to find and motivate voters. We might call this 'Type A' political communication. But consider the following news story taken from the middle of 2012, a far less obvious but much more complex example of our subject that illustrates what we might call 'Type B' political communication.

It is a mid-summer weekend in Dublin, the electronic dance music trio Swedish House Mafia is giving a final-tour concert, and 45,000 teenage fans are converging on the Phoenix Park for what should be a day of fun. But soon, the event is descending into chaos under the weight of under-age binge drinking, drug-taking and violence. YouTube footage captures images of bare-chested bellicose youths kicking and punching each other in a bath of mud, while on-lookers join in on a whim. When the mayhem is over, the toll is two drug deaths, nine stabbings, 33 arrests, and 70 charges brought by police. Now the media take note. Before the day is done, it has become a major mediated event, dominating news bulletins and projected across the country through a wide range of media channels.

Then it starts to become political. It initiates a maelstrom of political communication involving a wide range of actors and activating a range of public institutions. The police announce a comprehensive review of the violence, to make recommendations to the minister for justice. Other public bodies spring into action promising their own reviews: the city council that issues licenses for public events, the managers of the Phoenix Park, the director of public prosecutions. The media hold the event at the top of their agenda for the next 72 hours and start teasing out issues relevant to public health, the education of teenagers, and the nation's drink habits. The range of participants now includes radio producers, print journalists, leader writers, TV researchers, celebrity presenters, photo editors, current affairs teams, and on-air academic pundits. Online social networks are buzzing. Letters to the editor and vox-pop street interviews on radio stations provide their own approximation of the voice of the public, before the pollsters can start measuring opinion in a more systematic way.

At this stage, pressure begins to mount at another level, in the domain of politics proper. The minister of state for health, a member of the Labour Party in the coalition government, repeats her argument that government must finally decide on a range of alcohol marketing reforms in order to deal with a growing 'drink problem' in Ireland. These include minimum unit pricing, restrictions on advertising and sports sponsorship, and a 'responsibility levy' on alcohol sales to fund media campaigns about the dangers of alcohol aimed at young people. This in turn mobilises business lobby groups to challenge the idea of state intervention: the drinks industry, supermarket chains, and the Irish Business and Employers' Confederation (IBEC). Trade unions are ambivalent, since jobs could be lost. There is talk among backbenchers of increased strain between the coalition government partners, as another minister, thought to be heavily targeted by lobbyists, queries the Labour minister's proposals. Resistance to reform of alcohol marketing features in the resignation of the Labour minister a few months later in response to a different crisis.

So over the course of a single bank-holiday weekend, in a process not planned by any human agency, the visit of Swedish House Mafia has been transformed from a musical event into what could be described as a convulsion of political communication, just when the Dublin-based political system seemed ready to pack its bags for the summer recess and journalists prepared for the seasonal drop in 'Type A' political communication.

How do we begin to analyse the multifaceted nature and sometimes unanticipated range of political communication in contemporary society? The aim of this chapter is to present an overview of what is undoubtedly the most important of the many forms public discourse can take and to offer some insights into the distinctive field of knowledge about political communication that has developed over many years of academic analysis. Motivating this scholarly work has been the aim of developing a deeper understanding of how political power is distributed in society. Here we will try to map the major concepts that structure this interdisciplinary field and to focus on pertinent issues that have piqued researchers' curiosity about power and public communication.

Matters of definition

In a very loose sense, political communication developed over many centuries as both scholars and practitioners observed how people communicate about politics, speculated on the consequences of this and analysed how certain outcomes could be produced or avoided. Its early origins can be found in the writings of Plato, Aristotle, and Cicero in the classical world, but also in Machiavelli and other commentators in the Renaissance period, and in Enlightenment political philosophers, including Locke, Kant, and Hume.

It began to develop in a more disciplined way at the turn of the twentieth century, emerging as a sub-field of political science. Concepts were more carefully defined, the importance of the historical and socio-economic context of politics became evident and systematic methods of analysis were developed. The mainstream of the field crystallised around study of the strategic uses of communication by political actors and their impact on the attitudes and behaviour of the public. Communication scholars began to focus on the various processes through which political institutions, media organisations and citizens interact with each other when there is deliberate action to mobilise and transmit political influence.

In the contemporary era, media institutions and the technologies they deploy have become central to understanding the interaction that occurs between media and political systems at several levels: locally, nationally, and internationally. The focal points for scholarly analysis outlined by Franklin (1995) are a useful starting point for understanding the range of themes to be considered. He argues that we need to study at least the following, in order to make sense of the totality of political communication:

(a) the political context of media content (news and current affairs, coverage of elections and referenda, reporting of parliament, political cartoons);

(b) the actors and agencies – both political and media – involved in the production of media content (government ministers and press secretaries, press officers in political parties and pressure groups, journalists and editors, media owners, and broadcasters) as well as the nature of the relationship between journalists and politicians, whether that relationship is conflictual, consensual or collusive;

(c) the impact of media content on various audiences (both the general public and more narrowly defined business and political elites) as well as the impact of the media on policymaking and the role of the media in framing significant issues in public opinion;

(d) the impact of the political system on the media system (government media policy, party media policy, systems of regulation and censorship, attempts at news management and agenda-building by political actors, lobbyists, media owners and other significant individuals);

(e) the impact of the media system on the political system (structures of ownership of the press and broadcast media, locally, nationally, and globally, the effect of media partisanship on political outcomes, fourth estate functions of critique and accountability).

This useful five-fold division of the field of political communication was formulated in the mid-1990s, when the Web was in its infancy and social media had not yet appeared, so it needs considerable updating to deal with issues that arise, for instance, in the use of new media in election campaigns. But first we go back a little in time to provide historical perspective, to see how some important ideas emerged over the course of the last century and how they were used as conceptual tools to analyse political systems.

Communication as persuasion

Political communication as a formally organised academic discipline began to take shape early in the last century with the analysis of propaganda in the aftermath of the First World War. Harold Lasswell's seminal text *Propaganda Techniques in the World War*, published in the USA in 1927, established the mainstream framework for later research, using quantitative content analysis to understand how governments use persuasive messages to influence public opinion. Lasswell regarded 'content' as a set of 'messages' aimed at 'recipients' (Who said What to Whom with what Effect) rather than as 'texts' to be interpreted by 'readers' (a notion that would not fully emerge until the arrival of semiotics in the 1970s). This early propaganda model argued that media generally produce powerful, direct, uniform effects on people. It assumed a so-called 'magic bullet' impact on readers and audiences.

For most of the inter-war years, the prevailing approach in American universities emphasised the power of media effects on people, pointing to impressive examples like the role of the Hearst newspapers in shaping a pro-war public opinion and leading the USA into the Spanish–American war in 1898 (an event viewed by later historians as the defining moment in the launch of American global ambitions). Another example of media power was seen in the mass panic that followed the CBS broadcast of Orson Welles' radio play *War of the Worlds* at Halloween 1938, presented in the realist manner of a series of news bulletins suggesting to many listeners that an actual alien invasion was under way.

In sketching the early history of how political communication has been studied, mainly in the USA, it must be remembered that unlike many European countries, political marketing based on theories of persuasion became embedded early on in the American electoral system. Paid television commercials today are a major force in American elections, especially at the presidential level where they are used to shape the contours of each candidate's political campaign. Novice politicians with little name recognition must first establish their fund-raising credentials to pay for access to television. Early American academic interest in the psychological mechanisms governing how persuasive campaigns influence voters feed directly in to the contemporary fascination with marketing principles now routinely applied in Irish (and other European) elections in the twentieth-first century. These include the role of market research in party branding and the creation of specific imagery around a candidate, strategies for market segmentation and candidate positioning in the overall political landscape, and the search for consultants with the best track records and experienced commercial managers who can run a successful political marketing campaign.

By the 1940s, serious academic efforts were being focused on studying the effects of radio and print media on voters' choice of candidates. Both qualitative and quantitative methods – in-depth interviews, participant observation, content analysis and panel studies – were being refined by Paul Lazarsfeld, an Austrian émigré working at Columbia University. Carl Hovland and Kurt Lewin at Yale were making a credible case for using the experimental paradigm in a social scientific context, borrowed from the natural sciences where the experimental method had flourished for a long time. Their focus was on attitude change resulting from exposure to media stimuli, using careful measurement techniques, data gathering, and statistical analysis to study voter habits. They also studied less obvious aspects of political communication, such as wartime government use of domestic radio propaganda to urge Americans to buy war bonds, collect scrap metal, and plant 'victory gardens' to survive food shortages.

Only later in the 1940s came the realisation that what had been called the 'magic bullet' approach to media influence needed to be tempered by the realisation that people selectively avoid (or seek out) particular media content, then selectively perceive particular meanings in the content. Working out what a concept like 'selective exposure' or 'selective perception' means empirically – and operationalising it in the design of research projects – indicates a new emphasis on the psychology of personality variables and a sociological emphasis on demographics (which evolved much later in the century into the marketing terminology of 'psychographics'). Media influence could no longer be presumed to be either direct or uniformly powerful or involving always a passive audience. A more nuanced approach to communication theory, involving a search for a subtler understanding of how human beings persuade each other, was needed if theory was to guide more fruitful empirical research on media and politics.

One of the most comprehensive wartime studies of voting behaviour – how the 1940 presidential election campaign played out in Erie County, Ohio – produced the almost accidental insight that when people make decisions about political issues, interpersonal communication plays an important, complementary role, along with exposure to media content. Thus, a new emphasis was placed on the role of opinion leaders, that is, people with more than average exposure to media content, more involved in debating public issues and more centrally placed within interpersonal networks in their community. Opinion leadership became the focus of a long series of studies using a new approach, the so-called 'two-step flow' model of communication. The media primarily influenced opinion leaders, who then had an effect on networks of people linked to them through interpersonal contact.

This model was also applied in a Cold War context to study how innovations could be diffused by American development agencies eager to influence emerging Third World countries looking to either the USA or the USSR for help. American innovations being diffused to counter Soviet influence in the process of decolonisation included not only new methods of farming but also Western models for how media and politics should be organised. The emphasis on interpersonal networks in the 'diffusion' paradigm would emerge yet again in more recent studies, as we will see, with scholars going beyond an interest in 'old' mass media channels to focus on study of blog posts, Twitter messages, and other online social networks that serve as new platforms for political expression.

Public discourse

There is another significant tradition in the study of political communication that has developed alongside the American social scientific paradigm, one that is quite different from it in its concerns, its theoretical background, and its methodologies. It is strongly rooted in a humanities perspective and emphasises the concepts of rhetoric and discourse. Rhetorical analysis is built on qualitative approaches to research, similar to those found in English departments in the early twentieth century. The text is central.

Early precedents for reflecting on rhetoric and the role of public discourse in society can be found in the insights of Plato and Aristotle as they engaged with early forms of political communication in the fledgling Athenian democracy of their time. There is an emphasis on speakers' motives and oratorical style, the historical context of political events, and the rhetorical structure of significant speeches. This approach survives today in many American universities in the form of focusing critical attention on presidential speeches or on swathes of media content using conceptual approaches not too far removed from literary studies. These include dramatistic analysis, the exploration of 'fantasy themes', the analysis of narrative, myth, and ideology in political discourse, and Lakoff's (1996) influential work on the role of metaphor.

Rhetorical analysis has been very successfully applied to media coverage of political events including election campaigns, where the primary emphasis is on qualitative approaches to content or 'text'. The turn towards rhetorical analysis of political communication was enriched by the emergence of semiotics in the 1970s as a major new approach to analysing the workings of signification, the complex process that creates meanings in public discourse. Semiotics helped to underpin a critical view of how political meaning is created in publicly circulated texts such as news reports. Inspired by the emergence of the New Left and Cultural Studies movements in Britain, it was enriched by the neo-Marxian emphasis on understanding questions of power in contemporary culture by analysing and deconstructing ideology.

Ideology in this sense refers not to clearly articulated doctrine that might be promoted by a political party, but to something far more subtle flowing through society, erasing its roots as it moves, tacitly creating a 'common sense' that can frequently assume a hegemonic position in discussion of public issues. Stuart Hall defines ideology as 'the mental frameworks – the languages, the concepts, categories, imagery of thought, and the systems of representation – which different classes and social groups deploy in order to make sense of, figure out and render intelligible the way society works' (Hall, 1996, 25–46). Ideology often serves to protect the real material interests of a small section of society, justifying its activities and attitudes and promoting its interests, by creating a coherence of meaning and generating a widely held 'common sense' that gains traction far beyond its core group.

One of the most spectacular examples of ideology at work in recent times has been the influence brought to bear on the shaping of news discourse across the USA by right-wing, ideological think-tanks, many of them endowed by very wealthy patrons like the Koch brothers. These include Americans for Prosperity, the Heritage Foundation, the American Enterprise Institute, the Competitive Enterprise Institute and many others. These well-funded think-tanks devote substantial resources and skilled effort to promoting the ideas of wealthy industrialists and owners of capital. While keeping their political programme relatively invisible, they achieve high visibility for their solutions to national and global political issues by gaining favoured access to prominent mainstream news media and directly lobbying different arms of government. Their major achievement leading up to 2012 was the significant impact they made on presidential politics using conservative grass-roots movements like the Tea Party. Think-tanks shaped both mass opinion and elite attitudes (including senior journalists and editors and Congressional staff) towards a range of major political issues: healthcare reform, anthropogenic global warming, the (de)regulation of the banking, oil, gas, coal, nuclear, and chemical industries, the right of workers to collective bargaining with employers, the size of the military budget and the need for national involvement in foreign wars.

Whether we call the publicly circulated words and visual images that influence public opinion 'rhetoric' or 'discourse' does not really matter, if we have a sound method for analysing how power is exercised in democracies through public communication – both in electoral campaigns and in the long gaps between elections. The critical tradition in Western Marxism, represented by Gramsci, Althusser, and the Frankfurt School, is an important backdrop to what is one of the most fertile of contemporary approaches to analysing political discourse. Critical Discourse Analysis (CDA), seen at its best in the work of Van Dijk (2001), Fairclough (2003) or Wodak and Chilton (2005), involves a search for aspects or dimensions of reality that are obscured by an apparently natural and transparent use of language. Its use in political communication often centres on the role of journalism, considered as a discursive reconstruction of reality. Rarely do journalists get to know reality in an unmediated way, without heavy reliance on sources of information. The role of political sources has been widely investigated in the study of both popular and elite media. These include think tanks, public relations agencies, lobbyists, whistle blowers, government leakers, and spin-doctors.

As professional storytellers, journalists have effectively always naturalised the political and economic practices of their era by circulating the myths, ideologies, memories, and symbols from which people construct their political identities and justify their political actions. So a focus that becomes important for the academic analyst interested in news sources is the question of whose perspective seems to dominate in news reports and editorial comment (Louw, 2005). How does public discussion become structured by particular social actors who have the power to put a 'primary definition' on a problem? Who has 'framing power?' How is the overall meaning of a defined block of media discourse successfully shaped in one particular way rather than another, by the imposition of a particular frame on the texts that make up that block? Framing power is the capacity of one actor – a politician, an institution, a spin-doctor, a moral crusader – to convey his/her views through the media by having those positions represented either in the form of quotes or paraphrase or in the actual selection and arrangement of the elements of a text.

Framing is inherent in the construction of all political communication. A frame is a structure in a text – which might be a particular type of newspaper content or television broadcast – that organises and creates a meaningful and coherent picture of an unfolding series of events (Gamson and Modigliani, 1987). Frames are used in the production of media output to define problems, suggest diagnoses, make moral judgments and prescribe solutions (Entman, 1993). Teenage binge drinking in Dublin in 2012 was eventually framed as a deficiency in the regulation of the drinks industry. Alternative frames were either not used or withered away in the early stages of the media discussion. Some frames can have very deep historical roots. Rojecki (2008), for instance, uses frame analysis to study media elites' understanding of American post-9/11 foreign policy and George Bush's war on terror. He argues that Bush gained the support and moral cover of media elite opinion, especially in the *New York Times* and the *Washington Post*, for the invasions of Afghanistan and Iraq by successfully framing his foreign policy in terms of the moral component of American political culture.

His team constructed arguments and justifications in terms of 'American exceptionalism', the strong mythic commitment, rooted in the history of the United States, to an exemplary moral vision that many Americans are convinced is unique to the United States. Historians trace the ideological roots of this pervasive myth to moral and religious views embedded in early nineteenth-century Puritanism and its focus on the 'manifest destiny' of the United States.

Analysis of media discourse is often carried out by concentrating on what CDA analysts call 'critical discourse moments', where discursive positions that exist for some time start becoming more and more recurrent. These moments are usually centred on specific, socially relevant events that challenge well-established attitudes. The death of Savita Halappanavar from complications of pregnancy in a Galway hospital in 2012 is a case in point. Future studies of the politics of abortion in Ireland will undoubtedly investigate the 'discursive moment' that was triggered by her death and its initial reporting in the *Irish Times*. In this moment, an old debate about abortion emerges once more from social amnesia and marginalisation, and long sedimented positions are scrutinised afresh, despite the obvious reluctance of many politicians to allow abortion back onto the political agenda.

Agenda-setting

Just as we can ask which frames are privileged in a range of politically relevant news texts, or which frames are totally excluded, so we should ask what alternative issues, arguments and proposals are included or excluded from public agendas and why this is so. Agenda-setting research is centred on the question of whether (and how) the media can affect political agendas, and how institutional forces such as political parties or business interest groups can influence media agendas. A parallel concern is how either the media or the political system, and the agendas they adopt at any particular time, can shape public opinion by creating a hierarchy of issues that influences what people think about. This shaping of public opinion can sometimes be captured in a series of opinion surveys. A conclusion of the earliest research on agenda-setting in the 1960s is that the media may not tell us what to think, but they can certainly tell us what to think about. Quite apart from research findings, surveys of politicians and journalists frequently indicate a strong belief among both groups that the media are indeed important agenda-setters in politics and in public opinion.

ASINCA

DESDE 1945
LEATHER SHOP

ASIN

DESDE 1945

sa Foradad

Port de Valldemossa
Cala de Valldemossa

Mirador d'es Puig
de Sa Moneda
Ma-10

Cala Banyalbufar
Torre Talaia de Ses Animes
Banyalbufar
Plantció
303
Esporles
(196)

Cala Estellencs
Sa Granja
Ermitade Maristella
932

Estellencs
La Reserva
Mirador de R. Roca
Parc Natural
Establims
Esclop
Galatzó
926
1026
Puigpunyent
Ma-10
Galilea

Sa Dragonera
Sant Elm
S'Arracó
Capdellà
PAL
Castell de Sant Elm
Calvià
(Ciutat de Mar)
Andratx
Gènova
Ma-1
Sant Joan
Cala d'Egos
Port d'Andratx Ma-1
Costa d'en Blanes Bendinat Cala Ma
Badia d'Andratx
Peguera
Son Bugadelles
Hietas
Platja d'
Camp
Cala Platja de
de Mar Fornells Peguera
Portals Nous
Cala Llamp
Palma Nova
Santa Ponsa de Palma Nova
Santa Ponsa
Magaluf Platja de Magaluf
Cala Vinyes
Portals Vells
Illa del Toro

WWW.

ASINCA

ARTESANOS DE LA PIEL DESDE 1945
Modernidad y tradición. Amplia exposición de prendas, calzado, marroquinería, bolsos y complementos en piel.

....

LEATHER ARTISANS SINCE 1945
Modernity and tradition. We offer a wide range of clothing, footwear, leatherwork, bags and accessories made from leather.

....

SEIT 1945 IM LEDERHANDWERK TÄTIG
Innovation und Tradition. Vielseitiges Angebot an Kleidung, Schuhen, Taschen, Zubehör und sonstigen Lederwaren.

....

ARTISANS DU CUIR DEPUIS 1945
Modernité et tradition. Large choix de vêtements, chaussures, maroquinerie, sacs et accessoires en cuir.

Ctra. Palma - Alcúdia esq. Ctra. Manacor
07300 Inca (Mallorca)
971 50 12 50 / 971 50 12 54
asinca@telefonica.net
www.asinca1945.com

PARKING

ACCESO DIRECTO
A-27

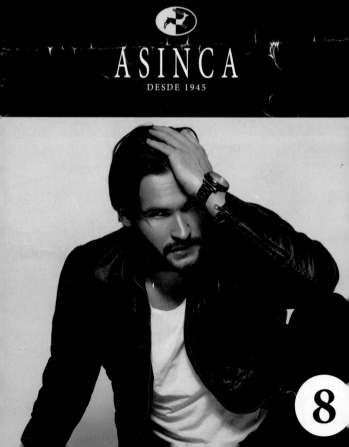

ASINCA

DESDE 1945

8

A key question for political scientists is the extent to which a political leader – a president, prime minister or Taoiseach – can successfully use one of the key weapons in their rhetorical arsenal in order to set the national agenda: the nationally televised speech. At the onset of the banking crisis in Ireland late in 2008, for instance, then Taoiseach Brian Cowan was heavily criticised for not attempting to use the power of television to set his imprint on the intense national discussion that was about to follow the collapse of banking in Ireland. Would it have made a difference? American research (Peake and Eshbaugh-Soha, 2008) on the effectiveness of presidential addresses in increasing news coverage of White House priorities and agendas, suggests that media attention can increase in the short-term following a major speech, but it tends to drop off quickly and is affected by such factors as previous media coverage, the level of public concern about an issue and the current presidential approval rating.

One of the strengths of agenda-setting as a conceptual tool in research on political communication is that it goes beyond the simple stimulus–response model that underpinned earlier attempts to understand the impact of the media on public opinion (McCombs and Shaw, 1972). It enables an institutional study of newspaper and broadcast media on the one hand, and government and political parties on the other, to see how they function in relation to making selected issues more salient in the public sphere.

In some cases, the public is totally excluded from the circular process of political influence, though it will of course have to live with the outcomes of policymaking. Aeron Davis studied the use of media by members of parliament in Westminster and concluded that intense media attention focused on particular issues can shift political agendas and create an impact on British government policy without involving public opinion at all. The elite political sphere based in London produces and consumes information within closed communication networks, in which a very small number of media play a crucial part, where 'the mass of consumer-citizens can be no more than ill-informed spectators' (Davis, 2007, 60). Elite journalism can play a significant social role by enabling politicians to negotiate different agendas and policy options within their small elite sphere, across government and opposition parties. Corcoran and Fahy (2009) conclude from their analysis of the role of the *Financial Times* in Brussels that a distinction must be made between a broadly based European public sphere and a more enclosed European elite sphere, composed of senior business people, national and EU politicians, lobbyists, public relations executives, diplomats, regulators, senior civil servants, and journalists assigned to Brussels.

In European politics, media institutions like the *Financial Times* seem to perform a role in accordance with the classical model of the public sphere (Habermas, 1989) except that public opinion actually plays little or no role and the sphere in question is an elite micro-culture. The decisions and ideologies of this special sphere have, of course, a significant, extended material impact on society in general in all member states, hence the complaint from some quarters about a 'democratic deficit' in EU politics. Likewise, Entman (2004) argues convincingly that a foreign-policy elite in Washington first debates and reaches a consensus on the direction American foreign policy should take and only then seeks to shape the news in mainstream media to create public acquiescence to the agenda already worked out by the policy elite.

The internet and political engagement

So far, we have been considering the role of traditional media in political communication. But what of the internet, which, since the emergence of the Web in the mid-1990s, has become a major force in contemporary culture? One of the first concerns that arose in the field of political communication, driven partly by the widespread influence of Putnam's book *Bowling Alone: the Collapse and Revival of American Community* (2000), was whether the internet has a positive or negative effect on civic and political engagement. The question is not a simple one, not least because of difficulties in defining the terms of the debate and then in deciding on what researchers call the direction of causality.

Putnam believed the internet will have a detrimental effect on citizen engagement with politics because it is used primarily for entertainment. People will have less time to devote to joining civic groups and engaging in other social activities (including bowling). However, the internet can also be seen as facilitating increased access to political information and more intense political discussion, especially on topics marginalised by the mainstream media. If social networks develop in the direction of creating a genuinely alternative space for political expression, this would invigorate rather than destroy civic life. What has research to say about this?

Boulianne (2008) undertook a meta-analysis of 38 studies published in recent years, all investigating people's use of the internet and their political behaviour or expression: voting, donating money to a campaign or political group, working for a campaign, attending meetings or rallies, writing a letter to an editor, talking politics, wearing a political button, etc. Her findings suggest that internet use and political engagement are positively related. Online political discussion, for instance, has a significant positive effect on offline political participation. But which can be said to cause the other? Could pre-existing interest in politics be a third variable influencing people both in their internet use and in their civic engagement, making the causal link between the internet and politics difficult to establish? Most of the studies analysed by Boulianne are silent on this. They assumed there was a causal direction of effects and did not attempt to test the possibility of reciprocal effects. Could those who are already more politically engaged use the internet more than the average citizen? Bourianne concludes from her meta-analysis that the effects of internet use on civic engagement are positive but not substantial. If internet use is measured mostly in terms of accessing online news, this tends to increase the likelihood of finding a positive and larger effect of internet use on civic engagement.

This body of research suggests that better access to a large, diverse range of political information may help to invigorate civic life by reducing the cost of participation in the public sphere in terms of time and effort. But more needs to be known about this increasingly important aspect of political communication and how it impinges not just on individual voters but also on pressure groups and social movements. Online social networking features strongly in contemporary political protest movements, as can be seen in the role of the internet in the so-called Arab Spring revolts of recent years. A great deal of political protest in the digital age manifests itself in rapid and dense network behaviour that crosses the boundary between issues and organisations much more easily than the often fractious coalition brokerage that characterised mobilising people against the Vietnam War in the 1970s.

The internet now plays a unique role in transforming the scope and scale of interpersonal political relationships. The mobilisation of protest is made easier, not least because online communication facilitates the emergence of horizontal, digitally distributed networks that operate beyond the reach of formal organisations, like the global social justice movement that emerged out of transnational demonstrations against the Iraq War in 2003 (Bennett et al, 2008). The internet enables sustainable, interpersonal network organising on a large scale, capable of acting upon conventional organisations such as churches, trade unions, political parties and peace groups. Some global protest movements, such as the Zapatista Solidarity movement in Mexico, or the Ogoni in Nigeria, have been more successful than other social movements in finding their voice in the arena of global civil society, where dozens of civil society groups seek to challenge power structures in their own countries and compete for active support from elsewhere in the world.

E-campaigning

Mainstream interest in political communication will continue to be centred on the influence of the media on electoral politics, or in the case of the internet, the impact of the Web in online election campaigns. We already know that Barack Obama's 2008 presidential campaign set a new standard for e-campaigning (Kenski et al, 2010). Like Howard Dean four years previously, Obama was highly successful in both fund-raising and building an online community of strongly motivated supporters. This inspired a scramble among politicians in many other countries who attempted to copy his success, believing the Web is revolutionising modern election campaigns as television did in the 1960s, with similar far-reaching consequences. A new slogan began to appear in political marketing circles: 'Politics is no longer local, it's viral.'

Systematic empirical analysis of e-campaigning is limited, however. The spectrum of research findings currently available range from the argument that there is no marked effect of e-campaigning on voter behaviour – since the internet reinforces rather than challenges contemporary political practices – to the contention that there are significant gains to be made by candidates utilising the internet in imaginative ways. Ten years ago, there was a growing consensus within the e-politics literature that the internet was leading to minimal or no change within wider institutions of governance and the citizen body as a whole. But as the Web itself evolved, evidence is emerging that the impact of online campaigns is moderated by the type of Web tools used. Most politicians, in Ireland and elsewhere, presently focus on attempts to capture mainstream media coverage on their websites and make very little use of Web 2.0 technologies. Yet these are now revolutionising the way the internet facilitates new forms of political communication: building websites that are genuinely interactive, posting videos on interactive video channels, establishing profiles on social networks, and blogging.

Recent evidence from the Australian general election of 2007 suggests that an exclusive emphasis on using Web 1.0 capabilities is not a wise strategy for ambitious politicians. Australia is one of the global leaders in levels of internet use. Facebook, YouTube and Google have enjoyed a growing popularity among the electorate over several years, and so it has provided a good context for research on e-campaigning. Use of new Web applications had more than doubled in the two months prior to the 2007 general election. The internet was still far behind TV as a source of election news but was rapidly catching up with radio and newspapers and was expected to surpass radio within a decade.

Against this background, Gibson and McAllister (2011) set out to systematically compare the impact of Web 1.0 and Web 2.0 campaigning on Australian voters' choices in 2007, while controlling for a wide range of other factors. Their goal was to interrogate growing academic and media orthodoxies about the effectiveness of the Web in securing votes. They conclude that Web 2.0 technologies certainly make a difference to voters and are much more effective in political campaigning than the more static Web 1.0 platform, with its emphasis on candidates placing their personal pages on party websites, sending out email newsletters and advertising their online addresses in traditional outlets. By contrast, the interactivity and dynamic interconnectiveness of Web 2.0 virtual spaces leads to messages being transmitted widely and virally via supporter blogs to very large numbers of people linked to Twitter, Facebook, online video and grass-roots activist sites. Gibson and McAllister conclude that this is where real political conversion and mobilisation may be taking place during election campaigns.

If these findings are replicated in future research, it means that it is Web 2.0 technologies that make the difference to voters and therefore the dominant narrative of Web research studies since the turn of the millennium will need to be challenged. This narrative privileges the idea that major political parties are merely reinforcing their offline dominance in the online sphere and nothing else is taking place. In the Australian election, it was the smaller parties that successively exploited the more grassroots-oriented types of new media that can create significant resonance and mobilising force with the electorate. In broader theoretical terms, it seems that direct Web effects are far less likely where voters convert to supporting a candidate after simply viewing his/her website in a passive way. A better model is one of indirect, two-step effects, where the Web becomes a source of information for political activists who go on to mobilise others, something like the 'opinion leaders' discovered in the US presidential election campaign in Ohio in 1940.

In order to understand the full gamut of public communication about politics, researchers in the past have sampled newspapers, analysed selections of television programmes, dissected documentaries or listened to radio news broadcasts, all perfectly legitimate endeavours in the age of the mass media. Since the emergence of the Web in the mid-1990s, the challenge now is to understand the impact of this quite different platform on political communication. New methodologies need to be developed for this, to analyse online social media as outlets for political expression and public debate that generate truly enormous data sets for the researcher. How do we grasp the significance of the massive network of people involved in Twitter, in terms of organised political campaigning? Answers to this are only just beginning to emerge (see Moe and Larsson, 2012). We have not yet begun to investigate 'Type B' political communication in online environments, though the savviest of politicians know that this is fertile ground for opinion formation.

Conclusion

New media developments obviously have great relevance for politicians and journalists reporting on politics. But they are also very relevant to the long-standing debate on the persistence of a political 'knowledge gap' in many democracies, despite the spread of new technologies and increasing access to the internet. Political knowledge is not equally distributed in society and there is plenty of evidence that the gap between the most and the least knowledgeable citizens is widening. This is due to a number of factors: socio-economic structures, disparities in educational levels, differences in rates of literacy and newspaper reading habits, and different patterns of media consumption. But it is also related to differences in media content between tabloid and broadsheet newspapers and between privately owned and public service radio and television channels.

The media environment of some countries creates conditions favourable to political knowledge gain, while in others, the media system leads to a widening knowledge gap. As Hallin and Mancini (2004) point out in their comparative study of three major media systems across Europe – the Mediterranean or Polarised Pluralist model, the Democratic Corporatist model in North/Central Europe, and the North Atlantic or Liberal model – regional differences in levels of political awareness can be traced to the relative dominance in the media sector of either market forces or strong traditions of public service media. These differences can have a serious impact on levels of political knowledge in the population and ultimately on the kind of democracy that emerges. It is surely in the public interest to foster policies that broaden and deepen democracy by providing all citizens with affordable opportunities for participation in political discussion that in these times surges through the public sphere in ever increasing volumes.

References

Bennet, W.L., Breunig, C. and Givens, T. (2008) 'Communication and political mobilisation: digital media and the organisation of anti-Iraq war demonstrations in the US' in *Political Communication*, 25: 269–89.

Boulianne, S. (2008) 'Does internet use affect engagement? A meta-analysis of research' in *Political Communication*, 26: 193–211.

Corcoran. F. and Fahy, D. (2009) 'Exploring the European elite sphere: the role of the *Financial Times*' in *Journalism Studies*, 10(1): 100–113.

Davis, A. (2007) *The mediation of power*, London: Routledge.

Entman, R.M. (1993) 'Framing: toward clarification of a fractured paradigm' in *Journal of Communication*, 43(4): 51–58.

Entman, R.M. (2004) *Projections of power: framing news, public opinion and US foreign policy*, Chicago: University of Chicago Press.

Fairclough, N. (2003) *Analysing discourse: textual analysis for social research*, London: Routledge.

Franklin, B. (1995) 'Political communication scholarship in Britain' in *Political Communication*, 12: 223–42.

Gamson, W.A. and Modigliani, A. (1987) 'The changing culture of affirmative action' in Braungart, R.G. and Braungart, M.M. (eds), *Research in political sociology* (vol. 3), Greenwich, CT: JAI Press.

Gibson, R.K. and McAllister, I. (2011) 'Do online election campaigns win votes? The 2007 Australian "YouTube" election' in *Political Communication*, 28: 227–44.

Habermas, J. (1989) *The structural transformation of the public sphere*, Cambridge, MA: MIT Press.

Hall, S. (1996) 'The problem of ideology: Marxism without guarantees' in Morley, D. and Chen, K.H. (eds), *Stuart Hall: critical dialogues in cultural studies*, London: Routledge.

Hallin, D. and Mancini, P. (2004) *Comparing media systems: three models of media and politics*, Cambridge: Cambridge University Press.

Kenski, K., Hardy, B.W. and Jamieson, K.H. (2010) *The Obama victory: how media, money and message shaped the 2008 election*, Oxford: Oxford University Press.

Lakoff, G. (1996) *Moral politics*, Chicago: University of Chicago Press.

Louw, E. (2005) *The media and political process*, London: Sage.

McCombs, M.E. and Shaw, D.L. (1972) 'The agenda-setting function of the mass media' in *Public Opinion Quarterly*, 36(2): 176–87.

Moe, H. and Larsson, A.O. (2012) 'Methodological and ethical challenges associated with large-scale analysis of online political communication' in *Nordicom Review*, 33(1): 117–24.

Peake, J.S. and Eshbaugh-Soha, M. (2008) 'The agenda-setting impact of major presidential TV addresses' in *Political Communication*, 25: 113–37.

Rojecki, A. (2008) 'Rhetorical alchemy: American exceptionalism and the war on terror' in *Political Communication*, 25: 67–88.

Van Dijk, T. (2001) 'Critical discourse analysis' in Tannen, D., Schiffrin, D. and Hamilton, H. (eds), *Handbook of discourse analysis*, Oxford: Blackwell.

Wodak, R. and Chilton, P. (2005) *A new agenda for critical discourse analysis: theory, methodology and interdisciplinarity*, Amsterdam: John Benjamins.

CHAPTER TWO

Elections and political communication

Donnacha Ó Beacháin

Election campaigns are sporadic events during which the apathy that the non-participatory political system engenders has to be momentarily surmounted to inject renewed legitimacy into organised political parties. How the citizenry are to be motivated to mobilise from their habitual passivity depends on the quality and quantity of political communication with the electorate. In short it is influenced, if not determined, by the character of the election campaign. This chapter provides a brief introduction to how those competing for votes have communicated with the Irish electorate since the foundation of the state.

Campaign slogans, techniques and candidates

As the revolutionary generation that had monopolised political power for the first four decades of independence exited the political stage during the 1960s, prospective candidates for election had to find new ways of getting on the ticket. For those not part of a political dynasty forged during the formative years of the state, sport proved another way of coming to the attention of the electorate, and the party leaderships. The 1965 general election returned 17 former Gaelic games stars (Whyte, 1966, 31) but a focus on GAA luminaries provides only a partial picture of the influence of the organisation. Brian Farrell (1971, 321–22) has noted that the 1969 election returned, in addition to 15 GAA stars, four GAA county officials and another 25 deputies who had been or continued to be active within the GAA as players or officials. The most significant figure of this new generation was Jack Lynch, who governed Ireland for most of the period spanning the mid-1960s to the late 1970s, and whose complete lack of a political pedigree was compensated for by having won six All-Ireland hurling and football medals.

The passing of the revolutionary generation also led to increasing localism. Almost a third of those elected to the Dáil on the back of their revolutionary exploits represented constituencies other than their home districts (Cohan, 1972, 61) and, initially at least, the most prominent represented more than one constituency with some elected to both the Dublin and Belfast legislatures. This feature of revolutionary politics freed representatives from dependence on a local bailiwick and allowed them to view issues from a national rather than a parochial perspective. Conversely, the localism that typified the post-revolutionary elite has had the opposite effect, restricting the manoeuvrability of deputies and encouraging a provincial outlook, a trend accentuated by the PR-STV electoral system. Whereas national prominence in the revolutionary era usually preceded constituency supremacy, for the post-revolutionary generations local dominance has been the only means towards achieving distinction at a national level. These contrasting routes to political eminence created different political creatures. Leaders of the revolutionary elite were politicians by accident, thrust into a political life that few had envisaged when taking up arms against the established regime during the 1916 Easter Rising or subsequent war of independence. Their successors were politicians by design and had to undergo a more gradual and less dramatic progression to high office.

The normalisation that followed the Irish revolution and the consequent localism that developed amongst the Irish political class is well illustrated by comparing the percentage of members of the revolutionary elite who had served on a county council with that of the post-revolutionary elite. Twenty nine per cent of politicians of the revolutionary elite had given such service at local level, the majority beginning their tenure shortly before their election as TDs. By the 1960s this figure had risen to 51% as service at local level rapidly became a *sine qua non* for entry to politics at national level (Cohan, 61). In addition, the absence of a revolution meant that the majority of aspiring politicians of the post-revolutionary generations have had to serve longer at local level before achieving Dáil success. This gradual progression to high office in a political system has inculcated a more gradualist approach to political problems. While the revolutionary elite was typified by its 'lack of connection with any formal governing apparatus that came before' (Cohan, 59), its successors grew up in a stable political environment that enjoyed majority support. This in turn made the concept of radical constitutional or political change more alien and unorthodox than it had appeared to many politicians of the earlier generation.

All of this has in turn contributed to changing political communication in Ireland. The political message has become increasingly moderate, the target audience local, and the support base less partisan. The balance sheet has become one of votes won or lost rather than policy goals achieved or postponed. Writing in the 1960s of the mass peoples' parties (*volkspartien*) of which Fianna Fáil was Ireland's prime example, Otto Kirchheimer (1966, 192) argued that 'there is need for enough brand differentiation to make the article plainly recognisable, but the degree of differentiation must never be so great as to make the potential customer fear he will be out on a limb.' Principles were revered but ultimately elastic and Fianna Fáil's main threat when in government was competition from a more attractively packaged brand of a nearly identical product.

Coinciding with the departure of the revolutionary generation was the advent of a national television service in 1961, which brought with it new challenges for those seeking election. The 1965 election campaign was the first to receive TV coverage, and in February 1973 RTÉ had another pioneering moment when Jack Lynch became the first Taoiseach to concede defeat live on television, bringing 16 years of Fianna Fáil rule to an end. Television's role during elections expanded thereafter. For the 2007 election RTÉ had, for the first time ever, an outside broadcasting unit in every one of the 43 constituencies (RTÉ, 2007a). From the beginning, senior politicians had been wary of television. In his televised address on the opening of Telifís Éireann, President de Valera had noted that while TV could contribute to the vigour and confidence of the nation it could also, if used unwisely, 'lead through demoralization to decadence and disillusion' (see McLoone and McMahon, 1984, 149–50). Insofar as political debate is concerned, parliamentary business has been televised since 1991, three decades after the idea was first mooted (Dunne, 1961). The impact that the arrival of television has had on Irish election campaigns should not be underestimated. As Olivia O'Leary (2006, 10) has pointed out, 'in a television age, most policy messages were too complicated, too confusing. You needed a single product with easy brand recognition. It was simple. You marketed the leader.'

Jack Lynch was better placed than Liam Cosgrave, or his predecessor James Dillon, to grasp the possibilities offered by new technologies, as evidenced by the razzmatazz generated by his presidential-style tour via helicopter in 1977. Cosgrave's performances were, by contrast, wooden and he was consistently ridiculed as miserly, authoritarian and uncharismatic in the hugely popular satirical programme *Hall's Pictorial Weekly*. Much of the innovative character of Fianna Fáil's 1977 election campaign can be attributed to the party's young general secretary, Séamus Brennan, who had spent two months with the US Democratic Party's presidential campaign during the previous year to pick up some tips from the Carter v Ford pre-race. There he learned the style of electioneering that parties in Ireland would have to embrace if they were to adapt successfully to a new age, increasingly shaped by television and consumerism. One of the many novelties that resulted from Brennan's brainstorming was the commissioning of Ireland's first election pop song. Entitled 'Your Kind of Country' and sung by Colm C.T. Wilkinson it contained some memorable lines, such as:

> We're more than just statistics, and black official ink
> We got our pride and feelings
> They're stronger than you think ...
> We need the kind of country where we can make our way
> That's why I'm voting for a change
> On this Election Day.

> So let's make it your kind of country
> Get out there and vote
> And show them that you're free
> Show them that you care a damn
> And that you'll win somehow
> Help us to make it
> Your country now

Dismissed by the Fine Gael–Labour Party government as an 'election gimmick' (Ryan, 1977) the record deliberately targeted the unprecedented number of first-time voters (the 1977 election would be the first in which voters from the age of 18 could cast ballots). Banned after a week by RTÉ and with a similar prohibition issued to CIÉ bus drivers, the song attained a subversive quality its producers could only dream of. 'Your Kind of Country' T-shirts proliferated during the campaign and while we can never know how many votes were won or lost as a result, it kept the party in the public eye. The initiative was considered such a success that in 1979, Cathal Dunne, nephew of Jack Lynch and singer/songwriter of Ireland's entry in the Eurovision Song Contest that year, recorded the single 'We're On Our Way to Europe' to coincide with the first direct elections to the European Parliament. Fianna Fáil produced another record for the June 1981 election but instead of being a song that spoke generally of youth dissatisfaction with the status quo it was an entreaty to the electorate to 'Arise and Follow Charlie', a reference to party leader, Charles Haughey:

Hail the leader, hail the man
With Freedom's cause, it all began
With Irish Pride in every man
We'll Rise and Follow Charlie

Though widely played throughout the campaign and appreciated by supporters, 'Arise and Follow Charlie' marked the end of the brief experimentation with party election campaign songs. An attempt to revive the idea in the mid-1990s with the penning of 'The Man They Call Ahern' failed to take off. While commissioned by the party and premiered at a major rally at the National Stadium on 7 March 1995, the song was never recorded but was, instead, sung occasionally by party activists at social gatherings (Lord, 2007 and *Dáil Debates*, 1995).

The personalisation of politics that television encouraged was in keeping with the 1980s, much of which was characterised by a political Punch and Judy show between Fine Gael leader Garret FitzGerald and his Fianna Fáil counterpart Charles Haughey. Capitalising on opinion polls that found that FitzGerald was more popular than Haughey, Fine Gael election posters asked voters, in November 1982, to 'Put the Right Man Back' and emphasised that FitzGerald had 'a strong team united behind his leadership' hinting at the contrasting disunity in Fianna Fáil. With a failing economy and a divisive leader, the Fianna Fáil leadership responded by playing the green card and questioning FitzGerald's patriotism. A Fianna Fáil election leaflet in one constituency adapted the famous British army First World War recruiting poster with the slogan 'Thatcher wants Garret. Do you? Safeguard Irish neutrality. Vote Fianna Fáil.'

This electoral cult of personality extended to the smaller parties. When the Progressive Democrats (PDs) contested their first general election in 1987 they adopted (apparently against the wishes of their leader, Des O'Malley) a presidential-style campaign, though they made it clear (and their candidate numbers indicated) that they were seeking the balance of power. The campaign slogan – 'Dessie Can Do It' – involved the reinvention of Des O'Malley from errant Fianna Fáil TD of almost two decades' standing to a new visionary with fresh ideas. In keeping with this dynamic image, O'Malley embarked on a helicopter tour of the country. The PDs made a virtue of the fact that many of their candidates were political novices by stressing that they were not tainted with the failure of governments past. They were also instrumental in depriving Fianna Fáil of overall majorities in 1987 and 1989, which, in turn, prompted Charles Haughey to abruptly and unilaterally jettison his party's anti-coalition 'principle'. Since then all parties have contested elections with the working assumption that some kind of coalition arrangement will need to be negotiated after the election and have tailored their election messages accordingly.

The three elections that took place during the economic boom (1997, 2002, 2007) were dominated by the irrepressible success of Fianna Fáil leader Bertie Ahern and his inner circle. The first leader since de Valera to win three successive general elections, Ahern withstood the challenges of three different Fine Gael leaders – John Bruton, Michael Noonan, and Enda Kenny. By the time of the 1997 election Ahern had discarded his trademark anorak for well-tailored suits and his party's election poster depicted a shot of a pensive leader over the banner 'people before politics'. Ahern represented a new type of leader in Irish politics – the 'everyman' whose popularity stemmed not from his exceptional qualities but from his very ordinariness, informality, and accessibility. Few commended his intellect, or his oratory, and yet he commanded widespread approval and affection, bordering on devotion. Government setbacks or crises never dented Ahern's enduring popularity. So great was his ability to retain his personal approval-ratings irrespective of how grave or high-profile the scandal might be that he was dubbed the 'Teflon Taoiseach'. Buoyed by a booming economy Ahern could not be touched by political or journalistic adversaries. In 2007, after a decade in power, Ahern was still deemed Fianna Fáil's strongest card with all party candidates depicted on their election posters as being part of 'Bertie's Team'. Ahern was photoshopped into pictures that contained different target sections of the electorate and the campaign slogan – 'the next steps'.

The volume of elections influences the amount that parties can raise to communicate their message. The holding of a snap election in September 1927, just three months after the previous one, meant that only the larger parties could mount two campaigns while smaller parties like Sinn Féin and Clann Éireann fell by the wayside. Similarly three elections in 18 months during 1981–82 resulted in a progressive reduction of expenditure. The estimated spending of Fianna Fáil and Fine Gael declined from £1.6 million (June 1981) to £1 million (February 1982) to £500,000 (November 1982) (O'Leary, 1982, 366; 1983, 175). It was not beyond the ingenuity of political leaders to try to extract political capital from these cutbacks; driving home the point that political parties, like the nation, had little to spend; Garret FitzGerald did much of his campaign travel by scheduled trains (RTÉ, 1982a). The costs of electioneering proliferated during the years of the Celtic Tiger, with lamp-post posters costing €6 euro apiece and billboards €1,000 a fortnight for the 2007 contest. Despite these costs, 450 tonnes of posters were produced for the campaign (RTÉ, 2007b).

Smears, scares and slurs

Negative campaigning has a long history in Ireland. The civil war provided the material for much of the election literature of the Irish Free State's first decade. Confronted with a resurgent Fianna Fáil, Cumann na nGaedheal (the predecessor of contemporary Fine Gael) presented themselves during the 1932 campaign as Ireland's 'bulwark against the terrorists' in a country that lay 'in the shadow of the gunman'. The government portrayed Fianna Fáil as the instigators of a communist revolution under the guise of patriotism. As one advertisement, which took up the entire front page of the *Irish Independent*, famously put it: 'The gunmen are voting for Fianna Fáil. The Communists are voting for Fianna Fáil. How will you vote?' (Ó Beacháin, 2010, 126). Similarly, on election day the *Irish Independent's* editorial warned voters that 'the very life of the State' was at stake, and that should they choose Fianna Fáil the verdict of the world would be 'suicide during temporary insanity' (*Irish Independent*, 1932).

Once ensconced in office, Fianna Fáil employed the same electoral scares in an effort to maintain power. During the 1940s, its message to the electorate could be reduced to an assertion that as the only organisation able to offer a single-party government (considered synonymous with stability), Fianna Fáil was the only defence against anarchy. 'If you vote Fianna Fáil, the bombs won't fall', the party proclaimed during the 1943 election. Fianna Fáil tried to whip up anti-communist hysteria by describing the mild-mannered William Norton as 'the Kerensky of the Labour Party', who, despite his innocuous rhetoric, was in reality 'preparing the way for the red shirts' (MacEntee, 1943). The scare worked; the Labour Party obligingly split in two early in 1944 on the issue of the level of communism within the party and during the election later that year the rival factions were too busy attacking each other to land many blows on de Valera's government.

Clann na Poblachta replaced Labour as the target of electoral red scares during the 1948 election. Taking out expensive half-page advertisements in national and local newspapers headed 'A Plan for Safety', Fianna Fáil warned of forces working for the overthrow of democracy, 'disguised [...] perhaps even under names in the Irish language'. Their methods would be 'to destroy confidence in the motives of the Government, and, if possible, by slander and abuse of political leaders, to weaken public faith in the democratic system'.

The advertisement concluded in apocalyptic terms by claiming that the free election that would bring 'the enemies of Christianity and democracy' to power 'is always the last free election ever held'. Predicting that revolutionary danger was 'on the horizon', the advertisement maintained that a vote for Fianna Fáil's opponents would signal the end of Christianity and democracy in Ireland and the triumph of revolutionary communism:

> The 'cells', whose task it is to exploit temporary causes of public discontent, and to promote social unrest are at work. The chance of destroying the Fianna Fáil Government, which the General Election gives them is being fully used [...] Fianna Fáil means safety. It means the preservation of democracy [...] which is the alternative to dictatorship. This is why these elections in Ireland are so important. That is why Fianna Fáil must win. (*Connacht Tribune*, 1948)

A comparison of the 1932 and 1948 elections demonstrates how close Fianna Fáil had come to the Cumann na nGaedheal party it had reviled. So great was the campaign in 1932 to portray Fianna Fáil as Bolsheviks that the party manifesto stated that they had 'no leanings towards communism and no belief in communistic doctrines' (Fianna Fáil, 1932). By 1948, Seán MacBride, like de Valera before him, was forced to claim that his policies coincided with Papal encyclicals and that there were 'no Communists' in his party (*Irish Times*, 1948). Cumann na nGaedheal's 1932 election slogan of 'Safety first' differed little from that adopted by Fianna Fáil after 16 years in power: 'Play safe'.

The 1969 election brought the return of the 'red scare' to Irish politics. Having temporarily overcome its phobia about the word 'socialism', the Labour Party boldly entered the election asking the people to 'peel off the tattered rags and battered image of the old Republic of the conservative Civil War politicians'. Instead electors were exhorted to vote for 'the new Republic', a land of communal responsibility, full employment and equal opportunity (*Irish Times*, 1969a). Few could imagine a more unlikely standard-bearer of socialism than Brendan Corish, who throughout the 1960s had displayed a greater knowledge of Papal encyclicals than many a parish priest. However, Fianna Fáil portrayed Corish as a man in the thrall of Marxist intellectuals eager to seize power and eradicate civil liberties. In keeping with traditional policy, Fianna Fáil did not issue a manifesto. In practice this was to allow the party the maximum flexibility after taking office, but Charles Haughey, as director of elections, offered a new ideological pretext. 'Manifestos', he claimed, 'have a Marxist ring about them' (*Irish Times*, 1969b). With characteristic gusto, the veteran red-baiter Seán MacEntee claimed that the Labour

Party stood for Lenin, Stalin and the 'red flames of burning homesteads in Meath' (*Irish Times*, 1969c).

In full-page advertisements in the national newspapers, the traditional argument espousing the virtues of a united single-party government (i.e. Fianna Fáil) as against a divided coalition of irreconcilables was extensively employed. Particular emphasis was given to those in the Labour Party who constituted a 'group of extreme left-wing socialists [...] preaching class warfare and who want total state control and all that goes with it' (*Irish Times*, 1969d). Neil Blaney warmed to this subject, accusing the Labour Party of promoting the 'failed system of atheistic socialism' of the Soviet Union, Cuba, North Korea, and Vietnam, where 'the freedom of man is a myth, where democracy has been trampled down and brutal dictatorship is supreme' (*Irish Times*, 1969e). The Labour Party programme, he concluded, was not for 1969 but for 1984 (*Irish Times*, 1969f). Jack Lynch claimed that by voting for Fianna Fáil the people would demonstrate 'that they prefer the reality of progress and prosperity to the Cuban myth' (*Irish Times*, 1969g). Anti-intellectualism was also much in evidence. Mícheál Ó Móráin, the minister for justice, condemned the 'left-wing political queers from Trinity College and Telefís Éireann', while another candidate, Joe Dowling, declared that 'the intellectuals had never done a day's real work in their lives' (*Irish Times*, 1969h; 1969i). Failing to make a major breakthrough, the Labour Party reverted to its default position of cautious moderation. The red scares snuffed out what little prospects there were for left-wing or radical ideas to flourish during the early decades of the state.

Opinion polls

Political parties and commentators only began to understand that opinion polls provided an accurate reflection of voter sentiment after these same polls correctly predicted a Fianna Fáil landslide in 1977, despite the ill-concealed confidence of the government and media that the ruling coalition would be returned. Though the first opinion poll in Ireland seems to have been conducted as early as 1961 this was considered a novelty. The Labour Party had conducted a major internal poll in 1969 and there were sporadic efforts at party polling during the early 1970s but, as Garret FitzGerald recalls, most politicians viewed these as 'unreliable'. His party leader and Taoiseach Liam Cosgrave was 'known to be particularly dismissive of polls preferring rather oddly to be guided on public opinion by individual letters [...] extracts of which he sometimes read to us in Government' (FitzGerald, 1991, 320).

Cosgrave's hostility to polls had had a public airing at the 1972 Fine Gael ard fheis, when he attacked a market research company that had conducted a recent poll saying that 'those who organised it could now give back the thirty pieces of silver', which seemed to suggest that the pollsters produced the results desired by their paymasters (FitzGerald, 1991, 105–6). When Cosgrave indicated that he wanted an election in June 1977 there were some ministers who favoured a later date – when economic reforms would have taken greater effect – and considered conducting a poll but, as FitzGerald recalls 'we were inhibited from suggesting it by the dismissive reaction we believed we would have met from most of our colleagues, including the Taoiseach' (FitzGerald, 1991, 320).

Indifference to polls extended to the media. On their eve-of-poll front page the *Irish Times* proclaimed that according to their team of reporters, who had covered all 42 constituencies, 'the Coalition will win the election by a fairly comfortable margin' while the following day the banner headline was 'Coalition set to take election' (*Irish Times,* 1977a; 1977b). So great was the media consensus on the outcome that Seán Duignan said that if Fianna Fáil won the election it would be 'the greatest comeback since Lazarus' and that the elite corps of political correspondents would have 'a lot of egg on their faces' (Farrell, 1978, 97). Following Fianna Fáil's victory – the biggest in Irish electoral history – Garret FitzGerald, in an opinion piece published in the *Irish Times* (1977c), urged a reconsideration of attitudes to opinion polls:

> The failure of most commentators and politicians to detect the change in mood and to evaluate its political consequences has been aggravated by what might perhaps be described somewhat paradoxically as a naive cynicism of most people in Ireland with regard to public opinion polls [...] Perhaps the result of this election will encourage all concerned to take these polls more seriously in the future.

After 1977, opinion polls would become an integral part of the electoral landscape to the extent that they have become stories in themselves and frequently frame election debates. Indeed, there is some currency to the criticism that, as Christopher Hitchens (2010) put it, 'to be able to cite a poll is now the shortest cut to economizing both on thought and on research.' While poll results are always welcomed by those who are reported to be performing well, politicians have developed an arsenal of well-rehearsed responses to poor showings. These include the rejoinder that the poll is just a 'snapshot in time', that it 'doesn't reflect what is being said on the doorstep', and/or that 'the only poll that counts is that held on election day.'

Polls not only reflect but have also come to greatly influence what people think and how they will vote. Candidates and parties can, consequently, become a victim of good poll results. During the 2002 general election campaign, Fianna Fáil's march towards an overall majority was thwarted in large part by the burden of glowing opinion polls, which put party support at 59%, prompting its coalition partners, the Progressive Democrats, to launch a campaign under the banner of 'One Party Government – No Thanks'. Though Fianna Fáil spokespersons did their best to dampen speculation that they could form a single party administration, and Bertie Ahern even went so far as to state a personal preference to maintain the coalition should his party secure an overall majority, the PD campaign, assisted by influential media commentators, provoked a significant portion of the electorate to reflect on whether Fianna Fáil could indeed be trusted to govern alone. Consequently, the PDs, as self-appointed guardians of Fianna Fáil's morality, doubled their parliamentary representation to eight seats, despite a dip in their vote, and Fianna Fáil fell just short of a majority (Collins, 2005, 211–13).

Presidential elections

Presidential elections are fundamentally different from general elections in that candidates are not competing for power. The lack of influence is all the more anomalous considering that the president is considered to personify and represent the nation and is the only political position that is elected nationally. This need to appeal to the national electorate for an office with very few competencies has produced increasingly surreal struggles in which candidates engage in a popularity contest to prove that they are needed to fill a position that, however desirable, many appreciate is politically superfluous.

Hard as it is to believe today, opposition in 1937 to the constitutional provisions establishing the presidency centred on the charge that it would become the platform for dictatorship, a fear dampened by the selection by parliamentary consensus of 78-year-old Dubhghlas de hÍde (Douglas Hyde) as first president. A Protestant cultural nationalist, with no identifiable party preference and certainly no political ambition, de hÍde defused the controversy and subsequent presidential elections were, with some minor exceptions, characterised by mild-mannered competition between senior citizens. Since 1938 the presidency has been determined without a contest on six occasions, when the major political parties have conspired to block a number of candidates. For example, after the premature death of one president, and the resignation of another in rapid succession, the Irish political elite, eager for a safe pair of hands, agreed, in 1976, on the candidature of Patrick Hillery, who served a full two terms and 14 years as president without ever submitting himself to the electorate.

Presidential elections since 1990 represent a second era. These were the first contests that incorporated opinion polls, TV debates, and other features of modern electioneering. The Fine Gael 1990 presidential campaign was debilitated from the start by the knowledge that candidate Austin Currie was asked to run after several party notables, including Garret FitzGerald and Alan Dukes, had demurred. Nominated by the Labour and Workers' parties Mary Robinson embarked on an impressive six-month door-to-door campaign but opinion polls suggested that she was still likely to lose to the frontrunner, Fianna Fáil veteran Brian Lenihan, until a media ambush transformed the campaign. When an interview given by Lenihan to student and Fine Gael member, Jim Duffy, several months before the campaign, contradicted a question asked by another Fine Gael activist on the current affairs programme *Questions and Answers*, his campaign was dealt a severe blow. He hoped to revive his fortunes by agreeing to a televised interview with RTÉ's political correspondent, Seán Duignan, but it backfired. Lenihan's key defence, that 'on mature recollection' he had erred in the interview he had given to Jim Duffy, attracted ridicule and his tactic of staring into the camera failed to assuage voter incredulity. His support recovered as he garnered sympathy after being fired from his ministerial post, not least because he was a visibly ill man still recuperating from a liver transplant operation. It was not enough, however, and despite Lenihan outpolling his rivals on the first count, Currie's transfers ensured Robinson's triumph.

Robinson's election campaign proved that a door-to-door campaign, combined with generous media coverage, could challenge the more established political dynasties. So successful was Robinson's presidency considered to be that all parties and ambitious independents sought to emulate the 'model'. Whereas in 1990 Mary Robinson had been the first female candidate ever for the presidency, the 1997 contest saw four women seeking the office (a solitary male candidate ran as an independent and came last). Despite a dirty campaign during which her critics charged her with being 'soft on Sinn Féin' (this was encapsulated by Eoghan Harris, the *Sunday Independent* columnist and manager of Derek Nally's presidential campaign, who referred to her as a 'tribal time bomb'), Mary McAleese won easily, becoming in the process the first president from Northern Ireland.

The presidency lapsed back into the bad old ways when, in 2004, all the major parties conspired to avoid a contest. However, the 2011 election witnessed a return to competition with an unprecedented seven candidates who debated on the national airwaves on eight occasions (also a record) over a 25-day period. Cognisant that the constitution prevented presidents from exercising real power, prospective candidates could not advocate policies as such, which reduced the contest to one between personalities. Most candidates had an Achilles heel that the media targeted. It is Seán Gallagher's candidacy, however, that best illustrates how glowing opinion polls and a media ambush can conspire to deny victory.

Throughout the campaign, Gallagher exuded confidence, ability, focus, and determination. Consequently in the month before election day his poll ratings almost quadrupled from 11% to 40%, and as polling day beckoned, Gallagher's lead over his only realistic rival, Michael D. Higgins, appeared insurmountable. His stellar performance in the polls prompted journalists and commentators to cast a more critical eye over Gallagher's candidacy. Though broadcast media are legally bound to afford each candidate fair and balanced coverage, Gallagher was the target of more hostile questions than any of his rivals during the final TV debate and an unverified tweet from a bogus Twitter account was read out, which depicted him as a Fianna Fáil bagman. With a blanket ban on electioneering and campaign reporting on the verge of kicking in, Gallagher had only a day to manage the crisis. His Icarus-like performance demonstrates the dangers of peaking too early in opinion polls. Gallagher's complaints regarding the disproportionate amount of hostile questions he was subjected to in the end-of-campaign debate and the failure to authenticate the controversial tweet were ultimately upheld by the Broadcasting Authority of Ireland (BAI, 2012) but this vindication did not compensate for the loss of the presidency.

From television to Twitter

As early as 1958, Key (1958, 375–76) observed in the United States that 'the doorbell ringers have lost their function of mobilising the vote to the public relations experts.' The ascendancy of media advisers came later to Ireland. As long-time Fianna Fáil minister, Kevin Boland (c.1989, 6), reflected:

> Consultation with the grassroots was, of course, an antediluvian practice outdated by the advent of the Think Tank. The organisation had been brought up to date, rationalised. There was a new tier of professionally

qualified advisers available now, financed by the contributions of big business, which believed in requiting services rendered. The role of voluntary workers 'on the ground' was simplified. They were for putting up posters, carrying out the National Collection which was a public relations exercise rather than a significant source of revenue, and for comprising awe-struck audiences to hear the words of wisdom relayed to them from the Think Tank via the local deputy.

With the advent of television came criticisms that politics had been trivialised, as the tyranny of the sound bite ruled supreme. Political life became more about choreography. Ard-fheiseanna (party conferences), now televised, are more for public consumption than the party faithful, who largely view them as social occasions. In these circumstances, strict discipline is expected and motions are carefully monitored lest they alienate the viewing public. Inevitably, the intellectual calibre of debates has greatly declined. Moreover, party tasks – particularly at elections – are increasingly remunerative.

Ireland had to wait until the early 1980s for election debates on national television. Ever since the famous Nixon–Kennedy debate in 1960, analysts have attempted to assess the impact of election debates in influencing voters in consolidated democracies. Fresh from his fact-finding mission to the USA in 1976, Fianna Fail's then party secretary, the young Séamus Brennan, returned to Ireland armed with an array of new ideas including TV ads, campaign battle-buses, and billboards, and persuaded Jack Lynch to challenge Liam Cosgrave publicly to a TV election debate (Lahiffe, 2009, 7–8). Cosgrave's dismissal of the offer as a gimmick only assisted his rival and was true to form. Lynch and Cosgrave represented two very different styles of political communication, and as Olivia O'Leary (2006, 11) has pointed out,

Lynch [...] suited an age which was moving away from megaphones and chapel-gate meetings. Ireland's public debate now happened on the national television service which had expanded and moved from black and white to colour, and people had got used to the shorter, feel-good messages of commercial advertising. Lynch's avuncular, pipe-smoking presence suited the more intimate atmosphere of a television studio. People watching from their armchairs at home felt reassured [...] Cosgrave's bristly moustache and his stiff military bearing looked out of place on television. He was uneasy with the informal style of television interviewing and refused to allow any intrusion into his private life. He avoided the limelight as much as he could and let the many stars in his cabinet shine instead. He belonged to another age.

Their successors as leaders of Fianna Fáil and Fine Gael, Charles Haughey and Garret FitzGerald, did not immediately agree to a TV debate and during their first contest in June 1981 there was no direct one-to-one confrontation, but rather a panel of journalists interrogated the three main party leaders. Ireland had to wait until February 1982 for its first television showdown. Two days before election-day the Fianna Fáil and Fine Gael leaders participated for the first time in a live television debate moderated by *Today Tonight* host, Brian Farrell (RTÉ, 1982b). A TV debate between FitzGerald and Haughey was also the highlight of the November 1982 election campaign. Haughey, the more aggressive on the night, emphasised that, unlike Fine Gael, his government had produced an economic plan and he stressed the impossibility of any party but his securing an overall majority and the dangers of unstable government. FitzGerald contrasted the unity of his own party to the well-known internal dissensions within Fianna Fáil. Though no clear victor emerged from the debate, FitzGerald was able to form a Fine Gael–Labour Party coalition government after election-day.

During the 1997 election, the format of TV debates had to adapt to the slow proliferation of parties. The governing 'rainbow coalition' of Fine Gael, Labour, and Democratic Left was being challenged by a rival Fianna Fáil–Progressive Democrats combination, though there were considerable disparities in party strength and their places in opinion polls. Consequently, the new Fianna Fáil leader, Bertie Ahern, debated with John Bruton in what might be dubbed as the Taoiseach debate while the PD leader Mary Harney took on Dick Spring in a contest between prospective Tánaistí. The Democratic Left leader, Proinsias de Rossa, was left with no one to debate and so was instead interviewed by RTÉ presenter Eamonn Lawlor.

Despite becoming an integral part of election campaigns, securing large audiences and attracting extensive media analyses, TV debates have never become the game-changers that many believed they might or can be. The media consensus that Michael Noonan had demolished Bertie Ahern in the 2002 debate (the analysis on RTÉ alternately described Ahern as 'stuttering', 'stumbling', 'nervous', 'in flight', 'uncomfortable', 'on the back foot', 'on the ropes', and 'wide-eyed with terror') did not reflect the election result; Fine Gael reached an historic low while Ahern led Fianna Fáil to within a whisker of an overall majority (RTÉ, 2002). The 2007 debate between Bertie Ahern and Enda Kenny favoured the incumbent while a debate for the leaders of the smaller parties produced some memorable one-liners as when Labour's Pat Rabbitte depicted the PD's Michael McDowell as a 'menopausal Paris Hilton [...] an inveterate attention-seeker' and McDowell responded that the opposition was composed of 'the left (Labour), the hard left (Sinn Féin) and the leftovers (Greens)' (*Irish Examiner*, 2007). The 2011 election produced two firsts. Apart from the debate between the leaders of the two main parties, Micheál Martin and Enda Kenny, there was also a five-way debate including the leaders of the Labour Party, Sinn Féin, and the Green Party. And on TG4 Martin, Kenny, and Eamon Gilmore conducted the first TV election debate exclusively through the medium of the Irish language.

In recent years, Facebook and Twitter have become core communication platforms for politicians and their parties. According to one survey of 48 TDs conducted shortly before the February 2011 general election, less than one third (32%) had used social networking tools during the 2007 election but over three quarters (77%) would do so during the 2011 contest. Facebook was the most popular social media tool for the TDs (86%) with Twitter lagging some distance behind (42%). While a substantial majority (60%) of those politicians surveyed maintained that door-to-door canvassing and face-to-face communication were the most important means of communication during an election campaign, almost nine out of ten (88%) believed that social media is changing the dynamics of politics and communication with voters, and almost all believed they would be using these media (blogs, YouTube) more frequently and expansively in the future (O'Keefe and Cunningham, 2010).

There was certainly no correlation between the numbers of followers of the Twitter accounts of politicians, or the volume of Tweets sent, with the number of votes garnered on polling day 2011. For one thing, followers are not geographically concentrated; ultimately, it is not the number of supporters globally but, rather, in one's constituency that carries a candidate into office. Moreover, to follow a candidate on Twitter does not necessarily imply an endorsement of their political views. Prior to the 2011 general election, the Green Party was unique in that all six of its TDs had Twitter accounts compared to 75% of Labour TDs, 37% of Fine Gael TDs and a mere 27% of Fianna Fáil TDs (siliconrepublic.com, 2010). The minister for communications, energy, and natural resources, Eamon Ryan of the Green Party, had the most followers of any Oireachtas member and those following Green Party leader John Gormley outnumbered those of the then Taoiseach-apparent, Enda Kenny, who tweeted daily as election day approached. History records, however, that the Green Party was annihilated in election

2011, losing its entire parliamentary representation in the process, while Enda Kenny led Fine Gael to an historic victory, attaining more seats for his party than at any time in its 80-year history.

The 2011 election was the first to involve Twitter and it is quite clear that the use of this social medium was very much in transition. On the eve of the 2011 election, only 38% of TDs (63 out of 166) had Twitter accounts. Within a year of the February 2011 election, however, this number had risen to 139 (84%) and in June 2013 the figure was 147 (88.55%). Fine Gael now has the highest percentage of TDs on Twitter (93%) followed by the Labour Party (82%) and Sinn Féin (64%) with Fianna Fáil still lagging (58%), in particular when compared with independent TDs and those of the smaller parties, 89% of whom have Twitter accounts. Sometimes it is the man and not the message that has attracted followers. In February 2012, Taoiseach Enda Kenny had the highest number of followers despite not having tweeted since July 2011, while the minister for education, Ruairí Quinn, ranked 15th in terms of followers despite never having tweeted (Murray Consultants, 2012). The rising star has undoubtedly been Sinn Féin president, Gerry Adams, who only joined Twitter in February 2013. As of May 2014, his account had more followers than the leaders of all other parties represented in Dáil Éireann combined.

While it is too early in the evolution of these types of social media to determine the influence they will exert during elections, a few trends are already evident. While there are four times as many Facebook accounts in Ireland as those for Twitter (approximately two million compared with 500,000), the number of Facebook and Twitter accounts attached to TDs is relatively even (297,000 v 234,000), suggesting that Twitter is more politicised (candidate.ie, 2012b) and, therefore, likely to be of greater importance in forthcoming elections. This is underlined by the fact that, as of the end of 2012, the number of individuals following the flagship accounts of the political parties was over 25% greater on Twitter than on Facebook (candidate.ie, 2012c). Facebook is more suited to detailed press releases and dissemination of photos and videos, whereas Twitter has a more immediate news value, its terseness more in tune with the age of the sound bite. Smaller and challenging parties along with independents have, initially at least, shown most enthusiasm and success in embracing new media (candidate.ie, 2012a; 2012c) but this edge is already being eroded as the bigger and more established parties direct their assistants to manage Facebook and Twitter accounts as part and parcel of the routine political activity of disseminating policies, publicising achievements and criticising opponents. However, new social media will most likely complement rather than replace traditional election tactics, which in the Irish context rely very much on face-to-face encounters.

Conclusion

The passing of the revolutionary elite combined with technological advances has ensured that the way in which politicians communicate with the electorate has evolved over the decades. Despite the ascendancy of the media as a means of communicating political messages during election campaigns, and irrespective of the fact that journalists and broadcasters generally prefer gladiatorial, adversarial contests, election campaigns today are much less confrontational than they were during the early decades of the state. The rival eve-of-election monster meetings have given way to TV debates, though these have never been decisive. Opinion polls, once considered akin to political astrology, now play a major role in framing debates and, along with focus groups, help parties fine-tune and tweak their policies. The door-to-door, house-to-house style of campaigning has not died, however. All indications are that voters still need to feel they 'know' a politician before voting for them and this can only be satisfied by the candidate making all efforts to come to the voter, be they in shopping malls, on the street, or at home. Social media will undoubtedly make greater inroads in coming elections. It will, however, most likely complement rather than replace the existing emphasis on personal interaction. As a people living in a small state, with multi-member constituencies and an electoral system that encourages clientalism while placing a high premium on 'preferences', Irish voters are not quite ready for an exclusively virtual relationship with their political representatives.

References

BAI (2013). See <http://www.rte.ie/news/2012/0307/bai_gallagher_ruling.pdf>

Boland, K. (n.d. / c.1989) 'The unnecessary coalition', published by the author.

candidate.ie (2012a) 'Mid-term report for Leinster House – Facebook & Twitter analysis' (3 November). See <http://candidate.ie/?p=1942>

candidate.ie (2012b) 'The 31st Dáil on Facebook and Twitter' (3 November). See <http://candidate.ie/?p=1934>

candidate.ie (2012c) 'Party Flagship Accounts' (31 October). See <http://candidate.ie/?p=1905>

Cohan, A.S. (1972) *The Irish political elite*, Dublin: Gill & Macmillan.

Collins, S. (2005) *Breaking the mould: how the PDs changed Irish politics*, Dublin: Gill & Macmillan.

Connacht Tribune (1948) 'A plan for safety' (24 January).

Dáil Debates (1995) vol. 450, col. 451 (8 March).

Dunne, S. (1961) *Dáil Debates*, vol. 192, cols 820–21 (23 November).

Farrell, B. (1971) 'Dáil Deputies: the 1969 Generation' in *Economic and Social Review*, 2(3): 309–27.

Farrell, B. (1978) 'The mass media and the 1977 campaign' in Penniman, H.R. (ed.), *Ireland at the polls: the Dáil election of 1977*, Washington, DC: American Enterprise Institute for Public Policy Research.

Fianna Fáil (1932) Manifesto dated 9 February, Fianna Fáil Archives, ff/789.

FitzGerald, G. (1991) *All in a life*, Dublin: Gill & Macmillan.

Hitchens, C. (2010) 'All the views fit to print', in *Slate* (1 November).

Irish Examiner (2007) 'Sorry but Pat doesn't do apologies' (24 August).

Irish Independent (1932) 'A fateful choice' (16 February).

Irish Times (1948) 'Intruders steal C. na P. scroll before meeting' (15 January).

Irish Times (1969a) 'Views of traditional politicians rejected' (3 June).

Irish Times (1969b) 'Haughey talks to press' (4 June).

Irish Times (1969c) 'MacEntee fears Marxist influence' (14 June).

Irish Times (1969d) 'The Choice' (17 June).

Irish Times (1969e) 'Marxist infiltration warning by Blaney' (17 June).

Irish Times (1969f) 'In the field' (10 June).

Irish Times (1969g) 'Choice is reality or Cuban myth – Lynch' (17 June).

Irish Times (1969h) 'F.G. – Labour wedding warning by Ó Móráin' (7 June).

Irish Times (1969i) 'Councillors charged with play-acting' (4 June).

Irish Times (1977a) 'Coalition to win comfortably' (15 June).

Irish Times (1977b) 'Coalition set to take election' (16 June).

Irish Times (1977c) 'Swing to FF is large only in context of recent past, says FitzGerald' (21 June).

Key, V.O. (1958) *Politics, parties, and pressure groups*, New York: Crowell.

Kircheimer, O. (1966) 'The transformation of the western European party systems', in J. LaPalombara, and Weiner, M. (eds), *Political parties and political development*, Princeton, NJ: Princeton University Press.

Lahiffe, F. (2009) *Séamus Brennan: a life in government*, Dublin: Liffey Press.

Lord, M. (2007) 'Miriam Lord's Week' in *Irish Times* (7 April).

MacEntee, S. (1943) speech made during the 1943 general election, UCD Archives, MacEntee Papers, P67/364.

McLoone, M. and McMahon, J. (eds) (1984) *Television and Irish society: 21 years of Irish television*, Dublin: RTÉ/IFI.

Murray Consultants (2012) 'Twitter Followers League Table 2012'. See <http://www.

murrayconsult.ie/professional-insights/wp-content/uploads/2012/02/2012-TD-Twitter-Followers-01.02.2012.pdf>

Ó Beacháin, D. (2010) *The destiny of the soldiers: Fianna Fáil, Irish republicanism and the IRA, 1926–1973*, Dublin: Gill & Macmillan.

O'Keeffe, M. and Cunningham, S. (2010) '77 per cent of Politicians to embrace social media in next election'. See <http://irishmediawatch.com/77-per-cent-of-politicians-to-embrace-social-media-in-next-election/>

O'Leary, C. (1982) 'The Irish general elections of 1981 and 1982' in *Electoral Studies*, 1(3): 363–74.

O'Leary, C. (1983) 'The Irish general election (November 1982)' in *Electoral Studies*, 2(2): 171–75.

O'Leary, O. (2006) *Party Animals*, Dublin: O'Brien Press.

RTÉ (1982a). See <http://www.RTÉ.ie/archives/exhibitions/688-elections/696-general-election-1982-november/139431-garret-fitzgerald-takes-the-train/>

RTÉ (1982b). See <http://www.RTÉ.ie/archives/exhibitions/688-elections/695-general-election-1982-february/139438-first-televised-leaders-debate/>

RTÉ (2002). See <http://www.RTÉ.ie/archives/exhibitions/688-elections/701-general-election-2002/287735-laweb_general-elections-tonight-with-vincent-browne-leaders-debate-noonan-ahern/?page=1>

RTÉ (2007a). See <http://www.RTÉ.ie/archives/exhibitions/688-elections/702-general-election-2007/139421-RTEs-largest-ever-coverage-of-election/?page=1>

RTÉ (2007b). See <http://www.rte.ie/archives/exhibitions/688-elections/702-general-election-2007/139414-how-important-are-election-posters/>

Ryan, R. (1977) Minister for Finance, Richie Ryan speaking on 'Election '77 Special' with John Bowman, available at <www.RTÉ.ie/archives/exhibitions/688-elections/692-general-election-1977/287919-general-election-1977/>

siliconrepublic.com (2010) '40pc of TDs among the Twitterati' (14 October). See <http://www.siliconrepublic.com/new-media/item/18313-40pc-of-tds-among-the-twitterati>

Whyte, J. (1966) *Dáil Deputies* (Tuairim pamphlet 15), Dublin: Tuairim.

CHAPTER THREE

A pragmatic partnership: politicians and local media

Sarah Kavanagh

The relationship between TDs and the media in Ireland is little studied, with existing analyses tending to focus on general election campaigns (Brandenburg, 2005, 298). This narrow focus fails to acknowledge that in the era of the 'permanent campaign' what happens between elections also merits scrutiny. In Ireland, national parliamentarians are strongly embedded in the life of their constituencies. Therefore, having a high profile in the constituency is *expected* of TDs, and a strong presence in the constituency is vital for TDs who wish to retain their seats. In this sense, local media represent the most effective conduit through which TDs can communicate to their electorate that they are out there in the ether working hard for the interests of the constituency. Local media allow them to articulate their policy positions, their views and what they consider to be their achievements. Moreover, because the media may be viewed as neutral, publicity in local media implies that a gatekeeper (an editor or head of news) has deemed the work of the TD to be worthy of mention. By contrast, a TD's newsletter may be considered as simple marketing.

This chapter examines the interaction of TDs and the local media in the period between general elections using a series of face-to-face interviews with seven TDs as well as parliamentary assistants, newspaper editors, and heads of news at local radio stations in two case-study constituencies. The interviews, granted on the basis of non-attribution, were conducted in 2007 with a view to establishing the approaches to, attitudes towards, perceptions of, and the practices inherent in the models of political communication that exist at local level. The chapter begins by outlining the perceived importance of local media to TDs by reporting the views of TDs, their Parliamentary Assistants (PAs) and local media editors / heads of news. It then considers the personal relationships that exist between TDs and local media personnel and the particular paradigm that this creates. The capacity of TDs to agenda-set in the local media is also considered and the journey of a press release from origin to publication/non-publication is examined in this context. Finally, the issue of bias in the media is analysed from both the political and media viewpoints.

The importance of local media for TDs

Blumler and Kavanagh (1999, 216) define the contemporary political communication epoch as 'the third age' – an era demanding for politicians and journalists due to the accelerated news cycle, more news outlets, and increased competition. An increasingly adversarial politician–journalist relationship has led politicians to seek to bypass the national media and use alternative means of political communication, including the favouring of regional press. Negrine (2005, 109) and Franklin (2004, 157–58) point to the advantages of the local media for politicians in terms of achieving name recognition among voters, of creating a perception that the politician is working and in getting coverage that the national media would never give them. Negrine's research suggests that for British MPs in the early stages of their careers the national media is not a priority concern, unlike local newspapers, which are perceived to be read by constituents. In Ireland, where multi-seat constituencies mean that the relationship between TDs and constituents is closer, high visibility in the constituency is considered essential for election and re-election. Local media can provide this visibility; 58% of Irish adults tune in to their local or regional radio stations on an average day (JNLR, 2012/13) while almost 40% of the population buy regional newspapers, increasing to 57% when Dublin and Cork cities are excluded (JNRS, 2011/12).

In interviews, the TDs felt that it was vital to have a presence in the local media as this provided the most effective mechanism for communicating with their constituents. TDs perceive a presence in the local media to be necessary in terms of attracting political support and believe that their constituents want to see evidence of their ongoing attempts to resolve salient local issues. The following quotation from a TD is illustrative:

> Absolutely essential [to have a presence in the local media] and the reason why is that, when it comes to politics, if you don't have a presence in the local area [...] then you're not likely to get support – so I would say [...] local media [...] creates a perception of somebody who is in touch,

somebody who is capable of identifying what the issues are, and somebody who is working to resolve those issues – so perception is hugely important in politics and the local media is a central element of creating that positive perception.

When asked whether they thought it is important for TDs to have a presence in their local media, the responses of media professionals revealed that they recognise the dependency of TDs on local media. One newspaper editor observed:

> It's hugely important. I think the desire to get re-elected seems to be there from once they enter the Dáil […] and they need to have the link with what's going on in Dublin and the relevance to [the constituency] […] they won't get [that coverage] in the nationals.

Here, reflecting Negrine's (2005) findings, the editor acknowledges three reasons why he believes TDs perceive local media to be important: that media coverage at local level is inextricably linked to the desire to be re-elected, that the local media offers a channel through which TDs can make sense of the link between their position as a national legislator and a defender of the interests of a particular constituency, and that TDs simply will not get the volume or style of coverage in the national media that the local media generally affords them.

TDs and PAs were asked whether local media or national media were more important to them. Three of the seven TDs interviewed expressed the view that local media were more important while the rest stressed the need for a balance between targeting local and national media. The priority for TDs appeared to depend on the stage that they had reached in their careers. The research suggests that TDs, in their public relations with the local and national media, are targeting two distinctive audiences. At a local level the target audience is the electorate, and the purpose of political communication is to encourage the electorate to vote for that TD at the next election. At a national level the audience is often the party hierarchy: for a backbencher the message to articulate is: 'promote me'. The national audience can also be what can loosely be described as 'opinion leaders'; this would include, for example, newspaper columnists. The aim for TDs is to establish themselves as people capable of being significant players on the national scene, as the following observation from a TD suggests:

> [The] national media would be very, very important so for a young TD aspiring at some stage to holding ministerial office, commanding high

ground on the national level is very, very important because it's not just sufficient to be well known in your own constituency, you have to try to broaden that [...] you're demonstrating a capacity to be able to command high ground on a particular subject which means you're noticed – you're noticed by higher civil servants, you're noticed by editors of the paper, you're noticed by people in politics so there's a wide range of things [...] I'm connecting the national media with promotion, with ambition, with higher office and all that kind of thing.

In contrast, all of the PAs expressed the view that local media coverage is more important than national media coverage for their TD. As one PA observed:

For a TD, I think it's without doubt the local media and the local stories, the stories which are specific to certain areas will go down better than trying to put out the message of a national issue which is probably at times too wide.

This finding may reflect the fact that political party press offices usually handle national media while PAs usually liaise with local media. The PAs interviewed stated that between 70% and 90% of their media attention is focused on local press releases. A majority of the TDs interviewed indicated that their offices spend a significant amount of their media time (75%) on local press releases each week, with an average of four press releases issued weekly, the vast bulk of which targets local media.

Local radio, local newspapers and social media

Under the Broadcasting and Wireless Telegraphy Act 1988 radio stations are required to dedicate a minimum of 20% of their output to news and current affairs. This creates a demand for news that has served politicians very well at local level. Local radio has been heavily targeted by the bigger political parties from the 1997 general election onwards (Holmes, 1999, 46; Collins, 2004, 207). Both media and political interviewees were asked which was more important for TDs in coverage terms: local radio or local newspapers. Of the TDs who addressed this question, three felt radio was more important, one asserted that local radio and local newspapers were of equal importance and one felt that print media was more important. The TDs who argued that radio was more important cited a number of reasons, including that it is easier to get one's message across on the radio; the resonance of a sound bite; and the fact that unlike most newspapers, one could listen to the radio for free:

> What I notice about local radio [...] is that you get your name on it by issuing a statement, but the one thing that I have noticed consistently is there are a number of people that would say 'I heard you on local radio this morning' – your voice is coming across and that is the chord with local radio.

Print media professionals seemed aware that they have fallen down the list of political public relations priorities for TDs since the introduction of local radio. As one newspaper editor observed:

> Local radio is their [TDs'] first port of call now. If there's a big announcement, they're straight onto the local radio and sometimes if it's late on, close to printing time, you could end up recording what they're saying on local radio and using that [...] We know we're down the line in terms of priority. The priority now is local radio.

The sole TD who believed print media was more important provided the following rationale:

> [When] something is written down it can be read a second and third time and can be read by a number of members of the family who didn't hear the radio so the paper then has this advantage [...] I suppose for the elderly population, certainly, the attachment to the [local newspaper] and to local media is very strong – they tend to read the whole paper.

For many TDs, particularly those who have a concern about political bias in the local media, radio is viewed as a fairer medium. As one TD put it:

> I think you can represent yourself possibly better on local radio. At least what you say is what you mean whereas print media can change a story and they don't often represent exactly what you mean.

As the above illustrates, there is a concern that politicians are misrepresented in the print media; this is somewhat unusual given that the majority of political interviewees conceded that it is relatively easy to have press releases reproduced verbatim in newspapers. It appears that politicians feel they have more control when they are speaking live on air; however, some asserted that with radio the stakes can be higher compared to the print media. Political interviewees observed that an interviewer can sometimes catch out an interviewee and it is not always clear who will be brought on to counter the politician's views:

> TD: [The public] tend to be pass-remarkable about the performance of somebody on local radio. In other words, if you're on it, you're up there and people do scrutinise what you say and how you perform. I think people are more critical of your performance on local radio. For instance, they'd see something in the local paper and they read it and they don't seem to care as much about it, so from that point of view, the local radio is more important.

> PA: With the content for radio, you've got to make sure that you're way more accurate [because] you're going on straight away and it's going out to a wider public who can ring in and can ring a forum to publicly disagree with you so you have to be more careful with radio. Local radio is far more important than any of the others [...] That is what we would feel – certainly what [the TD] would feel.

To measure the importance of local newspapers and local radio in an era where social media is growing in importance as a political communication tool (Wall and Sudulich, 2011), in 2012 TDs from the same case-study constituencies were asked to rank, in order of importance, a series of political communication tools including local radio, local newspapers, leaflet/information drop, Facebook, Twitter, and others (to be specified by the interviewee). The results confirmed the pre-eminent place of local radio in TDs' public relations priorities. Five out of seven TDs identified local radio as the most important tool for ongoing political communication with constituents while the remaining two TDs placed it in second or third place. Local newspapers continue to be considered very important for a majority of TDs (four of seven placed local newspapers in first or second place in order of priority).

While Twitter was at the bottom of the list of priorities for the majority of TDs, three out of seven TDs placed Facebook ahead of local newspapers in order of priority. All three stated that local newspapers were politically biased. While social media undoubtedly provides a useful, unmediated political communication tool for TDs, questions remain as to the extent to which social media is a valuable tool for communicating with constituents, whether it provides too great a platform for opponents to publicly attack TDs, and whether the amount of time that social media can take up is merited in terms of the political support it yields (Lilleker and Koc-Michalska, 2013; Jackson and Lilleker, 2011).

The relationships between TDs and local media

It is important to recognise the 'local' nature of the milieu that local journalists and national politicians from the same locality inhabit. Both journalist and politician are part of the local community and this produces particular outcomes. Neveu (2002, 53–54) argues that local journalism cannot be considered a variant of national journalism; rather it occupies a distinctive territory and is ruled by a relationship of dependence between journalists and their sources. Such journalist–source relationships produce 'comprehensive', often friendly coverage of events, as long as this does not trigger the opposition of powerful challengers in the local arena. Murphy (1976) argues that politicians and local journalists tend to have a relationship of trust as local journalists frequently rely on politicians, among others in the community, to act as official sources. Similarly, Franklin (2004, 157) states:

> Locally, politicians and journalists seem to be locked in an exchange relationship in which 'insider' political information is traded for access to editorial space to disseminate messages congenial to a particular candidate, policy or ideology [...] Each side gains from this exchange and has a clear interest in sustaining collaborative rather than conflictual ways of working. In this sense, news becomes a negotiated outcome of this carefully packaged exchange between politicians and journalists.

The interviews suggest that, in all cases the editors were very well acquainted with the TDs in the local area, often knowing them for many years. Many TDs work hard to cultivate a positive relationship with local media personnel for two reasons: firstly, they hope that this will help to increase their access to favourable coverage; secondly, having a good relationship with senior local media personnel allows politicians to telephone them when they are unhappy with their levels of coverage and ask that perceived imbalances in coverage are addressed. As one TD put it:

> I would have placed a lot of emphasis on having a good personal relationship with the key journalists. I think that they need to know you as an individual; they need to trust you [...] and I think that you're also more likely to get favourable coverage if you're on a one-to-one with them.

Cultivating a positive relationship with local media can benefit a TD in a number of ways. The interviews indicate that when a positive relationship is in place, the TD can persuade a journalist to carry his/her statement. It also suggests that politicians can use the media to discredit an opponent.

One editor stated that half the time, TDs telephone the media organisation with news that could discredit an opponent and the other half of the time, TDs call to promote their own statements. The interviews also indicate that TDs do not hesitate to engage directly with media personnel if they feel they are being treated unfairly. They believe that they must do so given what they perceive to be the media's significant power at local level. The media generally react positively to such reprimands. Neveu (2002) highlights the pressure that local journalists are under not to antagonise powerful local voices upon whom they are highly dependent for news. The following statements are revealing in this context:

> TD: If there's a problem from time to time I do call up the local editor or the local radio station [...] I believe that it's important to address the problem if there is one rather than actually being in confrontation with the local distributors of information.

> Newspaper editor: [We] do tend to even put [slightly irrelevant press releases] in boiled down versions because if you don't the phone starts to ring and this kind of 'oh, we're not getting coverage, he's getting more coverage' begins.

Thus the personal relationships that TDs cultivate with local media personnel provide them with a mechanism to exert a certain pressure to ensure that their press releases are carried by the local newspaper/local radio station. This is a huge advantage where TDs wish to agenda-set – that is, seek to prioritise some stories while de-prioritising others. Bennett (1996) has found that the routine practices inherent within journalism allow skilful political communicators to set the agenda.

The importance of press releases

The primary tool in a TD's agenda-setting arsenal is the press release. In 2005, TDs were given the option of appointing a Parliamentary Assistant (PA); this allowed them to employ a staff member with competence in a number of areas including media and public relations. This important development facilitated the professionalisation of public relations activities by TDs within their own offices and resulted in a steady stream of press releases flowing from TDs' offices to local media. As already noted, the PAs interviewed indicated that they spend 70%–90% of their media time working on local press releases, issuing an average of four each week.

Press releases are a highly effective mechanism for attaining local media coverage. In an analysis of one local newspaper in a constituency during the 1992 UK general election, Franklin (1994, 166–72) found that 29 press releases from the Labour Party generated 28 stories in that local newspaper. The newspaper published at least one story based on a press release every day of the campaign. Journalistic revision of these press releases was minimal – in fact one-third were reproduced verbatim and one-fifth were published with modest revisions with between 50% and 75% of the original text remaining. As McNair (2003, 131) notes, this dependence on press releases is a huge asset for politicians as it constitutes free advertising but disguises their authorship role, instead placing editorial responsibility on the journalist. Franklin (2006, 13) suggests that local journalists are 'no longer engaged in critical or investigative journalism'; rather they are on low pay, over-worked, and reliant on tools such as press releases for news. Within this context, political communications experts have identified the most effective way of attaining favourable political coverage in the local press: statements are written in a journalistic style and constructed as a news story incorporating the political party's spin on the subject. This allows newspapers to print the press releases verbatim under the by-line 'local journalist' or 'political correspondent' (Franklin, 2004, 156).

The timing of press releases differs depending on whether the TD is a member of a government or opposition party. Government party TDs have privileged access to news of departmental announcements in advance and can therefore always be first in with the news. While this gives them a huge advantage with the media, as they are able to supply bona fide fresh news, in constituencies where there are a number of government party TDs this can lead to a race to be first on the radio with fresh news. As one radio head of news observed:

> [Government party TDs'] offices tend to be very competitive because they will obviously have contact with the various government departments and particularly when there's a cabinet meeting on a Tuesday or Wednesday in the afternoon it's often 20 seconds between the two [press releases arriving].

Generally, the impetus for other political press releases tends to derive from issues highlighted by constituents. In the case of the opposition parties, the press offices frequently circulate standard press releases that can be adapted to fit into the context of the relevant constituency. Press officers were asked whether they issued generic press releases to their Oireachtas members and election candidates and, if yes, how often. The following statement was among the responses:

> We do that at least once or twice a week. We'd send them to our candidates in each of the constituencies. It's generally a national issue though that can be adapted for local use.

However, the success of this approach is questionable, as outlined by Negrine (2005) and as illustrated by the quotation below from a radio head of news:

> We get quite a lot of generic press releases [...] as in they are personalised from the local TDs but they are basically a press release that fits all and then they just stick the name of the local TD on to it. And they get kind of fairly short shrift from us now really because they're very recognisable, very often they come from the political party.

In the case of Fianna Fáil, in early 2007 the press office preferred to handle or at the very least be made aware of the majority of statements that TDs were issuing to local media. At that time, the Fianna Fáil press office provided a press officer to deal with all local public relations for Oireachtas members; an approach that the Fine Gael and Labour parties did not adopt during that period. However, the success of the Fianna Fáil approach is questionable as several media interviewees referred to the failure of this strategy by claiming that when press releases were authored by someone who was not 'on the ground' in the constituency, it showed, and these press releases were of far less value than those that emanated from the TD's local office.

Most press releases issued by TDs to their local media make it into the paper or on to the radio news as fillers. Most are not ranked very highly but they serve a useful purpose: for radio they are a useful fallback when nothing more newsworthy is happening in the locality and, for newspapers, they help to fill pages where necessary. The low level of importance attributed to press releases by media personnel explains why, in the print media at least, press releases can make it into newspapers without being altered – editors have no interest in wasting a journalist's time on such tasks. This may also explain why political press releases are not always given the prominence that politicians feel they merit within a newspaper. Asked what happens when a political press release comes in, the following were among the responses given by media personnel:

> Radio head of news: We look at it. We grade it in terms of importance [...] Obviously we want to achieve maximum listenership. We say 'is this

very important to somebody?' [...] We'd often leave it in the in-tray if we had a good news day [...] I mean, political stories, most of them are 'in case of emergencies break glass' [...] to be honest, that's what they are.

Newspaper editor: First of all [...] I would download them, I would read them, I would decide where they would go in the paper, you know, depending on the nature of what it was. If it was something that I would consider very newsworthy I would allocate it to a specific page, if it was an ordinary kind of thing [...] I would put into a general news file – they may get in, they may not get in.

Thus, TDs can have a high level of control over the content of their media coverage as statements are formatted in a way that requires little journalistic intervention. This gives them the capacity to agenda-set as their statements are generally carried – despite the low level of importance the media attaches to them.

Perceptions of political bias

Semetko (1996) argues that 'objectivity' and 'balance' demand contradictory practices: to be objective is to let news values determine the coverage an event receives; to be balanced is to give equal coverage to all parties in an event. This is a struggle that journalists must contend with, particularly in the local radio sector in Ireland, which is required by law to be impartial, fair, and unbiased. Bennett (1996) is critical of some calls for journalists to be less biased, because, he claims, the bias in question is usually 'in the eye of the beholder'. Schmitt et al. (2004) approach bias from the point of view of the reader, concluding that partisans use a process of selective categorisation in their approach to the media and that this results in their conclusion that the media is biased against their partisan point of view.

Local radio in Ireland is expressly prohibited from engaging in political bias under the Broadcasting and Wireless Telegraphy Act 1988 (as amended by the Broadcasting Act 2009), which created regulated independent local radio in Ireland. However, the vast majority of political interviewees felt that the local media was politically biased in a way that diminished coverage of their statements. There were contradictory elements to this assertion, as bias was asserted by TDs from different party backgrounds in the same constituencies and also, when asked what factors determined coverage, no politician cited bias as a factor. The following replies were among those given by TDs when asked if they believed the local media exhibited political bias:

TD 1: It is [biased], without doubt. That's why there's so many PR people in place – to spin the message and to get your own share of the airwaves and the print media.

TD 2: [There] are some people in the media who just don't like Fianna Fáil [...] and that's their prerogative.

TD 3: [I] might have very strong views about for example, [a local paper] who [sic] would be [...] very anti my party even though we'd be the dominant party in the country. They would have an ethos going back the other way and they're being challenged now and I can get my point across in other media outlets so I don't have to really depend upon them. Now they have the biggest circulation but they don't dominate and control like they used to.

As is evident in the responses, Fianna Fáil TDs felt particularly aggrieved in 2007. However, when asked to clarify whether they felt the bias was anti-Fianna Fáil in a broad context or whether they felt that they were given a harder time than their Fianna Fáil colleagues, one TD admitted that he felt the bias was more geographical than political (i.e. press releases relevant to an area where a newspaper did not have a significant readership might be ignored) and another TD felt that bias was directed towards individual politicians, rather than political parties:

It's got to do with the person, I think. Some of them [...] have no difficulty coming out and being very supportive to one [fellow Fianna Fáil] TD in our area.

However, Fianna Fáil politicians were not alone in feeling that the media was biased against them as the following response from an editor demonstrates:

[At] the last election [2002] [one opposition political party] threatened to pull their advertising, their general election coverage, because they felt that some of them were getting a raw deal.

The Parliamentary Assistants also tended to link certain papers with certain political parties:

PA (Fianna Fáil): I would find the [local paper] would be traditionally Fine Gael orientated but it's actually beginning to push a Green agenda as well and very much a Green agenda and if it's not pushing those agendas, editorially, it's certainly pushing an anti-Fianna Fáil agenda.

One PA described how this perceived bias manifests itself, outlining a typical scenario where a press release was sent into the print media and followed up with telephone calls to promote it as important but, rather than being given the prominence the PA felt the statement deserved, it would appear buried on a page with advertisements of planning notices and require real effort to find. However, as already mentioned, from the media perspective, it may be the low level of newsworthiness in a political press release that results in its relegation to a less prominent location in the newspaper and the sole reason for its inclusion may be because of the personal relationship between the TD and editor.

Media professionals were also asked for their views on whether political bias was present in the local media. The majority expressed the view that bias was not one of the factors that prevented a TD from getting coverage but that TDs did not understand this. They pointed instead to constraints such as news values and the newspaper's size. Interestingly, while five out of six PAs believed that the media were politically biased, when asked to identify what factors determine coverage they often echoed the media professionals' views, citing space constraints, having local content, having controversial content, when the TD last appeared in the paper, and timing. When asked if the local media were biased, media personnel responded as follows:

> Newspaper editor: I don't know; it seems to me that to succeed in politics, you basically have to have a very high paranoia and then politics makes you more paranoid [...] they study the media closely, and Fianna Fáil are convinced that I'm a Blueshirt, the Blueshirts are convinced that I'm Fianna Fáil or Green or whatever, they all have their pathetic little theories [...] It's about stories [...] And that's the mistake that the poor old TDs can't quite understand; they think that we're there to give everyone a fair crack of the whip; we're not.

> Radio head of news: [We're] driven by news values and in terms of the talk programmes [...] we're driven to some extent by people who are going to be interesting and are going to say stuff that's interesting but we're always reviewing and balancing and, you know, it's swings and roundabouts.

> Radio head of news: We very much strive for balance [...] it's different to a newspaper – a newspaper can take a political stand but a radio station has a licence from the government to provide information and we have to, I take that very seriously and any suggestion of political bias I would take very seriously because I try to be fair.

While radio heads of news pointed to the legal requirement for balanced coverage, the three newspaper editors interviewed gave varied responses. One stated that he tried to be balanced and fair; the other two stated that newsworthiness won out over the need to be balanced. One editor pointed to the fact that newspapers did not have the same obligations as radio to be balanced:

> I don't believe a newspaper is there – we're not a public broadcaster, we aren't – thank God – funded by the taxpayer so we've no obligations. If I decided tomorrow that I wanted to pursue a Sinn Féin policy, I would. That's totally my prerogative and the only consideration is whether the readership would get annoyed and leave in droves so, no, if anybody gave us five good stories I would use them. I'm interested in news stories I don't care about their provenance.

The point was also made that it was difficult to reconcile being politically balanced when some TDs were excellent and proactive sources of news while others were not:

> Radio head of news: [People] who give you particularly good hard information and hard stories and have something to say about it, over the period or a political and a broadcasting year, you'd have to say that if they're creating news [is it fair to limit their coverage?] because to balance it artificially would actually be artificial.

In general, sending in a large number of press releases appears to be a successful strategy:

> Newspaper editor: [There] is no doubt that the TDs who put out a regular stream of press releases get much more publicity than those who don't. It's indicative of a mindset you know [...] People who put out press releases, it's indicative of somebody who wants to reach out to the community and naturally that kind of a personality is going to get more coverage than a hermit.

Local news is the currency of local media, a point emphasised by Franklin (2004), Negrine (2005), and Chantler and Harris (1997). All the media interviewees emphasised that the more local a story is, the more likely it is to be printed or broadcast for a variety of reasons, including the role of national media in reporting national news, the news value of local news for local media, and the potential legal and financial risks associated with reporting more controversial issues:

Newspaper editor: You see sometimes we would get a press release on maybe the Taoiseach says something in such-and-such a place – say for example the Northern thing was going on – we would get press releases from local TDs or Oireachtas members welcoming the announcement of what happened in the North and complimenting Bertie [Ahern] and, to me, for a local paper, that isn't of great news value because that has been paraded in all the [national] papers.

Newspaper editor: Our role is to celebrate the community, to hold a mirror up to it, to inform people about what's going on, and the local panto is just as important and just as likely to move and excite people as the knowledge that a councillor has taken £100. Both belong in the newspaper but, you know, that's what the national newspapers are there for – they have the resources, they have the lawyers to protect them and they have the funds to pay out the outrageous libel amounts that they have to pay out. We don't.

Conclusion

It is clear that, even with the advent of social media, local media, particularly local radio, remain at the heart of the local political communication process. TDs view a strong presence in the constituency as a vital component of electoral success and the local media offer an excellent conduit through which TDs can publicise their views on a range of topical issues affecting the constituency and highlight their work at constituency level and at national level when it is relevant to the constituency. Local media constitute a subtle and somewhat covert publicity tool for TDs who, by and large, are able to have their press statements reproduced verbatim in local newspapers. The factors that combine to facilitate this process are: the low level of importance generally attached by media personnel to political press releases and their concomitant willingness to use them as 'fillers', and the politician's ability to exploit their knowledge of newsrooms by taking into account factors such as local content, time, newsworthiness, and formatting. Politicians demonstrate the value they place on local media by sending in a steady stream of press releases each week. This practice has become consistent and professionalised since the appointment of Parliamentary Assistants in 2005, the majority of whom dedicate a notable proportion of their time each week to public relations with the local media. These appointments, therefore, constitute a key juncture in contemporary political communication at constituency level.

The interviews that I have conducted suggest that politicians are highly attuned to their media coverage and while they recognise the importance of news values, many are convinced that political bias exists in the local print media and that this bias diminishes their coverage. Such sensitivities persist despite there being scant evidence that political press releases are altered by local journalists. Despite the pitfalls of local radio (a difficult interview or an unknown opponent), TDs feel more in control in such immediate media encounters. The importance of local media from the point of view of TDs and political parties generally points to a pressing need to conduct more research into its practices and culture. Transparency in respect of practices and procedures will enhance democracy by facilitating a more informed electorate that is aware that there is often more to what appears in the local newspaper or on local radio than meets the eye or ear.

References

Bennett, W.L. (1996) *News: the politics of illusion*, Washington: Longman.

Blumler, J.G. and Kavanagh, D. (1999) 'The third age of political communication: influences and features' in *Political Communication*, 16: 209–30.

Brandenburg, H. (2005) 'Political bias in the Irish media: a quantitative study of campaign coverage during the 2002 general election' in *Irish Political Studies*, 20(3): 297–322.

Chantler, P. and Harris, S. (1997) *Local radio journalism*, Oxford: Focal Press.

Collins, S. (2004) 'The parliamentary lobby system' in Garvin, T., Manning, M. and Sinnott, R. (eds) *Dissecting Irish politics: essays in honour of Brian Farrell*, Dublin: UCD Press.

Franklin, B. (1994) *Packaging politics: political communications in Britain's media democracy*, London: Arnold.

Franklin, B. (2004) *Packaging politics: political communications in Britain's media democracy* (2nd edn), London: Arnold.

Franklin, B. (2006) 'Attacking the devil? Local journalists and local newspapers in the UK' in Franklin, B. (ed.), *Local journalism and local media: making the local news*, London: Routledge.

Holmes, M. (1999) 'Organisational preparation and political marketing' in Mitchell, P. and Marsh, M. (eds), *How Ireland voted 1997*, Oxford: PSAI Press/Westview.

Jackson, J. and Lilleker, D. (2011) 'Microblogging, constituency service and impression management: UK MPs and the use of Twitter' in *The Journal of Legislative Studies*, 17(1): 86–105.

JNLR (2012/13). Figures available at <http://www.bai.ie>

JNRS (2011/12). Figures available at <http://www.jnrs.ie>

Lilleker, D. and Koc-Michalska, K. (2013) 'Online political communication strategies: MEPs, e-representation and self-representation' in *Journal of Information Technology & Politics*, 10(2): 190–207.

McNair, B. (2003) *An introduction to political communication*, London: Routledge.

Murphy, D. (1976) *The silent watchdog: the press in local politics*, London: Constable.

Negrine, R. (2005) 'The role of the UK local press in the local constituency campaign' in *Journalism Studies*, 6(1): 103–15.

Neveu, E. (2002) 'The local press and farmers' protests in Brittany: proximity and distance in the local newspaper coverage of a social movement' in *Journalism Studies*, 3(1): 53–67.

Schmitt, K.M., Gunther, A.C. and Leibhart, J.L. (2004) 'Why partisans see mass media as biased' in *Communication Research*, 31(6): 623–41.

Semetko, H.A. (1996) cited in Street, J. (2001) *Mass media, politics and democracy*, Basingstoke: Palgrave.

Wall, M. and Sudulich, M.L. 'Internet explorers: the online campaign' in Gallagher, M. and Marsh, M. (eds) (2011), *How Ireland voted 2011: the full story of Ireland's earthquake election*, Dublin: Palgrave MacMillan.

Ireland has a long tradition of prisoners who go on to have successful political careers.

Since the foundation of the state, security threats have frequently provided a backdrop to Irish elections.

CHAPTER FOUR

Political communication and the 'loony left'

Bryce Evans

For small political groups the challenge of getting their message across is essentially one of resources and imagination. This chapter outlines the challenges and successes of one such small political grouping, the United Left Alliance (ULA), in doing just that. During the 2011 general election, a coalition of left-wing candidates contested seats under the ULA banner. The Alliance comprised members of the Socialist Party, the People Before Profit Alliance, a number of independents, and members of smaller activist groups such as the Tipperary Unemployed Workers' Movement. Often disparaged by hostile media elements as the 'loony left', the ULA put forward 20 candidates in that election and achieved relative success: five of its candidates were elected. But what is the nature of this new political movement and its relationship with the Irish media, and how well did it communicate its message during the 2011 general election?

Beginnings

The ULA was formed in November 2010 prior to the widely anticipated announcement of a general election by the outgoing Fianna Fáil government. Following the Green Party's withdrawal from power, which signalled the final mobilisation towards the ballot box, the Alliance was announced at a press conference held in Dublin's Gresham Hotel. The ULA's website gave its raison d'être:

> [We are] opposed to the government's bailouts and the slash and burn policies which are only making the crisis worse. In the general election we aim to provide a real alternative to the establishment parties as well as Labour and Sinn Féin, who [...] refuse to rule out coalition with right wing parties. (ULA homepage)

The movement was thus founded as an umbrella group for those who viewed austerity measures as an unjustified attack on working people. Yet from the outset – as the above excerpt makes clear – the Alliance had one eye trained on the likely coalition that would follow the expected mauling of Fianna Fáil and the Green Party at the polls. The ULA, which viewed the Labour Party as little better than a quisling to socialism, had little doubt that Labour would plump for shared power with Fine Gael once the votes were counted. The longer-term goal was clearly to occupy at least some of the opposition political space vacated by Labour.

Shortly after its announced intention to run candidates, RTÉ's *Six-One News* programme carried an item that focused on the two men viewed as the movement's leading lights. Then-MEP Joe Higgins of the Socialist Party, the one real political heavyweight of the ULA, stated that working-class people should not be expected to pay for the mistakes of the wealthy; Richard Boyd Barrett, then a councillor representing People Before Profit, told viewers that the ULA favoured the heavy taxation of the wealthy as an alternative to the austerity agenda (RTÉ, 2010).

The harmony that was expressed in the initial bout of coverage for the ULA across the visual, print and auditory media masked the difficult task that the very foundation of the Alliance had posed. The ULA aimed to appeal to voters as a broad anti-capitalist movement capable of attracting and representing a broad range of people. Yet the two main parties behind the Alliance – the Socialist Party and the Socialist Workers Party – had a history of each doing their own thing. This is perhaps surprising, given that both parties have historically only achieved a tiny share of the vote in Ireland and that the ideology underpinning both is Marxist, but, to paraphrase the writer Brendan Behan's famous quip, the first item on the agenda for the Irish left has (all too often) been the 'split'.

It was the Socialist Workers Party that signalled a more ready willingness to embrace 'united front' leftist politics in response to the gravity of the state's financial crisis. In 2009 it ran a number of candidates in the local elections under the People Before Profit (PBP) banner. Although represented by some sections of the online media as a 'front' for the Socialist Workers Party, People Before Profit was founded as a non-sectarian leftist venture, and some of its candidates were not Socialist Workers Party members (politics.ie). The Socialist Party, which emerged from the old Militant Labour, was initially slower to engage in this style of politics, but signalled its accommodation with 'Alliance' politics in time for the 2011 general election. After their election in 2011, the five ULA TDs – Joe Higgins, Clare

Daly, Richard Boyd Barrett, Joan Collins, and Seamus Healy – formed its public face through exposure in live parliamentary debates and television magazine programmes.

In terms of the Alliance's birth, a less-publicised force behind the ULA was university lecturer Kieran Allen. With an impressive output of sociological books and articles and a media profile of his own, Allen has been instrumental in orienting the Irish left away from not only home-grown neo-liberal economic policies but also any reversion to flag-waving Irish socialism with its 'neo-colonial' focus on British perfidy. In the long run-up to the 2011 general election Allen was a leading light in the moves to achieve a long-desired electoral compact between the Socialist Workers Party, the Socialist Party, and other Irish socialists.

While it is important, then, to take account of the occasional antagonism between its two dominant political components, it is also evident that facing into the 2011 election the Alliance had achieved a historic unity of policy. And one common attitude that united these potentially disparate leftists was a resoundingly dim view of the mainstream Irish media. With the growth of the ULA in late 2010 it seemed that Ireland's left had overcome at least some of its reservations about the ability of liberal parliamentary democracy, as opposed to popular action, to effect meaningful social change. If this was the case, reservations about the concentration of Irish media ownership were not similarly jettisoned. With its membership commonly informed by a materialist conception of politics and society, the saturation in ownership of Ireland's mass media by entrepreneurs such as Tony O'Reilly and Denis O'Brien did not signal an easy ride for the ULA in terms of electoral coverage. As the ULA prepared for the election, its attitude towards the traditional media was characterised by the long-held belief that it would receive no favours from either the privately owned press, with groups such as Independent News and Media historically inclined against socialism, and the national broadcaster, RTÉ, regarded as possessing a thinly veiled catholic–nationalist agenda.

On the other hand, the Irish left faced the communications challenges of election 2011 with quiet confidence on two fronts. First, there was the potential of 'new media' techniques. Barack Obama's 2008 US presidential election was greeted with cynicism by most on the Irish radical left, who pointed to the vacuity of Obama's message of 'Hope'. But with Obama's victory famously appealing to 18–29-year-olds through internet communication, the democratic potential of new media was obvious. At the same time that Obama's online communications strategy was building, the Irish left was using similar techniques to help defeat the Lisbon Treaty referendum of 2008. While the 'yes' campaign struggled to find a common voice, figures on the Irish left, such as Richard Boyd Barrett, Joe Higgins, Hugh Lewis, Mick Barry, Kieran Allen, and Peadar O'Grady, explained their opposition to the treaty in simple terms via short YouTube clips and the popular voteno.ie website.

Secondly, owing to the evident gravity of the state's financial crisis, the men and women who would go on to establish the ULA had enjoyed increased exposure from the established media. The galvanising effect of common left-wing opposition to Lisbon I in 2008 should not be understated. As an *Irish Times* journalist put it after the 2012 referendum on the EU fiscal treaty, 'to groups on the far left, EU referendums are the political equivalent of a lottery bonanza or a licence to print money' (de Bréadún, 2012). Such was the case with the Lisbon treaty referenda of 2008 and 2009, when the proto-ULA benefited in terms of access to the news media, using this as a platform to tap in to the growing working-class alienation across Ireland and establish itself as a coherent political force for 2011.

During the 2011 election campaign, the ULA's political communications were managed by a four-person media sub-committee of the Alliance's national steering committee. The media sub-committee was composed of unpaid activists Michael O'Brien, Sinéad Kennedy, Eddie Conlon, and Cian Prendiville. Their brief for the campaign reflected the internal challenges and opportunities listed above. The media sub-committee was charged with working out a succession of ULA-themed press events during the campaign focusing on various policy areas around which there was agreement among the ULA components; sharing information regarding press events being organised by the individual components so that there was not a clash; the maintenance of the ULA website, Facebook and Twitter accounts during the election; lobbying editors for coverage; and the 'sharing out' of high profile media opportunities (O'Brien, 2012).

New media and the election

For all the hype about the new media, delegates at pre-election ULA meetings stressed that old fashioned doorstep communications would prove the most fruitful. In the 2009 local elections the Socialist Party had won four seats, the same number as in the previous local elections; but as an example of a new type of socialist electoral alliance, People Before Profit had performed particularly well, winning five seats – a marked improvement on the 2004 county and town council elections. This strong showing in 2009 vindicated the Alliance approach, which initially had its many detractors and doubters within the Irish left. The internal consensus was that this relative success had primarily been achieved through many hours of honest hard work pounding the streets and knocking on doors. At planning meetings for the 2011 election, some ULA candidates professed to having worn the soles of their shoes thin in canvassing for the local elections, an effort that would have to be redoubled if the left was to make an impact in the general election. If there was something of the 'pious protestor' identified by acerbic journalist John Drennan (2011) in these claims, they also reflected the consensus within the movement that as a 'new' option on the ballot paper, ULA candidates needed to put in the hard work if they were to shake up voters' habits.

This did not rule out the use of new media. The ULA launched a new website complete with links to video clips of its candidates, events, and campaigns. Each of its 20 candidates used Twitter, Facebook, and YouTube to communicate with voters, and some communicated with constituents through online live chats and blogs. While 'entryism', the bogey associated with the radical left through which neutral organisations are infiltrated by secret agitators, was not encouraged as a communications tactic by the ULA, message boards on internet political fora such as politics.ie were used by supporters to drum up support for socialist candidates. The ULA received positive coverage on left-leaning but non-partisan political websites such as politico.ie and indymedia.ie. Candidates undertook several innovative attempts at online publicity. Socialist Party Cork North Central candidate Mick Barry uploaded dozens of short YouTube clips in which, reclining in his study, he gave his opinions on everything from the health service to the minimum wage. But arguably the most effective effort in this vein was from colourful People Before Profit Dublin Mid-West candidate Gino Kenny with his idiosyncratic re-mix of the Dexys Midnight Runners' 1980 hit 'Geno', a campaign song championed by the influential Maman Poulet political blog (Poulet, 2011).

The ULA did not use consumer marketing based on data about voters, but did canvas using their own databases, based on the electoral register and previous doorstep conversations. Supporters were regularly contacted throughout the campaign via personalised email and text messages. While the ULA was dismissive of compiling consumer data, the Labour Party embraced this tactic, spending €120,000 on market research alone during the campaign. At the same time, the ULA's conviction that new media and marketing techniques would take a second seat to tried and trusted electioneering was borne of a stoic awareness of the economies of scale at work in election 2011. As an outsider in the 2011 campaign the ULA could not avail itself of the large public funding, for example the first preference vote payment, which established parties use to part-finance their publicity campaigns (Sipo, 2011a). Moreover, as its website made clear, 'the ULA does not accept donations from big business' (ULA homepage). This refusal to accept large corporate donations meant that the ULA was at a marked disadvantage in getting its message across. The campaign war chest, consisting of small donations from raffles, quizzes, auctions, and fundraising gigs in the backrooms of pubs, was relatively empty. During the 2011 campaign a stock joke among activists lamented the fact that, unlike a rival left-of-centre party, the ULA did not have the booty from a bank robbery to use in promoting itself: a reference to the alleged involvement of the IRA in the Northern Bank robbery of 2004.

In coming to terms with these economies of scale, the record of electoral expenses published by the Standards in Public Office Commission is telling. Collectively, People Before Profit and the Socialist Party spent €132,881 on election 2011. This compares with €3 million spent by Fine Gael and around €2 million by the Labour Party (Sipo, 2011a). When these figures are broken down, the challenges of political communication for the ULA become clearer. Statistics for the 2011 election reveal that the Socialist Party spent just €653 on national publicity and the People Before Profit Alliance just €848: collectively, the two main parties behind the ULA spent a mere €1,500 on national publicity during the campaign (Sipo, 2011b). When compared with the parties that went on to form the coalition government, this figure demonstrates the paucity of resources apportioned to national publicity by the ULA. Out of all their election expenses, Ireland's main parties spent the lion's share on national publicity. The Labour Party, which spent around €2 million overall, allotted €800,000 to national publicity (roughly 40% of expenditure); Fine Gael spent €2 million on national publicity (roughly 66% of its full expenditure). In contrast, as a new-born political entity, the ULA spent just over 10% of its financial resources on building its national profile.

The amount listed above does not account for the ULA's total spend on media and communications. The Socialist Party, for instance, assigned €45,000 to individuals to spend on their own campaigns, the bulk of which was spent on communicating the ULA's message at local level. This reflects the ethos of the ULA, which rejects expenditure on marketing and remains cynical about political 'spin' techniques, confident that in time people will see through them. Shunning the use of communications experts, spin-doctors, and public relations consultants, the ULA instead pointed to its candidates' track record of local activism. With a number of its leading figures having been imprisoned during the 2003 anti-bin-tax campaign in Dublin, the Alliance based itself around a pedigree of grass-roots activity. In the 2011 election campaign the movement's commitment to 'bottom up' action was repeatedly stated. Following the dictum that 'all politics is local', the ULA focused on community action such as opposition to bus route cuts and the closure of public amenities that it viewed as the local manifestation of the EU–IMF austerity programme that it opposed. The track record of local causes emphasised in ULA election literature in the 2011 election (all of which was accessible online) included active opposition to mobile phone masts, water charges, the closure of public baths, and the closure of a children's hospital (irishelectionliterature). To underline their identification with workers, ULA candidates pledged that if elected they would only accept the average industrial wage – €35,486 – as their salary in place of the TD's salary of €90,000.

These campaign pledges were repeated across Twitter and Facebook. Nationally, only 57.4% of candidates engaged Twitter and 78.8% Facebook in their campaigns, with the ULA comparing favourably to other parties in this respect. A Dublin Business School study found that while Fine Gael and Labour candidates had the highest ratio of Twitter users to non-users, Socialist Party and People Before Profit candidates had the next highest Twitter usage. ULA candidates also outperformed all the other parties in their Facebook visibility (McMahon, 2011).

But if the ULA put a lot of energy into engaging with social media, its candidates were still at a competitive disadvantage in promoting their online profiles. Records show that neither the Socialist Party nor the People Before Profit Alliance spent any money on web advertising. By comparison, Sinn Féin spent €15,041 on Google and Facebook advertising alone while Fine Gael paid US internet consultants Election Mall €149,435 and spent €98,616 on Google and Facebook adverts (Sipo, 2011b). Once again, these figures illustrate the disparity in the economies of scale of political communication and highlight a shortcoming in the online visibility of the ULA during the 2011 election campaign. As a new political entity, the lack of recognition for the ULA as a national political option proved a major teething problem. While both of the two main parties behind the ULA uploaded dynamic online material such as the series of short video clips on the website people-beforeprofit.ie, due to timing and resources the ULA's national online profile remained underdeveloped.

The traditional media

When it came to televised news coverage, the ULA's most successful coup was an unplanned ambush of former Taoiseach Bertie Ahern. Ahern was in the middle of a gentle RTÉ interview outside Leinster House on his last day in Dáil Eireann in January 2011. As he reminisced on his 34 years in the house, People Before Profit candidate Joan Collins interjected. 'Have you no shame?' she asked Ahern in her thick Dublin brogue, referring to his stewardship of the economy. Ahern brushed off the intervention, claiming 'people come along here to try and get themselves on TV and radio.' If that was her goal, Collins was successful. The clip was repeated on that evening's radio and television news bulletins and soon became something of a cause célèbre for those who blamed Ahern for the country's financial crisis. Collins was later elected in Dublin South Central with 13% of the vote. Her ambush of Ahern was not the only unexpected television event of the 2011 campaign from which ULA candidates were able to benefit. Only days previously, Socialist Party leader Joe Higgins succeeded in getting underneath constituency rival Joan Burton's skin on TV3's nightly *Tonight with Vincent Browne* programme. While media commentators focused on Burton's shrill complaints of sexist treatment from Browne, the episode was grist to the Higgins campaign mill (TV3, 2011).

Both People Before Profit and the Socialist Party recorded party political broadcasts that were broadcast during the campaign, each of which aired before RTÉ's *Six-One News* programme. These recording costs accounted for well over half of the ULA's collective national publicity spend, with the filming of the People Before Profit broadcast costing €450 and the Socialist Party's broadcast €650 (Sipo, 2011b). This was hardly lavish expenditure, and the People Before Profit broadcast communicated a simple message via the simple format of speaking directly to the camera. It featured a typically dressed-down Richard Boyd Barrett on the banks of Dublin's Royal Canal, calling for a 'complete transformation in the way our society is run', and Joan Collins, who urged voters to protect public services by putting 'people before profit'. The broadcast ended with a list of People Before Profit candidates, mentioning that they were running as part of the United Left Alliance. The Socialist Party produced an election broadcast that conveyed a similar message, attacking 'casino capitalism' and advocating instead a major public investment programme. It featured Joe Higgins and Clare Daly canvassing door-to-door in Dublin and was narrated by Higgins. A more polished piece, it was interspersed with images of dole queues, ghost estates, Anglo-Irish

Bank, and street protests and was broadcast in both the English and Irish languages. Although the Socialist Party is less willing to be subsumed in any united front its broadcast made greater mention of the ULA, promising a 'new party for working people'.

When compared to the established parties, the money spent by the ULA in engaging print media was small. For example, excluding a full page advert in the *Northside People* for Dublin North candidate Clare Daly towards the end of the campaign, there was no major money spent on newspaper advertising or publicity. By comparison, the Labour Party spent €327,000 on advertising, Sinn Féin €22,000, Fianna Fáil €202,000, and Fine Gael €500,000 (Sipo, 2011b). While struggling against these odds, there were several sympathetic pieces in national newspapers in the run-up to polling day. Perhaps the most complimentary was a lengthy feature on Richard Boyd Barrett in the *Irish Daily Mail*, a newspaper for which Joe Higgins had once written a weekly column (O'Toole, 2011). Amongst other things, the article explored the tale of Boyd Barrett's relationship with his actress-mother Sinéad Cusack, a celebrity link he is keen to play down but which undoubtedly enhanced his human interest appeal. As well as the mainstream media, the ULA's cause was covered prominently in party newspapers *The Socialist* and *Socialist Worker*, which profiled candidates and outlined the ULA's programme.

As a natural consequence of being part of an alliance comprised of two distinct parties and a number of non-aligned members, ULA candidates had to engage individually with local radio and print media in the frequently vain hope of an interview or feature. Without the support of media professionals and national party office resources, this proved an uphill task. Occasionally there were breakthroughs for less prestigious candidates in the established media. On the eve of polling, for example, relatively unknown People Before Profit candidate for Dublin North Central John Lyons enjoyed a full page spread in the widely read free newspaper *Metro Herald* (2011) and polled fairly strongly the next day. Moreover, the ULA could count on publicity from at least one secretly sympathetic journalist within the *Irish Times* (private source).

Generally, however, there was a mounting belief that media coverage was inadequate. Media giants such as RTÉ, the *Irish Times*, and the *Irish Independent* lumped ULA candidates under 'Independents and Others' in party-by-party breakdowns and this, it was felt, diminished the ULA's status as a credible political force. The national media sub-committee addressed this lack of attention by organising a meeting with RTÉ's editorial staff in an effort to negotiate better coverage. According to Michael O'Brien, a member of the sub-committee:

> As the campaign wore on we found that the media were turning up to our press conferences in smaller numbers. To give an example, hardly anybody showed up to a particular conference which we had high hopes for around the issue of health where we obtained significant facts and figures from the Netherlands on the health insurance scheme that operated in that country and which was being promoted by Fine Gael. The research was done with the help of a Dutch Socialist MEP and a member of the European Parliament United Left staff came over for the event to share information which refuted claims being made by Fine Gael. At the press event also we had the ULA Carlow/Kilkenny candidate Conor Mac Liam. Conor's wife was the famous Susie Long who came to national attention when she went public about her fatally delayed diagnosis of colon cancer which arose because of cuts in the healthcare system. (O'Brien, 2012)

Much of this frustration stemmed from the ULA's failure to make it on to the ballot paper as a party in its own right because of the late timing of its formation. Nonetheless, in establishing visibility, the ULA – as a new political entity – certainly benefited from the unprecedentedly comprehensive coverage of the campaign across various media. If less established ULA candidates were not able to avail themselves of precious radio and television air time or national newspaper column inches, they were assured that their profiles were displayed on websites such as mycandidate.ie, Newstalk 106–108 FM's GE11 website, the RTÉ News election 2011 website, electionsireland.org, and irishpoliticians.com. Recent content analysis research conducted by Dublin City University has shown that the established media coverage of the election tended towards coverage of policy issues rather than the rather glib tendency to report the contest as a 'game' (O'Malley et al., 2012). As vocal opponents of national austerity measures (the biggest election issue) the ULA could be seen to have benefited from the print media's rejection of the 'game frame' and its representatives won air time on prime-time television programmes such as RTÉ's *Front Line*. On the other hand, the ULA's lack of Dáil representation before election 2011 meant that the anti-austerity voice in media discussion of policy often belonged to Sinn Féin and, to a lesser extent, the Labour Party.

As mentioned, most of the ULA's campaign money (held in separate party purses) was spent by individual candidates on the printing and distribution of leaflets and posters. In People Before Profit, the party coffers stretched to just one postal service leaflet per candidate; all other leaflets were circulated door-to-door, by hand. Campaign posters conformed to the usual type seen in Ireland around election time; significantly however, candidates were identified with the Socialist Party or People Before Profit and posters were not emblazoned with any 'United Left Alliance' logo or wording. Despite this recurrent lack of a ULA 'brand', it is clear that between them the ULA candidates spent proportionately more on posters than the established parties. As this expense took up the majority of ULA candidates' individual monetary allowances, there was a danger of the message being drowned out amidst the plethora of different posters adorning telegraph poles and lamp-posts. Again, economies of scale came into play. The established parties augmented candidates' individual posters with a number of 'national' posters advertising the party rather than the individual. Sinn Féin spent 32.5% of its national publicity expenditure on such posters, Fianna Fáil 30%, Fine Gael 15%, and Labour 13.75% (Sipo, 2011b).

As a matter of policy, the ULA's national media sub-committee divided media opportunities and campaign resources as equitably as possible. But with strong candidates such as Richard Boyd Barrett, Joe Higgins, Clare Daly, and Joan Collins polling increasingly well, sparse funds and volunteers were continually diverted from weaker candidates to these campaigns. As the campaign progressed, the ULA's media sub-committee had to be inventive in getting its message across. Reacting to a lack of media interest in press conferences, it abandoned the traditional indoor press conference mid-campaign, instead coming up with visually arresting stunts and photo calls. As Joan Collins' 'intervention' with Bertie Ahern had proven, political messages had to be 'inserted' in new ways in order to get some media attention. Of these efforts, a 'tug of war' stunt outside Anglo-Irish Bank's St Stephen's Green headquarters between the ULA's Joe Higgins, Brian Greene, Clare Daly, and Richard Boyd Barrett, on one side, and three people wearing 'Enda Kenny', 'Eamon Gilmore', and 'Micheál Martin' masks, on the other, was repeated across various media.

Conclusion

During the 2011 campaign, the ULA successfully established itself on the political stage. As Michael O'Brien, a member of the ULA's four-person media sub-committee, put it: 'the concept of the ULA as a factor in the election, albeit a small factor, was established and an impact achieved that simply would not have been the case had the components run completely separate campaigns' (O'Brien, 2012). Given its late formation, its financial constraints, the relative absence of a national profile, its aversion to public relations and the emergence of various rival 'anti-establishment' parties and candidates during election 2011, the achievement of five seats for the United Left Alliance was no mean feat even given that most of the winning candidates had come close to winning seats in election 2007.

As this chapter has shown, the Irish radical left prioritises resources for activism and 'fighting funds' over marketing and publicity. Enlisting the help of professional communications experts is seen as somewhat antithetical to its raison d'être. Action is favoured over 'spin' and this is integral to the movement's communications strategy. At the same time, as the ULA builds its support base and financial resources, it steps closer towards conventional party status. This is not a smooth process and faces significant opposition from those within the Alliance who want to preserve their independent status. A key consequence of this tension is the underdevelopment of a national identity for the ULA. This was felt during the 2011 election when, despite the best efforts of the ULA to engage with the media, communications for most candidates remained essentially grass roots and localist. ULA candidates overcame this lack of media attention and occasional derision as 'loonies' by promoting their ideas at public meetings and, significantly, through social media. Yet the disparity in national publicity spending, which this chapter outlines, demonstrates the challenges faced by the Alliance in getting its voice heard. A united left may have finally come of age in the general election of 2011 but, quite clearly, its voice was still breaking in the process.

References

de Bréadún, D. (2012) 'No camp will take a lot of positives from poll defeat' in *Irish Times* (2 June).

Drennan, J. (2011) *Cute hoors and pious protesters: traits and characteristics of Irish politicians*, Dublin: Gill & Macmillan.

irishelectionliterature. See <http://www.irishelectionliterature.wordpress.com> (United Left Alliance).

McMahon, C. 'Social media usage by candidates in the 2011 general election', accessible at <http://www.slideshare.net>

Metro Herald (24 February 2011).

O'Brien, Michael (2012) Interview (16 July).

O'Malley, E. et al. (2012) 'Mediating the 2011 general election: preliminary results from an analysis of newspaper and broadcast campaign coverage', Leinster House presentation (27 June).

O'Toole, J. (2011) 'The Jason O'Toole interview' in the *Irish Daily Mail* (13 February).

politics.ie. See <http://www.politics.ie> (both the 'People Before Profit/SWP' and the 'Candidates from the Left' threads).

politico.ie. See <http://www.politico.ie>

Poulet.ie. (2011). See <http://www.mamanpoulet.com/campaign-song-gino-kenny/>

RTÉ (2010) *Six-One News* (25 November).

Sipo (2011a) Standards in public office commission, report to ceann comhairle re Dáil general election of 25 February 2011, Dublin: Sipo. See <http://www.sipo.gov.ie>

Sipo (2011b) Standards in public office commission, summary of election expenses by party, Dublin: Sipo. See <http://www.sipo.gov.ie>

TV3 (2011) *Tonight with Vincent Browne* (24 January).

ULA homepage. See <http://www.unitedleftalliance.org>

PART TWO

Political Communication
and Journalism

CHAPTER FIVE

'Sources say ...':
political journalism since 1921

Mark O'Brien

While political journalism plays a central role in the political process it remains a hugely under-researched area of enquiry in Ireland. This is regrettable as political journalism holds those whom we elect to public account, it offers insights into the workings of political parties and governments, it is often the first draft of political history, and, occasionally it makes or breaks political careers. Taking the long view, this chapter presents a snapshot of how political journalism has evolved over the course of the last 90 years or so. Using digital newspaper archives it sheds some light on political journalism and political journalists in the early years of the state. Through interviews it examines the role that television played in transforming political journalism from passive reporting to critical analysis and commentary. Finally, amid a rapidly changing media environment, it examines the factors that impact on political journalism today.

A new state, a new parliament, 1919–61

When Dáil Éireann was established in 1919 it fell to a journalist, Piaras Béaslaí, to propose the adoption of the proclamation of independence. Béaslaí, who had worked on the *Freeman's Journal* and been imprisoned for his part in the 1916 Rising, was one of a number of journalists who combined newspaper work with republican activities. At the *Irish Independent*, reporters Michael Knightly and Hugh Smith had been active during the Rising and, along with Ned Lawlor and Paddy Quinn, reported the bitter and divisive Treaty Debates in December 1920 and January 1921 (Smyllie, 1948). Hugh Curran reported on these debates for the *Irish Times* and some months later, that paper's future editor, Robert Smyllie, first encountered Michael Collins. While Smyllie had expected 'a sinister, beetle-browed, scowling kind of anarchist, who would cut your throat as soon as he would look at you' he found Collins to be 'a big, jovial, open-faced young man with a great shock of black hair and a wide grin that explained to me, at any rate, the astonishing hold that he had on his followers' (Smyllie, 1948). The establishment of a new parliament and its move to Leinster House in 1922 entailed a process of negotiation regarding the facilities afforded to journalists. In June 1923 the political correspondents walked out of the Dáil halfway through a debate in protest at the lack of facilities provided for them. This had an instantaneous effect: the ceann comhairle wrote to them and the journalists agreed 'that the offered accommodation for tea-room etc. be accepted' (*Irish Times*, 1923a; see also *Irish Independent*, 1923).

The following October the journalists established the press gallery committee to liaise with the clerk of the Dáil on matters affecting the work of political journalists. Its first chairman was William Clarke of the *Belfast Telegraph,* and amongst its members was Frank Geary, later editor of the *Irish Independent* (*Irish Times*, 1923b). However, the return of the political correspondents was not universally welcomed. In 1924 the leader of the Labour Party, Thomas Johnson, suggested that the Dáil had not earned the electorate's respect and asserted that the political correspondents were to blame. The parliament had not, he declared, 'impressed the newspapers with the necessity of appointing people who will give an intelligent criticism or an intelligent summary of [its] work' (*Dáil Debates*, 1924). Unsurprisingly, the political correspondents expressed surprise that a TD 'be permitted to abuse the privileges of the House by making such sweeping and unfounded charges' (*Irish Times*, 1924).

As had happened prior to independence, politicians thought nothing of saying one thing in public and then criticising journalists for supposedly misquoting them in their reports. In 1926 the governor-general, Tim Healy, accused two journalists, William Buttimer of the *Irish Times* and Ned Lawler of the *Irish Independent,* of misreporting a speech he had delivered to Dublin's chamber of commerce. In his speech, Healy had made some choice remarks about Fianna Fáil's decision to remain outside parliament. Noting that the public never heard of certain politicians 'except in connection with explosions and assassinations' Healy concluded that they were 'quite welcome to stay out, and the further out they stayed the more welcome it will be, and the better some of us will be pleased'. When Thomas Johnson raised the matter in the Dáil, W.T. Cosgrave told the house that Healy had informed him that the reports of his speech were inaccurate. However, both journalists wrote to their respective newspapers and refuted Healy's assertion by releasing their full notes of his speech (*Irish Times*, 1926). Commenting on the affair, the *Irish Statesman* noted that Healy's reaction was 'a common form with politicians of all schools, who find themselves in an awkward corner'. If, it concluded, newspapers reported all that a politician said 'as he said it, with "hems" and "haws", un-concluded sentences, futile repetition and doubtful grammar' then allegations such as Healy's would cease to be made (*Irish Times*, 1964).

Relations between Cosgrave's government and political journalists seemed patchy at best: in October 1929 they walked out of a function that he was hosting in Dublin's Shelbourne Hotel for 23 overseas journalists who had travelled to Ireland to visit the Shannon Power Works in Co. Clare. The walkout occurred when the overseas journalists were seated in the main dining hall and the Irish journalists were instructed to take seats in an adjoining room. While some newspapers, such as the *Irish Times*, depended on Cosgrave's circulated speech as the basis for its report of the event, other newspapers, such as the *Evening Herald*, made no bones about telling its readers that the event was not being reported because of how its journalists had been treated. This contretemps prompted Cosgrave's secretary to write to the department of external affairs, which had organised the function, to record that Cosgrave was 'much perturbed at the comments [and was] very anxious that nothing should occur in regard to any future function with which he or any other Minister is concerned which might be made the subject of complaint or adverse comment in the Press'. The secretary also wrote a letter of apology to the editors of the national newspapers recording Cosgrave's 'sincere regret' that journalists 'should find cause for complaint in anything arising out of functions' with which he was connected (National Archives, 1929).

Cosgrave was, perhaps, sensitive to the move that Fianna Fáil was making in establishing its own national newspaper to counter the negative publicity of the *Irish Independent* and the *Irish Times*. First published in September 1931, five months shy of the 1932 general election, the *Irish Press* was a powerful addition to the political and media landscapes. It played a central role in bringing the party to power in 1932 and keeping it there; so much so that de Valera noted that 'if the paper were to disappear, the government would disappear with it' (de Valera, 1932).

The arrival of the *Irish Press* brought with it several new political correspondents, with Brendan Malin and Joe Dennigan joining the parliamentary lobby. Ironically, some months after Fianna Fáil had taken power, Dennigan was imprisoned for refusing to reveal the source of a story he had written. As political correspondent of the *Irish Press*, Dennigan was summoned to appear before a military tribunal where one E.J. Cronin was charged with membership of an illegal organisation, the Young Ireland Association or 'Blueshirts'. Sometime before this, Dennigan had written a story in relation to the Fianna Fáil government's plans to declare the organisation illegal and had reported that the government 'proposed to allow a short period to members of the organisation so as to provide them with an opportunity of ceasing their membership' (*Irish Press*, 1933). This information had only appeared in the *Irish Press* and it was part of Cronin's defence that, as a non-reader of that paper, he had been unaware of any such amnesty. When asked to identify the source of his story Dennigan claimed privilege and was gaoled for one month for contempt of court (National Archives, 1933).

Whoever Dennigan's source was, the political correspondents of this time did most of their dealing with ministers Seán Lemass, Jim Ryan, and Gerry Boland. As remembered by long-time *Irish Times* political correspondent Michael McInerney (1975), it was in the late 1930s that Lemass came under huge pressure from the political correspondents to hold a weekly press conference – pressure intensified no doubt by the rigorous state censorship adopted during the Second World War. As minster for supplies, Lemass briefed the journalists on a weekly basis between 1939 and 1948 and 'was also readily available on the phone'.

The first inter-party government of 1948–51 was, as remembered by McInerney (1975), easy to deal with on the basis that 'new governments always are easier to deal with.' While there was 'little official information about the famous Baltinglass Post Office case or the Noel Browne crisis', not only did the political correspondents 'know of Cabinet meetings, but they also knew the decisions made'. It was this government that began the process of holding press conferences, prompted in part by Taoiseach John A. Costello's announcement that the Free State was to leave the Commonwealth, which prompted a flurry of international press activity in Dublin (*Irish Times*, 1948). Perhaps the most startling act of political journalism in pre-1960s Ireland was the decision in 1951 by Robert Smyllie of the *Irish Times* to publish the correspondence between the inter-party government and the Catholic hierarchy in relation to Noel Browne's ill-fated Mother and Child healthcare scheme. When the hierarchy objected to what it viewed as state intervention in an area it controlled, the government backed off and Browne resigned as minister for health. Just before he did, he delivered the correspondence to Smyllie, who had promised to publish it. On 12 April 1951 the *Irish Times* reproduced the full text of the letters, forcing the other national titles to do likewise. For his trouble, Smyllie was condemned in the Dáil: the minister for defence, T.F. O'Higgins, described him 'as the "nigger in the wood-pile" who is causing irreparable damage to [...] this nation' (*Dáil Debates*, 1951).

Fianna Fáil's return to power in 1957 resulted in a shake-up of how governments handled political communication. Tánaiste Seán Lemass held weekly press conferences: as remembered by Michael McInerney, 'in one case a talk extended for nearly three hours: and the field was wide open [...] though much was non-attributable.' The government information bureau, long derided by political journalists as 'the bureau of no information', got a new director, Pádraig Ó hAnnracháin, who McInerney recalled, 'urged Ministers to talk to the correspondents, and they did'. Remarkably, according to McInerney, de Valera 'even began to hold his own press conferences'. The most open minister in this administration, McInerney recalled, was finance minister Jim Ryan: he 'broke the news about the Dev. retirement [in 1959] in the most casual way, so casual that one might almost miss it' (McInerney, 1975). But overall, political journalism in the first few decades of the state was, as described by journalist Michael O'Toole (1988, 11–12), characterised by 'an unhealthy willingness to accept the prepared statement, the prepared speech, and the handout without demanding the opportunity of asking any searching questions by way of follow-up'. There was, he concluded, a 'failure to apply critical analysis to practically any aspect of Irish life'.

Television and openness, 1961–79

Seán Lemass' election as Taoiseach was mirrored by the appointment of a new generation of political correspondents and the inauguration of a national television service in 1961 – a service bound in law to be objective and impartial in its coverage of news and current affairs. This stipulation was to have a profound impact on political journalism. Whereas previously the main media organisations represented or supported various interest groups, the new television service, through the requirement to be impartial, was bound to ensure more than one viewpoint on any matter was represented. While this was eventually to force the print media, to varying degrees, to move in the same direction, in the early days it gave a new generation of political correspondents a powerful platform, independent of their newspapers, to air their views and opinions. Amongst the new generation of political correspondents were Michael Mills of the *Irish Press* and Arthur

Noonan of the *Irish Independent,* while John Healy joined the *Irish Times* as a political columnist.

When offered the post of political correspondent of the *Irish Press* in 1963 Mills accepted it on the basis that he 'would try it for six months but would not write propaganda'. This condition was accepted by the Press Group's chairman Vivion de Valera who, influenced by the arrival of television, was trying to transform the paper's editorial ethos from its reverential coverage of the party to a 'fair to all, friendly to Fianna Fáil' approach (Mills, 1997). Arthur Noonan, who succeeded Paddy Quinn as the *Irish Independent's* political correspondent, was a regular television commentator on political events; in the 1970s he served as RTÉ's political correspondent, and later still, its political editor. But it was John Healy's 'Inside Politics' column, written under the penname 'Backbencher', that was to many people the most influential political column of the 1960s. It first appeared in the *Sunday Review* (Ireland's first tabloid newspaper) and from 1963 onwards in the *Irish Times.* The column was distinctive in that it often contained information, sometimes on government policy, sometimes political gossip, derived from Healy's large circle of sources and it was written in an irreverent style. As one commentator noted, 'until the arrival of the "Backbencher" column in the *Sunday Review* and later the *Irish Times,* which has in turn led to a similar licence in other newspapers, regular and provocative political journalism was almost unknown in Ireland' (Thornley, 1967, 223). Healy's column has inspired a long line of successors in the form of informed and sometimes irreverent parliamentary diarists.

The changing media scene was also helped by the appointment of a younger generation of ministers determined to use the media to help shape their public profile – a process dismissively described by Máirtín Ó Cadhain as 'pressomatosis' (Ó hEithir, 1983). Along with Charles Haughey and Brian Lenihan, Donogh O'Malley courted the political correspondents: as Michael McInenery remembered it, 'in the days of the "Golden Boys" Donogh O'Malley perhaps was the first "open Minister"' (McInerney, 1975). A gregarious individual, O'Malley would often sit with the political correspondents in the Dáil restaurant and revelled in his friendship with John Healy (Mills, 2005, 41). Besides O'Malley, Healy was enamoured with Charles Haughey and often referred to him in his 'Backbencher' column as 'The Golden Boy'. But Healy also had sources within Fine Gael and at least one commentator has hinted that his insider within that party was Patrick Lindsay, the long-time Co. Mayo TD (O'Dea, 1984, 29). Whoever his source was, in May 1964 Healy noted cryptically at end of his column, 'I share with Mr Declan Costello a passion for discretion just now, but I can be depended upon to speak at the appropriate time.' The following week Healy was the first journalist to reveal the new 'Just Society' policy programme that Costello had confidentially circulated within Fine Gael (Healy, 1964).

Healy also chaired the current affairs programme *Hurler on the Ditch* on Telefís Éireann. The programme consisted of a weekly overview of events by the political correspondents of the national dailies. The programme gave Michael Mills, Michael McInerney, and Arthur Noonan a platform from which to analyse and discuss the issues of the day, sometimes in ways that were not possible in their respective newspapers, a point recounted in detail by Mills:

> I had an advantage over previous political correspondents in that television had arrived and I appeared on several programmes and would often say on television what I might have difficulty saying in the *Irish Press*. There was opposition from sections of Fianna Fáil with many meetings passing resolutions trying to get the management to sack me. When the attacks came, Vivion [de Valera] resisted them and said he would stand by me. I used to get flak from TDs but I had regular access to television and radio which was a great help as I could reach a far greater audience there than by the *Irish Press*. (Mills, 1997)

Mills did, however, come under intense pressure to retract a story published in the *Irish Press* in October 1966. He had been 'given a tip off by one of his political friends' that Lemass was about to retire and the editor, Joe Walsh, accepted 'the veracity of the story and ran it as a lead in the following day's papers' (Mills, 1997). The article informed a stunned party faithful that 'sources close to the government were predicting that the Taoiseach would announce his retirement within the coming fortnight' (*Irish Press*, 1966). The scoop was news to most senior party figures and was vigorously denied. Pressure mounted on Mills and Walsh to retract it and by that evening Walsh 'began to have doubts as other political correspondents attempted to knock the story on the basis of contacts with reliable government sources'. After two days of denial and pressure from Fianna Fáil and the rebuttal of the story by the other newspapers, Walsh decided that the *Irish Press* would retract the story. However, Mills asked Walsh to 'hold off until the last minute in the belief that the story would be confirmed. Just before the deadline, a message arrived stating that a special meeting of the Fianna Fáil Parliamentary Party had been called for the following week' – a sure sign that something dramatic was about to happen. Lemass then announced his intention to retire (Mills, 1997).

The analysis and commentary by Mills, Healy, Noonan and McInerney in their respective newspapers and on television did not sit well with many politicians. During a 1966 Seanad debate on broadcasting Senator Patrick Quinlan criticised the prominent coverage given to the views of political correspondents. He noted that 'the political commentators who have appeared in GAA clothes, "The Hurler on the Ditch", have been given a place of importance in this country altogether out of keeping with a democratic country.' No other democracy would, he declared, allow 'a small group to get into their hands the power to make and break politicians and to make and break Governments that Telefís Éireann have given to the political commentators here' (*Seanad Debates*, 1966).

The arrival of television also created some competition between broadcasters and the political correspondents. While one commentator noted that 'Irish print journalists suddenly found themselves in competition with a new breed of interviewer, people like Brian Farrell and John O'Donoghue [who] were often better educated, more confident and more professional than their colleagues in the newspapers' (O'Toole, 1988, 11), simply by their longevity in reporting politics, the newspapers' political correspondents tended to have better sources, which occasionally produced tensions when they were interviewed by the newer broadcasters. Reviewing one current affairs programme in 1970, one television critic noted that 'Brian Farrell had got a bit testy with John Healy and Arthur Noonan because they seemed to him to be coy about their interpretation of Mr Ó Móráin's resignation as Minister for Justice and John Healy had, in turn ticked Farrell off for expecting them to provide sensational tit-bits specially for television' (*Irish Times*, 1970).

While the sudden resignation of Ó Móráin, a sociable minister with a history of health problems, raised a few eyebrows, a telephone call from the government information bureau asking the national newspapers to hold off printing the next day's edition until an important government statement could be released increased the suspense. The statement – that ministers Neil Blaney and Charles Haughey had been sacked by Taoiseach Jack Lynch because they did not fully subscribe to government policy on Northern Ireland and that another minister, Kevin Boland, had resigned in protest – finally reached the newspapers at 2.50 a.m. As remembered by Chris Glennon, who shortly afterwards replaced Arthur Noonan as the *Irish Independent's* political correspondent, 'in keeping with the style of the time, there was no explanation of why Mr Lynch had taken such a drastic step.

It was well into the day before newspapers were able to link the upheaval to an alleged attempt to import arms into the state for possible transfer to Northern Ireland' (Glennon, 2011).

The formation of the Fine Gael–Labour Party coalition in 1973 seemed to herald a new beginning in many ways and a new generation of political correspondents that included Dick Walsh of the *Irish Times*, Chris Glennon of the *Irish Independent*, and Seán Duignan and Donal Kelly of RTÉ entered the fold. Despite his dour public persona, as remembered by Dick Walsh, Taoiseach Liam Cosgrave showed 'more willingness than any of his predecessors to explain to commentators and the public at large what he and his colleagues are about'. Cosgrave was, Walsh remarked, 'positively garrulous and some of his colleagues embarrassingly loquacious [...] on all subjects other than security there is a frankness which, ten years ago, would have seemed startling.' As Walsh recalled, some ministers agreed to attribution of their remarks though 'in a minority of instances' they preferred the political correspondents to use phrases such as 'Ministers believe...' or 'A senior member of the Cabinet considers...'

The appointment of Muiris Mac Conghail as government spokesman was a key factor in the coalition's good media relations in its early days (Walsh, 1975). Mac Conghail met with the political correspondents daily and briefed them on developments and, as remembered by Michael Mills, 'this was a completely new development which removed much of the secrecy surrounding cabinet sessions and made the public more aware of the nature of government operations' (Mills, 2005, 112). Despite such progressive moves the coalition endured a sometimes fraught relationship with the media. Conor Cruise O'Brien's proposal to extend a Section 31-type ban to the print media and Paddy Donegan's description of President Cearbhall Ó Dálaigh as 'a thundering disgrace' soured media coverage of the coalition (O'Brien, 2001, 147–55).

At the 1977 general election Fianna Fáil romped home with a 20-seat majority, helped in no small part by Jack Lynch's popularity. Having hired Frank Dunlop as party press officer in 1973 in an attempt to play the coalition at the briefing game, Lynch appointed Dunlop as the country's first government press secretary. But it was the *Irish Press*, not the opposition parties, that helped bring Lynch's term as Taoiseach to an end. Despite the friendship that existed between Lynch and Michael Mills, the latter never let it interfere with his job. In 1979, following a harrowing day of violence north and south of the border and under intense pressure from the British government, Lynch conceded a ten-kilometre over-flight zone along the border; a concession shrouded in secrecy but which Mills revealed in a front page story (*Irish Press*, 1979). As Mills remembered it:

> We had a very good relationship until the story about the cross-border flyovers. Of course it upset the relationship, but I was a journalist with a good story and I could not sit on it. I knew new security arrangements had been made and there was only one place that it could be – the air. When I put my idea to certain people they were visibly upset by my knowledge. I ran the story but it was denied by the government (Mills, 1997).

At a stormy parliamentary party meeting, one TD asked whether Mills' report was true, to which Lynch replied 'as of now, the British have not permission to over-fly the border.' As Mills reported, much anger was directed at him and the *Irish Press* for running the story (*Irish Press*, 1979). By this stage a number of pressure points had built up: there were two by-elections in Lynch's native Cork but towards the end of these campaigns Lynch was on a tour of the USA. Briefing the political correspondents on the flight over to Washington, Lynch told them, off the record, that 'if he lost one it would be manageable, but if he lost two he would be "goosed"' (private source). The following day, in the wake of those two by-election defeats, Lynch let a fatal truth slip from his lips when answering questions about border security at a news conference in Washington (*Irish Press*, 1979). As remembered by Mills:

> It was at the Washington news conference that Jack slipped up. In reply to a question from Seán Cronin of the *Irish Times*, he replied that there was no change. He should have stopped there but then he said 'except in one slight respect'. This confirmed my story. The story appeared in the *Irish Press* and Bill Loughnane [TD] made an attack on Lynch. Lynch tried to have him expelled but failed. Of course our relationship suffered. He blamed me, but my duty was to the paper not to Jack. (Mills, 1997)

Lynch's resignation followed shortly afterwards. It was around this time too (1977) that Vincent Browne launched *Magill*, a magazine that, following in the footsteps of *Hibernia*, mercilessly dissected Irish politics. Its speciality was in-depth investigative pieces: its series on the arms crisis (1980), the relationship between the Workers' Party and the Official IRA (1982), and the Kerry Babies case (1985) came to define political journalism during the early 1980s.

The Haughey years

The politics and the reporting of politics in the 1980s were coloured by the events of the arms crisis a decade earlier. Having been sacked from cabinet in 1970 and having worked his way back to be elected Taoiseach in 1979, Charles Haughey was viewed with wariness by most, if not all, the political correspondents. He, in turn, viewed the group with undisguised suspicion. The appointment of the first female political correspondent, Geraldine Kennedy of the *Sunday Tribune*, in 1980 introduced a new dimension to political journalism. Kennedy made a name for herself by scooping the existing political correspondents: so much so that a tap was placed on her telephone by Haughey's minister for justice, Seán Doherty. In January 1983 the Fine Gael–Labour Party coalition revealed that the previous Haughey-led government had authorised the Garda Síochána to bug Kennedy's telephone and that of *Irish Independent* political columnist Bruce Arnold for most of 1982, presumably in an attempt to discover the sources of their stories on the heaves against Haughey then ongoing within Fianna Fáil. The coalition neglected to mention that the previous Fine Gael–Labour Party government had authorised a tap on the telephone of journalist Vincent Browne – a tap that lasted eight years. While Haughey denied any knowledge of the affair the revelations were followed by rumours that he was about to resign as party leader.

On the day of a much anticipated parliamentary party meeting, the *Irish Press* printed its infamous two-page political obituary of Haughey (*Irish Press*, 1983). The obituary, which carried a detailed account of Haughey's political career, had been prepared in line with the standard media practice of compiling biographies of national figures ready for immediate use should the need arise. By its context and content it was assumed by both Haughey supporters and critics alike as evidence that the paper believed he should resign. Haughey's survival badly wrong-footed the newspaper: as remembered by former minister, David Andrews (1997), 'it caused some ill-feeling within the party and the party took a very poor view of it. Of course Haughey was upset – who wouldn't be?'

While the coalition's press secretary, Peter Prendergast, who as general secretary of Fine Gael played a role in the government revealing the phone tapping scandal, had a good relationship with the political correspondents – one of them remembered him for his 'candidness' – he had a torturous relationship with the opposition. In 1984 he accused Haughey of 'gate-crashing' the departure ceremony for US President Ronald Reagan at

Dublin airport (*Irish Independent*, 1984). Fianna Fáil responded by pointing out the impropriety of the leader of the opposition being criticised by a public servant, and the coalition ultimately made the post of government press secretary a temporary one tied to the government of the day. While in opposition, Haughey appointed P.J. Mara as Prendergast's counterpoint: every day after Prendergast had briefed the political correspondents, Mara would brief them on the Fianna Fáil viewpoint. However, despite Mara's best efforts, the political correspondents remained suspicious of Haughey, and he of them. As remembered by Dick Walsh, this situation was exacerbated by Haughey's aloofness: 'he would carry on a very stilted conversation instead of having a relationship with people and talking normally. He was always conscious of who he was, and who you were' (Ryan, 1992, 60). Haughey's wariness of reporters was only reinforced by an indiscreet interview given to journalist John Waters that was subsequently published in *Hot Press*. Speaking freely, Haughey's frank assessment of political commentators left nothing to the imagination. When asked by Waters (1984) 'what aspect of Ireland or Irish society angers you most?', Haughey had responded:

> I *could* instance a load of fuckers whose throats I'd cut and push over the nearest cliff, but there's no percentage in that! (Laughs). Smug people. I hate smug people. People who think they know it all. I know from my own experiences that *nobody* knows it all. Some of these commentators who purport to a smug knowallness, who pontificate... They'll say something today and they're *totally* wrong about it – *completely* wrong – and they're *shown* to be wrong about it. Then the next day they're back, pontificating the same as ever. That sort of smug, knowall commentator – I suppose if anything annoys me, that annoys me. But I don't have sleepless nights about it!

Similarly, Mara's attempts to disarm the political correspondents with humour often backfired, as occurred in 1984 when he concluded a briefing with the words 'Uno duce, una voce' [one leader, one voice] and the quip was reported by Geraldine Kennedy in the *Sunday Press*. While Kennedy believed the quip was 'on the record', Mara disputed this by pointing out that she alone among the journalists present used the phrase in her report (Ryan, 1992, 63–64).

By this stage, the line-up of political correspondents had changed again: Seán O'Rourke replaced Michael Mills as political correspondent of the *Irish Press* in 1984 while Dick Walsh of the *Irish Times* was succeeded by John Cooney and later again by Denis Coughlan. In 1986 Mara adopted a new policy of inviting the political correspondents to travel with himself and Haughey to constituencies in advance of the upcoming election; a strategy that guaranteed media coverage while the Dáil was in recess. Activities such as these were viewed with suspicion by the coalition. As remembered by John Cooney, 'there was a far more independent line coming from a section of the political correspondents which was being interpreted in Fine Gael as pro-Haughey. By the end of my term I found the relationship with [Garret] FitzGerald quite strained' (Ryan, 1992, 88).

Haughey's return to power in the 1987 election (in which Geraldine Kennedy was elected as a Progressive Democrats TD) coincided with the arrival of several female political correspondents. Emily O'Reilly was appointed political correspondent of the *Irish Press* in 1989 and Una Claffey became RTÉ's political correspondent in 1991. The daily briefings by Mara continued though the political correspondents knew he was only imparting what Haughey wanted them to know, and that other than some off-the-record context, little else would be forthcoming. As remembered by Emily O'Reilly, the briefings consisted of 'a litany of atrocious gossip [...] You were left with a benign impression of Mara, which to a degree translated into a benign impression of Haughey' (Ryan, 1992, 101).

One person who ceased to have a benign view of Haughey was his former minister for justice, Seán Doherty. In January 1992 Doherty announced on RTÉ's *Nighthawks* programme that Haughey had known about the telephone taps in 1982, prompting Haughey's resignation and the election of Albert Reynolds as Taoiseach. Reynolds' decision to host a weekly, on-the-record briefing with political correspondents backfired when the 'X-case' controversy erupted. As remembered by one political correspondent, Reynolds found himself 'being pressed again and again, particularly by the women political correspondents on the issue about which he felt uncomfortable [...] It became a weekly briefing by the Taoiseach on the "X-case" and the abortion issue rather than a comprehensive run through of the broad range of issues facing the government' (Collins, 2004, 206). The weekly briefing was abruptly dropped when Fianna Fáil and the Labour Party formed a coalition in 1993 and, as Collins put it, 'the lobby system gradually became a less valuable vehicle for the transmission of information' (207).

Shifting priorities

By the 1990s quite a number of factors had changed the nature of political journalism. The establishment of a vibrant independent media sector from the late 1980s onwards and a more aggressive strategy on the part of British newspapers to establish their place more firmly in the Irish market in the early 1990s resulted in a large increase in the number of reporters being accredited as political journalists. As recalled by long-time political correspondent Steven Collins (2004, 217), this increase in numbers had a dramatic effect: 'with so many journalists in competition with each other for stories, the old off-the-record rule withered away and successive press secretaries became less and less willing to risk frank exchanges with the lobby.' In addition, the custom of having one press secretary per coalition party has led to different parties cultivating relationships with particular journalists. As Rafter (2009, 98) put it: 'The truth is that journalists do their business in private with their own sources. Politicians and their advisors also naturally brief journalists individually – and that is where the real business is done.'

Both Collins (2004) and Rafter (2009) have described in detail the changes they witnessed in the operation of political journalism. These include the hiring of private media consultants to work with journalists located outside parliament; the preference within some parties for local radio and tabloid newspapers, particularly at election time; the decline in time/space devoted to parliamentary reporting; the preference of political parties to make major announcements outside parliament; and an increase in the space/time given to commentary, opinion, and punditry. How much of this is media- rather than politically driven remains unclear: the proliferation of media outlets with more time and space to fill combined with digital technology has effectively created an instantaneous news cycle that cannot wait for parliament to convene and debate whatever issue is dominating the political and media agenda. As Collins (2008) recalled, Bertie Ahern, in his 11 years as Taoiseach, never met with the political correspondents in the Dáil to brief them: instead he communicated with the public through the 'doorstep interview' in which he answered questions as he moved from one function to another. While this created a public profile of a smiling Taoiseach willing to interrupt his busy schedule to answer questions, the technique prevented any serious questions being asked and facilitated short answers and sound-bites that suited Ahern's communication style.

What is certain is that the proliferation of media outlets has created more competition between journalists for a political scoop. For many years the media had turned a blind eye to Charles Haughey's extra-marital affair and a clear line divided what happened in the public and private lives of politicians, even if they did not practice what they preached. However, in March 1994 this long-standing tradition ended when the *Sunday Press* revealed that gardaí had instructed a prominent politician to leave a 'cruising' area of the Phoenix Park in Dublin. Some months later, at a press conference, journalists from *The Sun* questioned Fianna Fáil leader Bertie Ahern on the breakdown of his marriage. The *Sunday Independent*'s reportage on the death of former Fianna Fáil TD Liam Lawlor in a car crash in Moscow in 2005 caused controversy by inaccurately reporting that the crash had occurred in a 'red light district'. It was clear that a new era had arrived in which the private lives of politicians were now worthy of scrutiny.

It was also clear that the media would no longer shy away from revealing wrongdoing on the part of politicians. The tribunals of inquiry that began in the early 1990s revealed a litany of payments to politicians with the media often adding to the investigations. In 1996 the *Irish Independent* revealed the payments made by Ben Dunne to then Fine Gael minister Michael Lowry, prompting his resignation. The following year the media turned its attention to minister Ray Burke who, after confirming he had received a donation of £30,000 in 1989, resigned. Even Taoisigh were not immune: in September 2006 the *Irish Times* revealed that certain payments to then Taoiseach Bertie Ahern were being investigated by the Mahon Tribunal. While Ahern's initial explanation, that friends had given him loans following his legal separation from his wife, won him sympathy, his later explanation that he won some of the money on horse bets earned him ridicule. In 2009 the *Sunday Tribune* published the lavish expenses that had been enjoyed by ceann comhairle John O'Donoghue while a government minister. Despite an attempt to weather the storm, O'Donoghue resigned as ceann comhairle and later lost his seat in the 2011 general election. It is noteworthy that these stories were broken not by political correspondents but public affairs correspondents. Similarly, Alan Shatter's resignation as minister for justice in May 2014 followed allegations of policing irregularities first reported by the *Sunday Times* crime correspondent John Mooney. From all this, we can at least note that while political correspondents report on political controversies, it is very often their journalistic colleagues who first bring these controversies to light.

However, should this offer any validity to John Waters' (1992) assertion that 'political journalism in this country is both excessively conservative and far too close to politicians' it is equally clear that, in the battle for readers and viewers, some of the newer media outlets are more than willing to push the boundaries in terms of political coverage. In December 2009, TV3 revealed that then minister for finance, Brian Lenihan, had been diagnosed with a terminal illness. Despite repeated requests from Lenihan's staff not to run the story over the Christmas period, the station broadcast the story on St Stephen's Day. While the Broadcasting Authority of Ireland ruled that the story was in the public interest (see Rafter and Knowlton, 2013), it is difficult to imagine RTÉ having run that story, or at least having emulated TV3's sense of timing. It was also TV3's political editor, Ursula Halligan, who challenged then Taoiseach Brian Cowen on the cyber-based discussions about his sobriety that followed his less than impressive performance on *Morning Ireland* in September 2010. It was this action – asking Cowen to comment on the online debate – that fuelled much of the subsequent coverage. The ensuing, and heated, debate about the rights and wrongs of using online content to instantly challenge current or aspiring officeholders was a mere harbinger of controversies to come in a transformed media landscape.

Conclusion

In many ways, the development of political journalism in Ireland has mirrored the development of the state itself. The isolation engendered by economic protectionism, neutrality, and state censorship certainly did not lend itself to vibrant political journalism. The adoption of free trade and the advent of a national television service that was bound in statute to be fair and impartial in news and current affairs changed the political and media landscapes dramatically. National newspapers could no longer be seen to be handmaidens of political parties and television provided political correspondents an independent platform from which to analyse and comment on the issues of the day. The appointment from the 1970s onwards of government press secretaries to act as intermediaries brought mixed results but has not engendered a return to passive reporting. If anything, the greater proliferation of media outlets has changed the nature of political journalism. In the digital age politicians can be questioned on just-breaking news-stories and are expected somehow to articulate an instant and coherent answer to every political problem or controversy. Digital media also allow citizens to respond instantly to any politician's utterances. As the speed of technology increases so too does the speed of the news cycle and arguably the political process itself. What all this means for political journalism and attempts by politicians, journalists and the public alike to maintain a genuinely deliberative democracy remains to be seen.

References

Andrews, D. (1997) Interview.

Collins, S. (2004) 'The parliamentary lobby system' in Garvin, T., Manning, M. and Sinnott, R. (eds), *Dissecting Irish politics: essays in honour of Brian Farrell*, Dublin: UCD Press.

Collins, S. (2008) 'Cowen signals change of style' in *Irish Times* (9 April).

Dáil Debates (1924) Vol. 8, cols 2288–90 (25 July).

Dáil Debates (1951) Vol. 125, col. 940 (17 April).

de Valera (1932) De Valera papers, UCDA, File 1453/1 (letter to Archbishop D. Mannix).

Glennon, C. (2011) 'The big story' in *Irish Independent* (20 October).

Healy, J. (1964) 'Inside Politics' in *Irish Times* (9 May and 16 May).

Irish Independent (1923) 'Journalists protest – walk out of Dáil' (13 June).

Irish Independent (1984) 'Haughey guilty of discourtesy without precedent' (6 June).

Irish Press (1933) 'Letters recalled' (9 December).

Irish Press (1966) 'Mr Colley cuts short US trip' (31 October).

Irish Press (1979) 'Border air patrol plans' (5 October); 'Lynch gives assurance on sovereignty' (25 October); 'Lynch reveals border air plan' (10 November).

Irish Press (1983) 'C.J. Haughey – man of controversy' (27 January).

Irish Times (1923a) 'Reports of the Oireachtas' (23 June).

Irish Times (1923b) 'First Irish press gallery' (13 October).

Irish Times (1924) 'The Oireachtas press gallery' (2 August).

Irish Times (1926) 'The governor-general's speech' (17 November).

Irish Times (1948) 'Mr Costello meets pressmen in Dublin' (30 October).

Irish Times (1964) 'Informed circles' (21 May).

Irish Times (1970) 'Falling to the occasion' (11 May).

McInerney, M. (1975) 'Open government' in *Irish Times* (19 July).

Mills, M. (1997) Interview.

Mills, M. (2005) *Hurler on the ditch*, Dublin: Currach Press.

National Archives (1929) Tsch/S/5936 (various correspondence).

National Archives (1933) S2380 (Constitution: special powers tribunal).

O'Brien, M. (2001) *De Valera, Fianna Fáil and the Irish Press*, Dublin: Irish Academic Press.

O'Dea, T. (1984) 'The Great Khan of Cortoon' in *Magill*, 7(10): 24–33.

Ó hEithir, B. (1983) 'The ruthless rules of street fighting' in *Irish Times* (24 December).

O'Toole, M. (1988) 'The Roman Catholic Church and the media in Ireland' in Fahy, T. and Kelly, M. (eds), *Essays*, Dublin: MAI.

Rafter, K. (2009) 'Run out of the gallery: the changing nature of Irish political journalism' in *Irish Communications Review*, 11: 93–103.

Rafter, K. and Knowlton, S. (2013) 'Very shocking news: journalism and reporting on a politician's illness' in *Journalism Studies*, 14(3): 355–70.

Ryan, T. (1992) *Mara, P.J.*, Dublin: Blackwater Press.

Seanad Debates (1966) Vol. 60, col. 1492 (17 February).

Smyllie, B. (1948) 'An Irishman's Diary' in *Irish Times* (27 November and 4 December).

Thornley, D. (1967) 'Television and politics' in *Administration*, 15(3): 217–25.

Walsh, D. (1975) 'Telling like it is' in *Irish Times* (15 July).

Waters, J. (1984) 'Personally Speaking' in *Hot Press* (14 December): 9–11.

Waters, J. (1992) 'Breaking the shackles of political caution' in *Irish Times* (18 February).

CHAPTER SIX

In sickness and in health: politics, spin, and the media

Mark Byrne

Since the foundation of the state the relationship between politicians and the media has been characterised by the fraught, sometimes divergent, but ultimately symbiotic relationship between political communicators and journalists. This chapter explores, through interviews with journalists turned spin-doctors, the concept of political communication through the pejorative filter of spin. It considers the origins, connotations, and applications of spin in the context of the complex and interdependent relationship between media and politics and contends that the concept and effects of spin – positive and negative – are exaggerated. Specifically it argues that spin is an exercise shared, expected, and required by both politics and the media and that it is driven by a complex set of rules to which both sides are ultimately and increasingly bound.

The concept of political spin is so pervasive that it is easy to forget the term itself is less than 30 years old. In the course of that time it has become synonymous with mistrust of politicians and 'a euphemism for deceit and manipulation' (Andrews, 2006, 32). The term emerged from the sporting world, first from baseball in the USA, and later cricket in the UK. Moloney (2001, 125) notes that spin 'aligns the popular image of untrustworthy and scheming politicians with that of the wily spin bowler in a cricket match who, with the flick of a wrist, flights a curving ball of uncertain length and line towards the yeoman batsman defending his wicket'.

The term spin, personified later by the spin-doctor, entered the British lexicon during the 'age of spin' that characterised the electoral breakthrough and subsequent governments of Tony Blair's New Labour. Moloney (2001, 127) makes the case that 'spin [...] an aggressive, demeaning work of promotion and detraction by one part of the political class for another [...] began as a defensive response by Labour to editorial hostility shown by the

Murdoch media between 1979 and 1994, when Tony Blair became leader.' Lloyd (2008, 142) noted that the New Labour leadership is now 'regarded very widely – indeed world-wide – as something of a locus classicus when it comes to the political management of news. New Labour was created, after 1994, with the perceived need to manage its relations with the news media at the very heart of its project.' That period, personified by Alastair Campbell, presented the public with a new and not always pleasant caricature of the political spin-doctor: the shadowy, almost comically media-obsessed master of the dark arts. Spin then, has come to symbolise, at least in part, declining trust in the political process, but its definition depends on one's perspective. Regardless, the effects are such that, 'certainly we have now reached a time when any form of communications by a government is described as spin' (Andrews, 2006, 41).

If one accepts the contention that spin is a concept deserving of derision or suspicion, how should the bounty of blame be apportioned? One could make the case, as argued by the media, that spin is a reflection of the unattractive underbelly of the body politic; a symbol of dishonesty, manipulation, and coercion. One could equally contend, as politicians and spin-doctors regularly do, that spin is not spin at all; rather it is context and information, delivered for the welcome and greedy consumption of a news media that is driven and defined increasingly by celebrity, rows, and resignations to the detriment of policy and meaningful debate.

While there is much truth in these converse perspectives, each ignores the reality that one needs the other to survive. While the political side of this complex marriage can be seen to wear the connotations of spin more heavily – perhaps because the media has the power to frame the relationship – it is nevertheless reflective of a game to which both sides subscribe. Politics is played out through an interdependent and complex relationship between elected representatives (and their parties and agents), the media, and voters. To load the blame for increased scepticism of political communication entirely at the door of politicians and spin-doctors is to ignore the dynamics of that relationship. Lloyd (2008, 147) argues that spin is a 'joint creation by two classes of people who need each other, in some cases desperately; it was what one of these classes, the journalists, who had long lived by "spin", said was practised by the other, whose profession was also indivisible from it.' Similarly, McNair (2011, 63) argues that the relationship between politics and the media is defined by a 'relationship of mutual inter-dependence between politicians and journalists'.

From batsman to bowler

With the notable exception of P.J. Mara, spin-doctors in Ireland – in contrast to the USA and the UK – have been less to the fore of public consciousness. One could argue that the historical convergence of Irish political parties in the centre, devoid of the sharper ideological divide evident in the USA and UK, has facilitated a form of political spin particular to Ireland: more concerned with tribe than ideology and subject to an arguably less polarised and partisan news media. Since the late 1970s the government's communications infrastructure has grown and developed in an effort to meet the challenges of a divergent media and evolving political landscape. Since then successive governments have sought the assistance of journalists in the management of political communication and media relations, underlining perhaps, the interlocking relationship between media and politics.

Politicians employ former journalists as spin-doctors because of their insider-understanding of a sector with which they are obsessed and desperate to influence. One could argue however that the belief amongst politicians – that the acquisition of former journalists might equate to more positive coverage – misunderstands the nature of the potential 'pay-off'. The journalist turned spin-doctor does of course understand the media – and as a result he or she understands acutely the limits of spin and that the expectations of the political master are likely to be disappointed. Iarla Mongey, former political correspondent with Independent Network News (INN) and deputy government press secretary in the Fianna Fáil–Progressive Democrats coalitions from 2000 to 2005, described the attraction for politicians of employing a former journalist as follows:

> You know the people, you know the individuals, and you know the industry. You know that if you're dealing with a reporter from Today FM, what they're looking for is entirely different from what the chief political correspondent is looking for [...] you also put a human face on the government for journalists. You're one of their own, so they come to you for background, for context. You know instinctively what frustrates them having spent so much time yourself knocking on the door trying to get in. (Mongey, 2007)

The recruitment of former journalists as political communicators suggests a belief on the part of politicians and political parties that such individuals bring with them a knowledge and understanding of the media that might translate more effectively into that which is most elusive, valuable, and transient: public regard and popularity. Inside knowledge and an acute understanding of 'the rules of the game' is considered valuable, perhaps even essential. Cathy Herbert, former press advisor to the minister for tourism, sport, and recreation Jim McDaid and to the late minister for finance Brian Lenihan, believes that former journalists bring with them a set of skills that can counter the less media-savvy inclinations of attention-seeking politicians:

> Even though politicians live by the media and are absolutely obsessed by the media they are also notoriously inept at handling the media. In my experience they are extraordinarily naïve. You really do have to coach them; somebody who has worked in the media knows the way journalists think. (Herbert, 2013)

It is worth noting that while politicians undoubtedly recognise the nature of that interdependence – by virtue of their co-option of former journalists – it is a reality that is, perhaps, not entirely accepted by the media. Many journalists who moved from journalism to the post of government press secretary have experienced a 'poacher turned gamekeeper' reaction from their former journalistic colleagues. Shane Kenny, former RTÉ broadcaster, and government press secretary 1994–97, was disappointed by 'the level of antagonism and the gulf that was there, the coldness, the warm contact with colleagues that suddenly turned into this cold distance of people at conflict. Nothing can prepare you for that change until you actually experience it' (Kenny, 2007). Richard Moore, a former journalist with the *Irish Press*, spent 15 years advising government ministers, including Michael Lowry, Alan Dukes, Mary O'Rourke, and Dermot Ahern, on media relations. He too noticed an interesting change of perspective on the part of his former colleagues:

> Some of them reacted with this idea that because I was a journalist and now I was in this job that my function was to provide them with exclusives non-stop and to keep feeding them stories. One or two of them got quite nasty about it and then some of them had this idea that you're just a lapdog of the system and you've turned your back on the great noble tradition of journalism. (Moore, 2007)

He argued that the concept of spin is a myth 'wheeled out by journalists who consider public relations as something lesser or lower than journalism':

I find it highly entertaining that journalists are always on about spin this and spin that. In my experience, a journalist rings you up to ask you about a story. You tell them what the official government line is and then half the time, they're looking for extra information and interpretation from you. You have to give them a lot of background information, and that certainly isn't spin as far as I'm concerned. (Moore, 2007)

Dermot O'Gara, director of communications with the Labour Party since 2005 and a former journalist, similarly took issue with the presentation of political communication as something less noble than journalism:

I didn't even see it as a move to a different profession. As far as I'm concerned, what I used to do, and what I do now, is part of the same continuum, I just moved into a different part of it. Much like when I was a journalist, my job concerns communicating information to the general public. In my current role I try to control it or shape it, but journalists do that all the time as well. (O'Gara, 2013)

The negative reaction from former journalistic colleagues was not the only challenge faced by newly appointed press secretaries. Now firmly ensconced within the circle of power, many journalists turned spin-doctors reported an initial difficulty in de-tuning and realigning the focus of their knowledge and instincts. As remembered by John Downing, who worked as a journalist for 20 years before becoming deputy government press secretary in the 2007–11 government: 'I remember going to one meeting and filling a notebook; the devil in my head was thinking, go out that gate now and you've probably got three page one splashes and a half a dozen leads that you could feed out over the next few weeks' (Downing, 2013).

Iarla Mongey also agreed that the change was a shock to the system: 'there were occasions in my first few weeks that I was told about certain things and my eyes were as wide as saucers' (Mongey, 2007). Richard Moore concurred but also stressed the need to be wary of being fed a story to see whether it appeared in print: 'it took me a good while to adjust and you're thinking, Jesus it's great to be on the inside track. You had to be slightly wary as well [...] I'm not suggesting that this was the case but you were never sure if you were being fed a story to see if it might appear. You had to be very discreet, there was certainly a temptation' (Moore, 2007).

'Handling the media'

But while politicians may believe that a spin-doctor with experience of working in the media is more useful and effective, it is a contention that is not necessarily shared by those who made the move from media to politics. Seán Duignan, former RTÉ broadcaster and government press secretary 1992–94, observed that while journalists certainly bring useful attributes, knowledge, and qualities to the role, the tangible benefits are over-stated and often misunderstood by politicians:

> Politicians never understand that you can't 'handle the media', not really. They think that if they find the right person, the right spin-doctor that he or she will have the golden touch with the media. Because I worked so long in the media, I knew myself that this was impossible. You can feed and feed the media and the media will eventually bite your hand off. The media isn't in the business of saying 'good day for government'. The media is in the business of asking 'What's with these people? What are they at? What are they hiding?' (Duignan, 2007)

RTÉ broadcaster and former *Irish Examiner* journalist, John Murray, who worked as press advisor to Mary Harney from 1995 and served as deputy government press secretary from 1997 to 2000, agreed that the perceived benefits of hiring former journalists quickly dissipate upon assumption of the role:

> Once you cross the line, journalists think of you differently. It doesn't matter whom you were friendly with in the newsroom, their job is to make your life difficult. You could argue that the political benefit of having a former journalist in the role is over-stated. If you talk to a spokesperson in government they will inevitably say 'I'm trying to get stuff out that's positive and nobody's listening.' That's because the media has no interest – the media is interested in rows, resignations, and controversy. There is a complete divergence of interests and you realise after a while that you're at cross-purposes. I remember speaking with a former government press secretary and he said 'nobody wants to know about all the good we're doing.' And of course he was absolutely right; they don't. (Murray, 2013)

Iarla Mongey agreed that the notion of spin and news management is over-estimated and that most of the time, when a negative story breaks, the ability of a spin-doctor to manage or control the story is severely constrained:

You might get a call from the *Sunday Independent* or another newspaper on a Friday or Saturday evening to tell you that they have a particular story. When they ask you at that stage for a response, you know the story is already written and the best you can hope for is a paragraph at the end. They have already done judge, jury and executioner and they're just looking for a few final words. (Mongey, 2007)

If the powers of the spin-doctor are limited in the context of the day-to-day exchange with the media, the constraints of their influence can become even more apparent in times of crisis. This was certainly true of the Fianna Fáil–Green Party government of 2007–11 as it lurched from crisis to crisis. Liam Reid, former *Irish Times* journalist and media advisor to then minister for communications Eamon Ryan described the period from 2010 through to the end of the government's life in March 2011 as 'less a question of communications and more one of palliative care' (Reid, 2012). John Downing described the lead up to the EU–IMF bailout in November 2010 as 'absolutely hellish [...] In the autumn of 2010 things began to spin out of control and by early winter things were absolutely out of control [...] It was totally about damage limitation at that stage' (Downing, 2013). Richard Moore compared the final weeks of the administration to 'the crumbling and dissolution of an empire. It was like the fall of Saigon, the helicopter taking off from the top of Dáil Éireann with a few ministers swinging off the wheels shouting "get me out"':

> What happens in the kind of crisis that we saw in that government is that people get into a kind of a siege mentality [...] No matter what was said, they were in the bunker, and the hard hats were on. They found it very difficult, I suppose they were tired as well; they'd been there a long time. (Moore, 2013)

Cathy Herbert recalled that 'everyone was scared; nobody knew what was going to happen, as this was totally unprecedented. I remember a very senior person in the department [of finance] said to Brian Lenihan, "minister we don't know how to advise you – we've never been here before." This was an unprecedented crisis' (Herbert, 2013).

Ultimately, the move from batsman to bowler recognises the interrelated nature of the game played between and with media and politics. That there is still something of a stigma surrounding the move from journalism to public relations is evidence of the tensions that define the relationship: perhaps the media seeks to diminish the interdependence by marking the narrow and blurry division as one that cannot be crossed. While the skills and understanding are both valuable and transferable, one could make the case that the effects of the transition on politicians and politics are over-stated. Politicians recruit the insider – a star player – in the hope of a game-changer, but in fact the game continues in accordance with the rules. Former journalists understand that the expectations of their new employer – faced with the normal rules of engagement but also in times of crisis – are not based in reality.

If the ability to 'handle the media' is over-stated, particularly in times of crisis, then what other practical benefits might politicians expect from the employment of former journalists? One such benefit is the understanding, honed through years of experience in the media, that the age-old political maxim is true: a cover-up or mistruth is often more damaging than any initial misdemeanour. As Stephen O'Byrnes, a former journalist with the *Irish Press* and the *Irish Independent* and government press secretary 1989–92 put it: 'the golden rule of the job that I was in is that you can be economical with the truth but don't tell a lie. If you tell a journalist a downright lie you're finished' (O'Byrnes, 2007). One might cast a sardonic eye on the relationship between political communication and the truth, and yet, all those interviewed reported an instinctive understanding that it is usually lies, not mistakes, that sink political careers. As noted by former Fine Gael press secretary, Peter White, 'spin-doctoring, or massaging of public opinion, is a strange business because the truth has a funny old way of coming out in the end' (White, 1994). Thus, while spin is often presented as synonymous with dishonesty or even lies, both sides understand that to lie would be to derogate from the rules of the game, rules underpinned by mutual trust. As defined by John Dowling, spin is more about providing context and background for a hungry media:

> There is very little that you can do in the role other than begin and finish with the truth. There is an imperative to maximise your case of course, so one person's spin is another person's presentation. Often it's about background stuff. You'd say 'look, we're not saying anything whatsoever about that on or off the record, however since I know you, let's talk about it and I'll tell you what I do know.' That's where spin comes in, when you're explaining context and background [...] Peter Sutherland used the phrase 'deep background', and you are in Indian territory then. (Downing, 2013)

This requirement and expectation of trust between two apparently competing forces underlines the interdependent relationship that is in evidence between an attention-seeking political establishment and a content-hungry media. It is difficult to imagine how a spin-doctor could be effective once exposed as a person whose insights cannot be trusted. Such actions would disrupt the delicate interdependence that exists between the two camps. Seán Duignan observed that when spin and lies are synonymous, political disaster is quick to follow: 'if you lie to journalists then you're done. I'm not saying that from a moral point of view, but that is how it happens. Most of the great scandals in politics have been due not to the actual misdemeanour but to the attempted cover-up' (Duignan, 2007). Having worked as a reporter with the *Irish Independent* and as deputy government press secretary in the rainbow government of 1994–97, John Foley recalled that at no stage throughout the life of that government was it ever suggested that he should tell a lie to a journalist: 'it can be a very pressurised job in the day-to-day activity. In all that activity, it was never suggested to me that I mislead. I certainly tailored information; that was my job, but then you're dealing with adults who know the business' (Foley, 2007). The relationship is, perhaps, best described by journalist Sam Smyth: 'spin-doctors are like good head waiters. If you like and trust them you are prepared to take their advice. A bad spin-doctor, like a bad waiter, will try to flog you yesterday's stale item' (Foley, 1997).

A jester on the king's knee

As we have seen, the image of the spin-doctor as an all-powerful master of the political environment is at odds with the mundane realities of the role, which are determined to a large extent by the personal and political instincts and quirks of the spin-doctor's political master. Thus the spin-doctor can see his or her role reduced to that of the human shield; assailed daily in the trench between an expectant media and the media-obsessed politician. Seán Duignan recalled that while he had little or no influence on Albert Reynolds' thinking and was severely constrained by his political and personal style, he was never permitted to be too far away from him:

> The reason for that is the never-ending obsessive paranoia with the media in political circles; right up to the very top. That isn't just Albert Reynolds; it was Jack Lynch and Garret FitzGerald as well. The press secretary is like the jester on the king's knee; the king doesn't like the jester to be too far away from him at any stage. Why? Because the media drives him crazy. Who comes between him and the media? The press secretary. (Duignan, 2007)

John Murray similarly recalled the constraints of his role in the Fianna Fáil–Progressive Democrats government of the late 1990s:

> This was the time of the tribunals and what Bertie [Ahern] knew about Ray Burke and so on. I would say 95% of my contact with the media was journalists asking why we weren't pulling out over this or that. It was forensic and it was brutal [...] It got to the stage where I actually stopped proactively ringing journalists because there was no point; it was impossible to get the message out, they were only interested in discord and scandal [...] I remember at one of the political correspondents' dinners, Chris Glennon, former journalist with the *Irish Independent*, stood up and said 'I was going to say thanks John for all the help you've given us, but you've actually given us no help, you haven't even risen to a "no comment".' Mary Harney was laughing and sort of saying 'good man John'. It reflected the fact that I'd become a protector of the Progressive Democrats through saying as little as possible. It was akin to P.J. Mara's great quip, 'no comment, and that's off the record.' (Murray, 2013)

The grind of the role is underlined by Richards (1996, 8–9), who argued that, for much of the time, press secretaries 'deal with tedious logistics, they are dependent on elected politicians and often they face an unequal contest against the expanding media and the large number of political journalists'. Richards further contended that it is 'for the elected leader to decide the terms of the relationship'. The terms of that relationship can often dictate the extent to which spin and effective (or ineffective) political communication come to define a government's tenure and relationship with the media. As press secretary to the rainbow coalition of Fine Gael, the Labour Party, and Democratic Left between 1994 and 1997, Shane Kenny's experience was similar to that of Murray's in that he worked for a political leader who believed in government cohesion above all else:

> John Bruton was much more 'closed' in office than I thought he would be, and that became an issue. He said in the Dáil on becoming Taoiseach, before I became press secretary, that the government would conduct its business as if behind a pane of glass. He made it quite clear to me afterwards that government cohesion was the main issue for him and that his key concern was keeping the government together. In terms of the flow of information, he felt that it was the honourable thing to do to provide information only when government had discussed and decided on an issue. That doesn't suit journalists and I knew that I was going to be

in a very difficult position because the option of briefing (off the record) was entirely ruled out. He made it entirely clear to me that he didn't want any briefings to take place. (Kenny, 2007)

By reverting to a more restricted, and arguably more honest and ethical form of political communication, the rainbow coalition – through Kenny – disrupted the balance of the relationship between government and media and, as a consequence, changed the terms of the game: much to the chagrin of journalists. Writing in 1995, Geraldine Kennedy of the *Irish Times* argued that Bruton had placed an 'iron curtain around government operations' and had reduced the flow of information 'to a trickle of east European proportions' (Kennedy, 1995). While acknowledging that Bruton was more 'closed' than might have been expected, Kenny described Kennedy's claim as 'wildly over-the-top':

> Bruton could, of course, not control the information flow or briefings by the other parties in the coalition, but there was a distinct effort being made by everyone in the government to work in a harmonious way and [...] a very important part of that was that the three of us met the pol corrs together [...] This took place after the three of us met the Taoiseach to be briefed by him. This united front itself was very effective in demonstrating the cohesion of the government. The media loves conflict and was put out by not finding it. Differences in terms of handling issues were generally sorted out in the programme manager forum, but if not, then at a political level, by and large without being distorted and enlarged by media megaphone. (Kenny, 2007)

Seán Duignan reported a rather different experience with Albert Reynolds:

> For the full period of the Fianna Fáil–PD administration, which lasted less than a year, Reynolds gave an on-the-record news conference once a week. I went to Downing Street when I was appointed and when I told them what we were doing they told me that it was crazy and couldn't be done. 'You simply can't have people coming in and talking to the Prime Minister on any topic under the fucking sun; it'll do for you.' Well it nearly did for Albert. (Duignan, 2007)

Reynolds was arguably the most instinctively 'unspun' Taoiseach of recent times: he offered – in a refreshing if naïve nod to openness and transparency – a weekly on-the-record briefing to the political correspondents, and they, as remembered by Duignan, 'did their professional job and bored into him.

Very often we would have absolutely no idea what topic would be thrown in' (Duignan, 2007). Thus, the spin-doctor, constrained already by rules of engagement with the media, and by relative impotency in times of crisis, is further hampered by and subject to the whims and disposition of the political chief.

Team tactics

If the reputed powers of spin-doctors are over-stated in the face of crisis, the inability to lie, and the constraints applied by political masters, it is worth noting that effective political communication is further dependent on the mundane realities of internal communication. The history of political communication in Ireland lends credence to the suggestion that spin and its effectiveness is driven by political realities, rather than the other way around.

While the notion of coalition government is now the norm it originally came as something of a shock to Irish political parties; particularly to Fianna Fáil. Recalling the atmosphere that pervaded the formation of the first Fianna Fáil–Progressive Democrats coalition in 1989, Stephen O'Byrnes stated that 'the government had been conceived, born and reared in pure acrimony. The relationship was purely on the basis of a forced marriage':

> Here were a bunch of people who had left Fianna Fáil only a few years before – some of the best and brightest people like Des O'Malley, Mary Harney and Bobby Molloy [...] The tensions were appalling. I worked in government buildings and I'd meet Haughey in the corridor at least once a day, but for a long time he wouldn't even look at me. (O'Byrnes, 2007)

From a communications point of view, this marriage of inconvenience was a nightmare. O'Byrnes remembers that, due to inter-party tensions and distrust, he and his Fianna Fáil counterpart P.J. Mara rarely made any attempt to coordinate external communications:

> At critical times we would call each other and say look: broadly speaking this is my line on this particular issue. In that instance he would warn me if they were going with a different tactic. We might finesse the thing a small bit but generally we didn't. (O'Byrnes, 2007)

The bad blood between Fianna Fáil and the Progressive Democrats was something of a gift to the media, as both parties delivered separate, uncoordinated briefings to the political correspondents' lobby, as recalled by O'Byrnes:

> As a former journalist, I could write the script for that situation. P.J. Mara goes in and he is asked for the Fianna Fáil view on a particular issue. He says 'x' and then I go in later and I'm asked for the PD view on the same issue. Because I don't know what he has said, I might say 'y'. Inevitably the next day, all the headlines would shout about a 'major rift' between the government parties. (O'Byrnes, 2007)

Inter-party relations worsened when Albert Reynolds replaced Charles Haughey as Taoiseach in 1992. When Reynolds appointed Seán Duignan as government press secretary he encouraged him not to communicate with the PDs at all. In his memoir, Duignan recalls the reactions of Mara, who had agreed to stay on in a transitional capacity, and Bart Cronin (then head of the government information service) to the suggestion that he link in with his PD counterpart:

> I was quickly disabused of that notion. Both PJ and Bart told me that, since the formation of the government, contact between the government press secretaries had – 'by mutual consent' – been kept to a minimum. So, rightly or wrongly, I stayed clear of O'Byrnes. Nor did he seek to contact me. (Duignan, 1995, 12)

O'Byrnes recalls that, 'as bad as things were between P.J. and I, in terms of not briefing jointly, at least we did talk tactics occasionally and we both wanted the government to work.' O'Byrnes says that in the remaining nine months of that government 'Seán Duignan did not speak to me good, bad or indifferent' (O'Byrnes, 2007). Duignan, while eager to point out that there was no personal animosity between himself and O'Byrnes, noted that effective communication was made impossible due to the mutual antipathy and outright hatred between many senior people in both parties: 'Albert absolutely despised the PDs [...] they hated us and we hated them' (Duignan, 2007). As O'Byrnes remembered, 'it had to end sooner rather than later because there was absolutely no trust in that government [...] not only did we not brief jointly or talk tactics, we didn't actually talk at all. We were in the same building but one us might as well have been on the moon' (O'Byrnes, 2007).

The subsequent Fianna Fáil–Labour Party government of 1992–94 saw something of a new departure in internal coalition communication, a reflection of the recognised weakness of the previous administration's strategy, as well as the strong hand played by Labour in the formation of the government. Seán Duignan stayed on as government press secretary while Dick Spring appointed *Irish Press* journalist John Foley as deputy government press secretary. Foley recalls that 'we were a two-hander. Very unusually at the time we did joint briefings. I also did briefings on behalf of Diggy [Duignan] and vice versa. In previous governments there had been a clear divide' (Foley, 2007).

Improved internal communication between the parties, despite the government's eventual acrimonious disintegration, facilitated the effective operation of the administration for longer than might otherwise have been the case. It provided tentative proof (at least in the early stages) that if the age of single-party government had passed, then an emphasis on cohesive internal communication was essential for effective political communication and governance. These lessons were further woven into the fabric of Irish political communication with the formation of the 1994 government of Fine Gael, the Labour Party, and Democratic Left; the first in the history of the state to take office without the need for an election.

While RTÉ broadcaster Shane Kenny was appointed government press secretary, John Foley stayed on as deputy government press secretary and Tony Heffernan was employed to represent Democratic Left. Foley recalled that there was a 'deliberate attempt to maintain a homogenous government [...] I was there when the formation of the thing was being worked out so we attempted to continue that arrangement, and by and large we did. We would have been in touch all the time' (Foley, 2007). Kenny similarly recalls a 'strong professional relationship' between the three men, which led to coordinated internal and external communication (Kenny, 2007). This trend has remained – for the most part – at the heart of coalition government in Ireland. As John Murray remembered:

> For the most part, myself and Joe [Lennon, government press secretary] would have been a united voice [...] there was often pressure from the backbenches or the grassroots asking why did we sign up to this or why are we supporting that. There was pressure to brief separately or to make a break for it but after a while I realised that there was no benefit to the PDs of ploughing a lone furrow. You can only really do that once, and when you start creating that sort of mistrust and spinning against your partners in government then the government is doomed. (Murray, 2013)

Similarly, Iarla Mongey recalls of his time as deputy government press secretary of the Fianna Fáil–Progressive Democrats governments of 1997–2005,

> Even where there were different points of view or divergent opinions, I used to tease Mandy [Johnston, government press secretary], 'well regardless of where we stand on these issues we'll go river-dancing in here [political correspondents' lobby] together' [...] The last place you wanted to be discussing your differences was the political lobby. You might be doing it through other avenues, before or after that but you certainly didn't want to be there, and at odds with the person you had walked into the room with. (Mongey, 2007)

Similarly, John Downing observed:

> It is very, very important to present a government front [...] Journalists would have loved divide and conquer and part of the job was to minimise that and to downplay it. I had a very good personal relationship with Eoghan [Ó Neachtain, government press secretary] [...] We were a back channel of communication between parties when inter-party relations were rough. We spoke to each other and we spoke about how to minimise the damage and how to try to navigate through difficult situations. (Downing, 2013)

The experiences of successive Irish governments, and of the spin-doctors employed to represent them, lend weight to McNair's (2011, 123) contention that 'some of the great failures of party-political communication in recent years can be attributed to inadequate internal public relations.' The importance of internal communication adds another item to the long list of barriers and pitfalls around which the spin-doctor must navigate.

Conclusion

The notion of spin as a pejorative function of the modern political environment is, arguably, over-stated. Spin-doctors are subject to – and have limited influence over – the vagaries of the political landscape, and must work within the context and confines of public sentiment, inter-party relations, a voracious and expanding news media, and the political dispositions and personal inclinations of their political masters. The literature, and the experiences of journalists turned spin-doctors in Ireland, underlines the symbiotic and decades-old interdependence at play between politics and the media; each needs the other to survive. Media outlets, whether print, broadcast or digital, find themselves with ever more space to fill and limited resources with which to source and produce content. In this environment, the journalist is likely to need the spin-doctor all the more. Similarly, politicians are caught between the twin pressures of declining public trust in politics and institutions and the need to communicate through a fractured, divergent, and celebrity-fuelled media. The often fraught relationship between the body politic and the media is perhaps a reflection of this hyper-mediatisation. As Lloyd (2008, 144) argues, there is 'an extra cause of bitterness between journalists and politicians: both see their constituencies shrinking and are forced to cling to the other all the more, often blaming the other for the declining state of their fortunes.' Changes to the game – such as the altered media, political, or economic landscape – bring with them a sense of drift or panic for all concerned, but, as has always happened, the players will adapt and the game will continue as before.

References

Andrews, L. (2006) 'Spin: from tactic to tabloid' in *Journal of Public Affairs*, 6(1): 31–45.

Downing, J. (2013) Interview.

Duignan, S. (1995) *One spin on the merry-go-round*, Dublin: Blackwater Press.

Duignan, S. (2007) Interview.

Foley, J. (2007) Interview.

Foley, M. (1997) 'Spin Doctors' aim is to bewitch with images' in *Irish Times* (4 June).

Herbert, C. (2013) Interview.

Kennedy, G. (1995) 'A government closed to the release of information' in *Irish Times* (17 July).

Kenny, S. (2007) Interview.

Lloyd, J. (2008) 'The special relationship' in *Public Policy Research*, 15: 142–47.

McNair, B. (2011) *An introduction to political communication*, London: Taylor & Francis.

Moloney, K. (2001) 'The rise and fall of spin: changes of fashion in the presentation of UK politics' in *Journal of Public Affairs*, 1(2): 124–35.

Mongey, I. (2007) Interview.

Moore, R. (2007) Interview.

Moore, R. (2013) Email correspondence.

Murray, J. (2013) Interview.

O'Byrnes, S. (2007) Interview.

O'Gara, D. (2013) Interview.

Reid, L. (2012) Interview.

Richards, S. (1996) 'Despite widespread belief in their sinister powers, spin doctors aren't a new phenomenon and their influence is limited' in *The New Statesman* (6 September).

White, P. (1994) 'Spinning the right reactions' in *Irish Times* (1 August).

Above Political parties have traditionally reinforced rather than challenged gender inequalities in Ireland.

Above right The people have twice (1959 and 1968) defeated government efforts to change Ireland's electoral system.

Ireland's most successful politician of the twentieth century, Eamon de Valera, was the world's oldest head of state when he retired from the presidency in 1973, then in his 91st year.

CHAPTER SEVEN

Media advisers
and programme managers

Tom Clonan

On 29 September 2008, in a process shrouded in secrecy, the Irish government issued an unlimited bank guarantee to six banks. This would ultimately cost the Irish taxpayer billions of euros. Two years later, on 21 November 2010, Taoiseach Brian Cowen formally requested financial assistance for Ireland through the European Union's economic financial stability facility (EFSF) and the International Monetary Fund (IMF). One week later, the government, the European Union, and the IMF agreed to an €85 billion rescue deal, the EU–IMF bailout package. On that day, 88 years after the foundation of the state, Ireland relinquished its fiscal and budgetary sovereignty.

From that moment, Ireland entered one of the most prolonged and fraught crises of its political, fiscal, and social history. This chapter explores the communications role of politically appointed Irish government media advisers during this period of unprecedented national crisis from 2010 until 2012. This period encompasses a change of government in Ireland and the chapter includes a comparative analysis of the role of media advisers during the Fianna Fáil-led government under Brian Cowen and the subsequent Fine Gael-led government under Enda Kenny. The findings in relation to status and role, value for money, and ethical probity (in relation to the public interest) contained in this chapter are based on two sets of interviews conducted with Irish political correspondents in 2010 and 2013. In all, 15 political correspondents were interviewed – out of a total number of 46 in the Oireachtas press gallery. The interviews were conducted on the basis of anonymity. A variety of journalists were selected for interview with a mix of male and female interviewees working for both tabloid and broadsheet print media, along with correspondents (radio and television) from commercial and public sector broadcasters. In 2010, 11 out of a possible 13 politically appointed media advisers were also interviewed on the basis of anonymity.

Media advisors and programme managers

Politically appointed media advisers and programme managers made their first appearance on the Irish political landscape in 1993 when several such positions were created by members of the incoming Fianna Fáil–Labour Party coalition. Reporting at the time, Geraldine Kennedy (1993a), public affairs correspondent of the *Irish Times*, noted '[T]he majority of Ministers have appointed their new partnership programme managers, a new layer of advisers charged with the specific task of monitoring, implementing and coordinating work on the implementation of the programme for government in a continental-type *cabinet* system.' Kennedy also observed that whilst Fianna Fáil ministers 'by and large are appointing civil servants to the posts', Labour ministers 'seem to be appointing outside advisors'. Kennedy's article lists ten such appointments. However, shortly afterwards, Kennedy (1993b) reported that the number of politically appointed staff had grown to 135 and she raised concerns about the number of family members being appointed to the posts. She observed that in salaries alone, such appointments would cost over £3 million per annum. Concerns raised about the nomination of family members to such posts – many without 'formal job descriptions' – raised the issue of political cronyism. Funded exclusively by the exchequer, these posts were subsequently formalised by legislation.

Politically appointed media advisers and programme managers are now employed under Section 11 (1) of the Public Service Management Act 1997. Twenty years after their first appearance on the Irish political scene, it is appropriate to examine the status and role of contemporary politically appointed advisers with specific reference to the cost and ethical considerations associated with such appointments – most especially because their influence is not generally understood due to a lack of transparency in spheres of public affairs and lobbying within Ireland.

The political economy of communication explores the power relationships between print and electronic media organisations – traditional and digital alike – and other elite institutions within society. The most prominent power brokers recurrently examined include the executive, or government of the day, institutions of state, political parties, and powerful business interests. Indeed, in recurring analyses of public communication within the political economy approach, government is consistently identified as a major player in negotiating the range and scope of national discourses and narratives. The literature (Schiller, 1992; Mosco, 1996; Mc Chesney et al., 1998) suggests that powerful actors, such as government, invest their energies in seeking to shape a 'compliant' print and electronic media that will, ideally, constantly reiterate its views and positions.

Therefore, an entity as powerful as government, with constant and privileged access to what media professionals consider premium news content, is ideally placed to maximise a potentially mutually beneficial relationship with the media. Most government ministers and their media advisors enjoy privileged access to day-to-day departmental policy and operating issues that, by their very nature, are high in news value and often at the top of the news agenda. Media advisors regularly identify and target relevant media professionals and furnish them with an ample supply of authoritative news copy – on or off the record. In the case of each government department or ministerial portfolio, the relevant media correspondents and key opinion makers are targeted for supply with details of current policy initiatives at home and abroad. Providing journalists with information about issues high in news value in this way might assist the government of the day in its efforts to achieve 'primary definition' in relation to its policies. It might also function to divert media attention from peripheral and often negative issues affecting the government. It is arguable that successive recent Irish governments have shown themselves to be especially keen to control or influence public narratives around the ethical orientation and economic metrics of current fiscal and austerity policies.

Such a process, according to Hall (1978, 59), 'places the media in a position of structured subordination to the primary definers'. In this scenario, the media, by being overly reliant on the information provided by official sources assume a 'secondary role in reproducing the definitions of those who have privileged access'. This is especially so in an era of digital communication with increased pressure on media professionals to satisfy news deadlines in a highly competitive and time-sensitive environment. In other words, the operating environment within which media professionals now find themselves – with increased competition for access to privileged sources – functions to subordinate the media's role as primary definers. Commentators such as Keeble (2000, 43–44) further emphasise the negative aspects of this dynamic:

> At the heart of journalism lies the source. Becoming a journalist to a great extent means developing sources. As a journalist you need to know a lot: where to go for information and who to ask. And for career development, contacts are crucial [...] Media research suggests journalists use a remarkably limited range of sources.

Journalists dependent on a limited number of privileged sources and operating in a time-pressured environment would appear to be in an unequal power relationship with in-house sources, spokespersons, and public relations practitioners engaged by politicians. In the 1990s the levels of primary definition being achieved by government agencies and spokespersons in the West led some commentators such as Kellner (2001, 199–200) to describe the media as simply 'conduits for government policies and actions'. Given that the number and financial cost of politically appointed media advisers within Ireland is relatively high, their role in managing state–media relations deserves critical scrutiny.

Media advisers and the Cowen-led Fianna Fáil administration

On RTÉ television's *The Week in Politics*, on 14 November 2010, Fianna Fáil minister, Dermot Ahern described as 'fiction' international media speculation that Ireland was about to enter a bailout programme. Ahern, an insider at the heart of the government, stated that '[t]here are no negotiations going on [...] We have not applied.' One week later, Taoiseach Brian Cowen formally applied for financial assistance from the ESFS and the IMF. Ahern's performance on *The Week in Politics* seemed emblematic of the communications style of Cowen's government – patronising, arrogant, and misleading. Some months later, the minister for finance, Brian Lenihan (*The Journal*, 2011) stated that all ministers had been aware of the talks but that to admit the discussions were ongoing might have damaged Ireland's standing in the money markets. Within a year of the collapse of the Fianna Fáil-led administration, the communications profile of Cowen's government was neatly summed up by the business editor of the *Irish Independent*, Maeve Dineen (2011): 'The last crowd gabbed all the time and often ended up lying, as they did over the bailout talks, with the result that they left office with no credibility at all.'

As Cowen's administration lurched from crisis to crisis during the closing months of its term in office there was a growing consensus among politicians, journalists, and public affairs analysts alike that the government's media relations and communications style was going from bad to worse (O'Brien, 2009). In fact, notwithstanding the central issue of Ireland's unprecedented fiscal crisis, the communications style of Cowen's government had become a major news story, in and of itself. In March 2009, a satirical painting of a semi-nude Cowen was brought to the attention of the public by journalist Ken Foxe of the *Sunday Tribune*. The painting had been left on display in the National Gallery and the Royal Hibernian Academy. The matter received further national attention when RTÉ news broadcast images of the painting which featured a seated Taoiseach holding a pair of blue and white underwear in his left hand.

However, the story went international after RTÉ broadcast an apology the following evening. In the days that followed, An Garda Síochána also became involved: after an on-air discussion of the issue on Today FM's *Ray D'Arcy Show*, the radio station was visited by members of the force. It was widely reported that the gardaí visited the radio station in Dublin's city centre at the behest of 'the powers that be' (Cooper, 2009). What should have been a storm in a teacup in any mature parliamentary democracy – where political and artistic satire are accepted as normal, even civilised – government mishandling of the incident ensured that it became a major international news story. The sorry saga was re-told across the world from the BBC and the *Times* in London to Fox News and the *New York Times* in the USA. It even made headlines in Beijing's *China Daily*.

The following year, in September 2010, Cowen's government held a strategic 'think-in' at the Ardilaun Hotel in Galway. The think-in, which was later dubbed the 'drink-in' by the Irish media, would in turn spawn 'Gargle-Gate', an international news story prompted by Cowen's below-par communications performance at the event. On 14 September, Cowen gave a poor media interview to Cathal Mac Coille of RTÉ's radio programme *Morning Ireland*. The Taoiseach appeared irritable and at times misplaced words during the interview. This prompted Simon Coveney TD, a prominent member of the opposition, to tweet 'God what an uninspiring interview by Taoiseach this morning. He sounded half way between drunk and hungover.' Cowen's cabinet colleague Dermot Ahern explained the poor performance by stating that it was well known that Cowen suffered from 'nasal congestion' (Kerr, 2010). The opposition, however, felt that Cowen's interview performance was far less than inspiring. Róisín Shorthall (2010) of the Labour Party criticised the interview in no uncertain terms:

> Such a performance by a Taoiseach at any time would be a matter of concern, but at a time when the country is facing such huge economic problems, it must set serious alarm bells ringing [...] When the country is crying out for leadership, looking out for some optimism for the future, we had an interview from a Taoiseach that was semi-coherent and offered no hope or no vision [...] The point of no return has now been reached.

By the following morning the story had gone international and was reported as far afield as the *Huffington Post* in the USA and the Paris-based *Le Post*, which ran the headline 'Premier Irlandaise bourre sur le radio?' ('Irish prime minister drunk on the radio?').

'Cowen-Gate' and 'Gargle-Gate' demonstrated that the communications performance of Cowen's administration was bringing the state into disrepute. This questionable performance occurred, however, at a time when the hard-pressed Irish taxpayer was funding an ever-increasing army of government communications professionals. At Cowen's department of the Taoiseach alone, there were three separate government press secretaries – an unprecedented number, one each for Fianna Fáil, the Green Party, and the vestiges of the Progressive Democrats – along with a burgeoning government information service. Separately, at departmental level, there were approximately 35 press officers and assistant press officers employed at the public service rank of assistant principal officer with annual salaries ranging from €45,000 to €60,000.

In addition, almost all of Cowen's government ministers had appointed special media advisors to assist them with press matters and crisis communications. First introduced in the early 1990s, most were employed at principal officer level within the Irish civil service with salaries ranging from €85,000 to €110,000. Funded exclusively by the exchequer, they were employed under Section 11 (1) of the Public Service Management Act 1997. The *Irish Media Contacts Directory 2010* listed 13 of these special media advisors. Operating across almost all government departments, 11 of these 13 political appointees agreed to be interviewed by this author in relation to their status and role as special media advisors. One media advisor was unavailable for interview due to travel and one refused outright to be drawn into any discussion as to their status or role as a publicly funded appointee.

In terms of experience, the Cowen administration's media advisors combined an eclectic mix of professional and intellectual formation. Most had extensive media experience, some as journalists, and had university degrees, many to postgraduate level in areas relevant to their departmental portfolios. Just under half of the special advisors were members of professional bodies such as the National Union of Journalists or the Public Relations Institute of Ireland – which bound them to professional and ethical codes of conduct. Most, at the height of the Celtic Tiger, would have enjoyed far higher salaries as public affairs consultants in the private sector. On paper at least, the advisers would certainly have appeared to represent value for money.

However, a cursory examination of their actual roles as professional communicators – and crucially, their status as publicly funded consultants

– raises concerns as to whether or not such positions actually function in the public interest. Each of the eleven interviewees was asked to identify precisely their role as communicators – over and above those tasks carried out by the permanently appointed departmental press officers. In other words, they were asked to describe their role as politically appointed and publicly funded communicators vis-á-vis their public service counterparts. The responses were uniform, with the various media advisors indicating that politically appointed media advisors were there to deal with matters of a 'political' nature and to 'at all times seek to enhance the media profile of the minister in question'. One has to question whether, at a time of severe cutbacks in the public sector, it is morally problematic to use public funds in order to enhance the media profiles of individual government ministers. This is, by definition, 'spin' and an activity that ought to be funded solely from within party political resources.

In examining the status and role of the Cowen administration's media advisors, a number of political correspondents from the political press pool at Leinster House were interviewed. Out of a total of 46 journalists in the Oireachtas press gallery, approximately one-third or 15 journalists were interviewed to ascertain their experiences of dealing with politically appointed media advisors. Their responses were universally critical of what was generally referred to as the Cowen administration's confrontational communications style.

One senior political correspondent expressed the view that the Cowen administration operated a communications and public relations strategy that amounted to 'if not a culture of secrecy, then a culture of extreme discretion [...] to the point that we get nothing [...] no information'. Another political correspondent observed that the government's weekly press briefings given to journalists were 'almost completely devoid of hard, real-time information'; yet another described them as 'pathetic'. Most of the journalists identified a marked deterioration in government–media relations after Cowen's election as Taoiseach. One journalist stated that 'the house style has evolved into an abrasive and authoritarian approach towards media from the Taoiseach and the government press service.' Many of the journalists were of the view that the media relations strategy employed by the Taoiseach was 'incoherent' and based on 'cronyism', with certain journalists and media organisations deemed 'beyond the pale' and isolated – particularly if their coverage was critical of the Fianna Fáil-led government. According to one journalist, 'some of the government's media handlers seem to have taken it upon themselves to take personal offence at legitimate criticism instead of facilitating a professional communications relationship.' Another stated:

> It now takes a sledgehammer to get simple information. This cute-hoor approach, which seems to be coming from the top, is actually counter-productive for everyone in society including the government itself, business sentiment and even our image abroad.

On paper and in theory at least, the Cowen administration's team of highly qualified communications professionals should have been well able to provide the media – and the electorate – with clear communication, vital information and leadership at a time of unprecedented national crisis. However, at a cost of millions of euros per annum to the exchequer in salaries and expenses, as well as lucrative contracts to public relations consultancies, the collective abilities of these communications gatekeepers – according to the political correspondents interviewed – appears to have operated a culture of 'obfuscation', 'misinformation', 'obstruction', and spin. According to the journalists interviewed, this culture proliferated and persisted throughout the Cowen administration – becoming almost tragicomic in the days leading up to the EU–IMF bailout. Such a dysfunctional and ineffective communications regime ran counter to the assumptions contained within the literature (Miller, 2002; Gilpin and Murphy, 2008) about active engagement with journalists by powerful agencies during times of crisis. It also prevailed despite the electorate's need for dialogue and clear communication at a time of national crisis.

Media advisers and the Fine Gael–Labour Party coalition

In March 2011, after a landslide victory at the polls, Fine Gael leader Enda Kenny was elected Taoiseach. Though his party had promised in its election manifesto to 'deliver smaller, better government' during a time of austerity and fiscal crisis, it opted to continue the practice of appointing dozens of media advisors and programme managers. According to the *Irish Media Contacts Directory 2012*, there are now approximately 37 such political appointees. Funded exclusively by the exchequer, the salaries of at least ten of these advisors breach the austerity-related public sector pay cap of €92,672 per annum. Several of the coalition's key advisors receive salaries well in excess of €100,000 per annum. According to one newspaper report, the total cost of these advisors is just under €3.5 million per annum (Quinlan, 2012). In addition to this outlay, Kenny's administration also spends large amounts of public money on the services of public relations consultancies. In the 12 months between April 2011 and April 2012, coalition ministers spent approximately €200,000 on advice and speech-writing fees – despite having access to press officers in government departments (O'Brien, 2012).

The Irish government's spend on the services of communications professionals is high by EU standards. In comparison, the Conservative–Liberal Democratic coalition of David Cameron and Nick Clegg in the UK – in a parliament with 650 members and a population base of over 62 million citizens – spend an annual total of approximately £6 million on government advisers. (BBC, 2012) Whilst Britain's per capita spend on politically appointed advisors is approximately ten times lower than that of Ireland's government, the British electorate is, nevertheless, exercised by Cameron and Clegg's outlay on spin-doctors. In a submission to the public administration committee enquiry on special advisors, the Constitution Unit of University College, London, observed (Hazell et al., 2012, 3) that

Concerns about special advisors have been raised [... as to whether:]

They exercise improper and/or disproportionate influence
They marginalise the civil service
They lack transparency and accountability.

Against the background of this debate on the status, role, and cost of special advisors in Britain, the views of political journalists in Ireland were solicited on the 'house style' and communications performance of the Kenny administration's media advisors. Again, their responses were almost uniformly negative.

In comparing the communications style of the Fine Gael–Labour Party coalition with the previous Cowen administration, one senior political journalist stated that the situation was now 'worse'. He described the attitude of the government press service as 'guarded, secretive and paranoid'. Several senior political correspondents lamented the lack of 'proper ministerial briefings with off the record discussions of policy'. Another political correspondent expressed the view that a number of special advisors and their ministerial charges were 'childishly adversarial' and that there had been a marked deterioration in communication style. The unanimous view of the political correspondents interviewed was that the investment by the Kenny administration in special advisors 'did not represent value for money for the Irish taxpayer'. Several went further and stated that aside from representing a waste of public money, many of the special advisors were actually damaging

– rather than enhancing – the public profile of their ministerial charges. One of the most experienced of the political journalists interviewed elaborated on this point:

> Some of the advisors are incredibly defensive. They seem to have inherited a level of paranoia and hatred of the media from the previous adminis- tration. They don't engage with us. This is a pity because the new government ministers and office holders are earnest, honest people. However, they are being actively handled in such a way as to hamper openness. Only the shrewd ones among them are prepared to interact with journalists.

Out of the total number of journalists interviewed, only two offered an alternative view of the status and role of the Kenny administration's political media advisors:

> This lot are definitely better than the previous incumbents. There is a top tier of advisors who are genuinely helpful and try their best to keep us informed. This is particularly the case in the department of finance. There are a few duds, but you get them in every organisation.

Another journalist offered the view that:

> While the primary role of the advisors is to obfuscate and obstruct, they are slightly more impressive than the last lot. Despite this however, I don't believe that they act in the public interest. They act solely in the political interest of their minister – with varying results.

Based on the overwhelmingly negative views expressed by the political journalists interviewed, it would appear therefore, that at a time of national crisis – where clear communication is an absolute priority – the Irish taxpayer, Irish political journalists, and Irish politicians alike are ill-served by the communications culture fostered by politically appointed media advisors in Leinster House.

Conclusion

Given the high financial costs involved, it can only be assumed that the hiring of three dozen politically appointed media advisors by the Irish government is driven by its desire to harness the power of the media for its own ends. Whilst the number of politically appointed media advisers within Ireland is relatively high – with the Irish taxpayer, on a per capita basis, paying ten times what British taxpayers do for 'special advisors' – their effectiveness and value for money appear questionable. The relationship between media advisors and journalists is fractured and the facilitative symbiotic relationship between politically appointed media advisors and political correspondents appears to be absent. These advisors appear incapable of operating the 'optimum' strategic management of the news agenda as described by Hall (1978) to achieve 'primary definition' for their political masters. On the other hand, political journalists appear frozen out of what seems to be a dysfunctional and adversarial culture of media 'management' that alienates them and leaves the citizen ill-served by way of clear communication from government. This is compounding a growing disconnect and lack of trust between the citizenry and their elected representatives.

The electorate ought to be reassured that the growing plethora of media advisors and programme managers act in the public interest and provide value for money. This might be achieved if their status and roles were given significant clarification and rendered amenable to public scrutiny: in other words, if their work behind the scenes of government – and the work of lobbyists and pressure groups – were made transparent and accountable to voters and taxpayers. This would be consistent with the recommendations made to the UK public administration committee enquiry on special advisors:

> Special advisors need to be held accountable for their actions. This would be easier to achieve if there was greater clarity, advisor by advisor over the nature of their role. (Hazell et al., 2012, 1)

Without such clarity, transparency, and public accountability, the status, role, and value for money of politically appointed advisors may well continue to be treated with some scepticism. In the absence of such clarity, the potential for public suspicion and scepticism towards the role of such advisors remains:

> [S]pecial advisers [are] [...] treated with suspicion [...] [for] prioritising the minister's interests against those of his colleagues, favouring short term political advantage over long term policy gains; selective briefing of the media; negative briefing against rivals and opponents; favouring some interest groups over others; and cocooning the minister from unwelcome advice or different points of view. (Hazell et al., 2012, 1–2)

A thorough independent review into the functions, status and role of politically appointed advisors is imperative at a time of national crisis where effective government communication is a premium requirement. The taxpayer is entitled to the rigorous scrutiny and regulation of the activities of advisors, communications consultants, and all lobbyists and other stakeholders within the domain of public affairs and political communication. This might bring some clarity to the field of public affairs, lobbying, and 'spin' within the Irish political landscape. It might also remove obstacles to clear communication and end the disproportionate influence of back-room 'handlers' on public and political discourse. The system of government communication that currently operates is dysfunctional and inordinately expensive. It achieves little by way of clear government communication and is the result of an anachronistic system of political cronyism. Moreover, it is profoundly anti-democratic in that it functions to deepen the crisis of public confidence in our political system at a time of major national fiscal, social, and communication challenges.

References

BBC (2012). See <http://www.bbc.co.uk/news/uk-politics-18871984>

Cooper, M. (2009) 'Gardaí have better things to be doing than get painted into a corner' in *Irish Examiner* (3 April).

Dineen, M. (2011) 'Five reasons to believe the economy has started to improve' in *Irish Independent* (19 September).

Gilpin, D. and Murphy, P. (2008) *Crisis management in a complex world*, New York; Oxford University Press.

Hall, S. (1978) *Policing the crisis*, London: Routledge.

Hazell, R. et al. (2012) Submission of the Constitution Unit of University College, London to the public administration committee enquiry on special advisors, UK Public Administration Committee of Enquiry on Special Advisors.

Irish Media Contacts Directory (2010 and 2012), Dublin: Media Contacts.

The Journal (2011) 'Ministers had to lie about bailout talks admits Lenihan' (24 January).

Keeble, R. (2000) *The newspapers handbook*, London: Routledge.

Kellner, D. (2001) *Media culture*, London: Routledge.

Kennedy, G. (1993a) 'Labour appoints outside advisors' in *Irish Times* (29 January).

Kennedy, G. (1993b) 'Fianna Fáil and Labour appoint biggest staff in history of state' in *Irish Times* (20 February).

Kerr, A. (2010) 'FF troops jump to aid of "hoarse" leader' in *Irish Independent* (15 September).

McChesney, R.W., Wood, E.M. and Foster, J.B. (eds) (1998) *Capitalism and the information age: the political economy of the global communication revolution*, New York: Monthly Review Press.

Miller, D. (2002) *Crisis management and communication: how to gain and maintain control*, San Francisco: IABS.

Mosco, V. (1996) *The political economy of communication*, London: Sage.

O'Brien, C. (2012) 'Ministers paying PR firms out of secretary allowance' in *Irish Times* (14 April).

O'Brien, P. (2009) 'A single phone call brings master of spin into focus' in *Irish Examiner* (27 March).

Quinlan, R. (2012) 'No austerity for Taoiseach when it comes to staff' in *Sunday Independent* (10 June).

Schiller, H. (1992) *Mass communications and American empire: the emergence of a political economy approach to mass communications*, Boulder, CO: Westview Press.

Shorthall, R. (2010). See < http://www.breakingnews.ie/ireland/taoiseach-denies-being-hungover-for-interview-473530.html>

We've done the Groundwork—
NOW LET'S BUILD THE NATION

Fianna Fáil
THE REPUBLICAN PARTY

THE WAY FORWARD

Vote **FG** FINE GAEL

The 1980s was dominated by the rivalry between Charles Haughey and Garret FitzGerald, leaders of Fianna Fáil and Fine Gael respectively. These posters are from the 1982 and 1987 elections.

CHAPTER EIGHT

A limited focus?
Journalism, politics, and the Celtic Tiger

Declan Fahy

Journalists dominated the 2009 end-of-year bestseller lists with books castigating Ireland's financial and political elites for causing the financial crisis that would eventually claim the country's economic sovereignty. In *The Bankers* Shane Ross criticised bank executives and regulators for their close relationship that facilitated years of reckless property speculation, while in *Who Really Runs Ireland?* Matt Cooper laid out the elite nexus of bankers, developers, politicians, and media owners that he argued allowed a thriving economy to overheat. In *Ship of Fools*, Fintan O'Toole traced the entwined Irish histories of economic mismanagement, political corruption, and financial fraud that combined so disastrously in the crisis. In *Follow the Money*, David McWilliams described a panicked Irish government amid the 2008 global financial meltdown, as then finance minister Brian Lenihan, eating garlic to stay awake, paid a late-night visit to the columnist's house for advice. In *Anglo Republic*, Simon Carswell forensically examined the succession of high-risk financial decisions by Anglo Irish Bank executives that forced the government to guarantee bank debts and deposits. These books unflinchingly laid out the national systemic political and financial failure that found apt symbolism, among international media, in the half-finished 'ghost estates' that littered the Irish countryside.

These post-crash books were cutting and critical. But such comprehensive analyses, commentators noted, were mostly absent during the boom years, from the mid-1990s to the mid-2000s, when Ireland's economy expanded with unprecedented growth. Conor Brady, a former editor of the *Irish Times*, wrote that the country's journalists had failed in their fundamental duty to act as watchdogs over political and financial elites. 'Was the forming of this crisis reportable earlier? Were emerging trends apparent? Did they [the news media] do as good a job as they might have in flagging the approaching storm?' asked Brady (2010). He concluded that the criticisms of systemic problems in the Irish financial system were not reported 'in a form that was sufficiently sustained, coherent and authoritative'. In a similar vein, an examination of the coverage of the crisis in the Irish and British press found that reporters deserved an 'F for probing and predicting' (Marron, 2010, 274). Such critical sentiment was summarised in the conclusion to a study on the pre-crash performance of UK financial reporters: 'The financial media [...] did not warn us' of the impending economic turmoil (Manning, 2013, 187).

But such criticism overlooked the fact that there were repeated warnings from some journalists, economists, and news organisations. McWilliams was one media figure who argued consistently that the property bubble would burst. George Lee, then economics editor of the state broadcaster RTÉ, was another who sounded cautionary notes. *The Economist* predicted in 2003 that Irish house prices would plummet in the subsequent four years as part of a worldwide property crash. In 2005 *The New York Times* observed that regulation was perceived to be so lax in Ireland that 'Dublin has become known in the insurance industry as something of the Wild West of European finance' (Lavery and O'Brien, 2005). From 2006 onwards, University College Dublin economist Morgan O'Kelly wrote a series of op-ed articles warning that the property market would collapse. The 2007 RTÉ television programme *Future Shock: Property Crash*, presented by business journalist Richard Curran, detailed the excesses of the property bubble and asked whether or not financial institutions behaved responsibly towards borrowers. But as Carswell (2011, 72) noted, these few voices were ignored: for example, Bank of Ireland's chief economist Dan McLaughlin stated that *The Economist* article was based on 'specious' arguments.

These examples demonstrate that some journalists did warn citizens of the impending international financial catastrophe, but these voices were marginalised and were not given the appropriate sustained prominence in coverage that, in retrospect, they warranted. Against this background, this chapter offers a more fully developed explanation for the lack of systemic and sustained critical financial journalism during the economic boom. It synthesises published accounts of modern financial journalism, in Ireland and internationally, and in-depth interviews with Irish financial journalists to offer an insight into the production of financial news, a complex process influenced by the choices of individual journalists, their professional routines, the organisations for which business reporters work, and the political and legal contexts within which financial journalists operate. The eight interviewees were sampled to ensure variability in the type of media organisation (print, broadcast, wire service), the length of experience in financial journalism, and position in the editorial hierarchy. They were granted requested anonymity as they were frequently critiquing their peers and employers, and the views expressed were their personal opinions rather than those of their news organisations. The journalists were overwhelmingly experienced: six of the reporters had been reporting on financial matters for between five and ten years, one for between one and five years, and one for more than ten years (see Fahy et al., 2010).

This chapter argues that certain features of this journalistic specialism – undertaken in the particular Irish political, economic, and media culture – prevented the sustained systemic analysis that could have better anticipated the financial crisis. It examines how, amid a climate of rampant consumerism and auction politics – where candidates and parties compete to make financially attractive promises to voters – caused by the building boom, those who questioned the received wisdom (that this time it was different) were marginalised not just by the particular features of financial journalism but also by politicians and interest groups that benefited from the boom. It recognises also that media outlets themselves are financial entities that are not necessarily detached observers of, or immune to, economic booms and busts. The chapter concludes by arguing that the global financial crisis, coupled with seismic changes in journalism and political communication, has created novel opportunities and methods for systemic coverage of business and finance. These styles of financial journalism could broaden the range of journalism in Ireland, which has, as Cawley (2011, 600) has noted, traditionally been 'more comfortable reporting events than explaining processes', a characteristic that meant the media in general missed vital connections that would have helped predict the crash.

The historical tensions of Irish financial journalism

Specialist Irish financial journalists were not appointed until the 1960s. Before that decade, even though there was coverage of economic topics such as taxation and government budgets, financial reporting was largely limited to lists of share prices on the Dublin and London stock exchanges and reports of companies' annual general meetings. The rapid economic development that followed the switch to free trade in the early 1960s meant newspapers covered finance in more detail. Nicholas Leonard became the *Irish Times'* first financial editor in 1963, but he recalled that company directors did not welcome his appointment:

in 1963 it was quite commonplace for substantial companies, like John Power, the distillers, and Thomas Dockrell, the builders' providers, to ban reporters from their annual meetings. Maurice Dockrell, the chairman of the latter, used to personally bring me out a glass of sherry after the meeting and graciously inform me that all resolutions had been carried without dissent. (Leonard, 2006, 57)

From then on, media coverage of finance expanded considerably. *Business and Finance* magazine was first published in 1964 and *Hibernia* was reinvented in 1968 as a magazine with an editorial blend of politics, gossip, and business journalism. After it ceased publication in 1980, it was succeeded in 1983 by *The Phoenix*, which also featured substantive business coverage. The *Irish Times* and the *Irish Independent* had weekly business supplements by the mid-1980s while *The Sunday Business Post* was founded in 1989 and remains the country's only dedicated financial newspaper.

Yet tensions remained between business journalism and its source community. The Central Bank, for example, was contemptuous of reporters. George Lee, who worked there as an economist early in his career, described how the 'prevailing view was that journalists are not all that bright, never understand what they are told, will twist things to get a story, and should never be trusted.' Lee noted that RTÉ was first allowed to bring television cameras into Central Bank press conferences in 2001 – on the condition that the microphones were switched off, so as to prevent the broadcast of a potentially unguarded comment by an official (Lee, 2002, 68–69).

Brokers had a similar attitude towards the media. Martin FitzGerald, former group business editor of Independent Newspapers, recalled that in the 1980s an attitude existed among senior financial figures that they owned the financial pages. He recalled being at a lunch to mark the appointment of a new president of the Irish Stock Exchange when journalists and brokers began discussing the mutual dependence between reporters and sources:

'What do you mean, mutual?' a rubicund and slightly tipsy broker ventured. 'The business pages are ours. We own them,' he added [...] Trudging back to the office, however, I admit an icy feeling was coursing through my veins. Maybe, the chap with the English public school accent was right. He was implying that we were lazy, dependent and largely uncritical. More chillingly still, maybe our employers (who shared the same gentlemen's clubs with the brokers) were happy with such an arrangement. (Bourke, 2008, 61–64)

FitzGerald's reflections highlight two connected, fundamental tensions within financial journalism about its role and its audience. While journalism traditionally operates on the principle that it acts as a watchdog over the powerful in society, interpreting elite opinion for broad audiences, business journalism operates differently. The modern financial press has focused not on broad audiences but on the opinions and values of a narrow elite that reads the business papers. And business journalists themselves do not agree about their primary audience and their central role as reporters. For example, one journalist stated that he operated as a watchdog that held power to account. His job, he said, was 'holding business people and organisations to account and explaining complex events to people who are not experts in the field'. But another journalist expressed the widespread view that his job was to provide specialised market information to investors: 'the financial journalist is not paid to consider the wider consequences of commercial decisions, so hence the financial journalist has to be able to zone in on the strict commercial merits of big decisions.' As media critic Dean Starkman (2012, 26) observed in his analysis of pre-crash US business news, disagreements 'over what business news actually is has never been resolved within newsrooms, or even properly articulated'.

These different conceptions can depend on the target audience of the news organisation. Business reporters who work for the *Financial Times*, *Wall Street Journal*, *Business and Finance* and the news agencies Bloomberg and Reuters produce content aimed at highly financially literate audiences. Journalists who report on finance for outlets aimed at broad audiences, such as the *Irish Times*, the *Irish Independent* and RTÉ news, produce business and economics as part of their overall coverage of current affairs and frequently aim content at non-specialist audiences. But as Starkman (26) noted, these two audiences – investors and the public – need different news-gathering approaches. Reporting for broad audiences requires 'an accountability orientation – a frame broad enough to take in social and external costs, as well as the time and space to lay out a case'. But serving investors requires speed, access and 'a focus on internal metrics like earnings'. This tension is not always articulated or understood in criticisms of business news. Yet the result, Starkman (28) noted, was that 'the interests of investors, even small ones, should not be confused with the public interest, which is much larger and, by definition, more important. Business-news organisations often conflate these missions, leading to significant conceptual confusion.' Expecting systemic criticisms from reporters who do not see that style of reporting as their job is therefore unrealistic.

The second feature alluded to by FitzGerald is shared by all financial journalists: a reliance on a core set of sources. Business news is tied to the consistent daily stream of routine, market-focused corporate and government announcements. The majority of business news comes from regular sources, such as company results and announcements, bank announcements, regulatory business, consultants' reports, analysts' reports, brokers, economists, company spokespeople, and interviews with senior executives. The heads of public companies must communicate regularly with investors, brokers, pension managers, and fund managers. They do this frequently through media conferences, timed to occur as company results are announced to the stock market. The information relayed from these sources is usually crafted to appeal to specialists in finance, not general readers. As Matt Cooper (2009, 207–8), a long-time business reporter, observed,

> Unfortunately, these interviews are sometimes of little use to the radio listener or newspaper reader. The business leaders often lapse into jargon, sometimes deliberately, sometimes out of habit. They use terms familiar to their ilk but that confuse the general audience. They prefer to deal in specifics about their own company and talk in generalities about the economy – usually to condemn high costs, lack of competitiveness and excessive pay (for workers, not management). They also tend to steer away from criticism of, and confrontation with, the government or other authorities in the state.

This proximity to, and dependence on, a restricted range of sources presents difficulties for the journalistic critique of business and, as a consequence, the public understanding of finance. Not only do the core sources for financial news have a strong motivation to shape the news in a way that presents their organisation in the best light, but these same sources are also often the only sources of information for financial journalists. Moreover, the sources that provide expert commentary on financial news, such as economists and market analysts, are employed by banks and stockbrokers. As a result of this closeness to a set of sources, brokers and investors who supply information to journalists become definers of that information. The audience and source for financial news is often the same set of people. Financial journalism is produced with information from figures in the business community for the business community.

For the media sociologist Aeron Davis (2000, 285), this process harms democracy. His study of the production of financial journalism in the City of London, its financial sector, found that business news was produced and consumed in closed communication networks. Journalists moved in small circles that consisted almost exclusively of financial figures. For Davis, this flow of newsworthy information was not an example of elite to mass communication, as traditionally practised by journalists, but an example of elite–elite communication. That is, elites were at once the major sources, targets, and recipients of financial news. Excluded and absent from these networks were 'the mass of consumer-citizens [who] can be no more than ill-informed spectators'.

A feature of this closed elite–elite network is that business reporters must navigate an expanded layer of strategic communication professionals who aim to control the flow of information between companies and journalists. In Ireland, the number of public relations professionals has also grown and, between 1993 and 2003, public relations expertise has become a core part of the management of Ireland's top 300 companies (O'Dwyer, 2005). Companies employ these professionals because public image contributes to corporate reputation and revenue.

During interviews that I have conducted, financial journalists noted that one of the ways that these communication specialists seek to influence the content of financial news is to cultivate favourable relationships with some journalists while simultaneously excluding other journalists from the elite–elite communication network. One journalist observed: 'it was well known that some PR companies try to bully journalists by cutting off access or excluding journalists from briefings.' Yet reporters must maintain good relations with this set of core sources to access information. Another journalist noted that 'reporters operate within that system and within [or] on the fringes of certain circles of knowledge. If they are overly critical of those within those circles, they can lose out on access to that knowledge and therefore they lose stories.' An 'exchange relationship' exists whereby journalists get stories and companies get publicity, but this sets the conditions for less sustained critical reporting. One journalist noted this was evident in the boom years: reporters were 'reluctant to be critical of companies because they fear they will not get information or access in the future'. Another journalist stated that this support was 'justified editorially because many developers and bankers limited access to such an extent that it became seen to be better to write soft stories about them than to lose access'.

Celtic Tiger journalism: herding and groupthink?

Journalists, who cite independence and detachment as professional values, are reluctant to acknowledge that they are embedded within such elite–elite networks. When asked whether they operated within these elite–elite networks during the boom years, no consensus emerged. Yet they stated that their sources came from the business community, which formed a large part of their audience. More generally, such a closed network is a feature of the relationship between elites in Ireland. Former finance minister Brian Lenihan stated that the crisis in corporate governance was influenced by 'too many incestuous relationships', which the *Financial Times* interpreted as a small pool of people willing to take up non-executive roles in companies (Grant and Murray Brown, 2010, 14).

As well as operating within elite networks, some journalists during the boom years operated within the same intellectual framework as these political and economic elites – elites that pushed the message that regulation in any form was bad for business. In 2007 one prominent banker described the lax regulatory regime as 'corporate McCarthyism', which prompted little or no journalistic comment (Madden, 2007). Some journalists believed in the historical liberal economic view that financial markets were efficient, stable, and self-correcting. According to a government-issued report by Peter Nyberg, a former International Monetary Fund economist, this points to the role that an uncritical media played in the systemic financial crisis. Before such crises, the media were, he wrote, 'generally supportive of corporate and bank expansion, profit growth and risk taking, while being dismissive of warnings of unsustainable developments'. The media, Nyberg added, had a fairly 'large influence on how pre-crisis developments were perceived, discussed and acted upon' (Nyberg, 2011, 5–6).

Nyberg is describing here the media's agenda-setting function. At its simplest, this influential theory of media effects explains the process of the media presenting some issues often and prominently with the result that large segments of the public come to perceive those issues as more important than others. The tone of the coverage, furthermore, is the tone that will be foremost in the public mind when considering the issue. Communications researchers have demonstrated that the news media do have a degree of influence over how people view the economy (Hester and Gibson, 2003). Having looked at how the media covered the boom, Cooper (2009, 36) concluded that the pervasive media tone was that of 'wealth and consumption', while Carswell (2011, 31) found that the 'media enthusiastically supported the Irish preoccupation with property ownership and supported the profit growth at the banks while generally dismissing warnings that the property market was growing out of control.'

Due to their reliance on a core set of sources, business journalists found it difficult to find a range of dissenting views to this prevalent mood. Their sources, essentially, were all saying the same thing. Nyberg noted that 'herding' was prevalent within the banks: institutions uncritically followed each other's practices. Within institutions, 'groupthink' dominated; there existed little or no considerations of alternative positions or little critical analysis (Nyberg, 2011, 7). In communication terms, a spiral of silence – whereby people fear the isolation or exclusion that would result from speaking publicly against a perceived dominant view – appeared to operate within financial institutions. Warnings were dismissed as wrong. Staff members were afraid that their status or reputations would suffer if they argued a contrary view. Doubters stayed silent to avoid sanction or isolation. The oppositional viewpoints that were expressed came from what Nyberg (2011, iii) called 'a handful of identified vociferous contrarians'.

Similarly, financial regulators did not provide consistent dissent. As Carswell (2011, 74) found, the Irish Financial Regulator was 'under-resourced and out of its depth' as it had just three people supervising Anglo Irish Bank in 2005; the same three people who were responsible for monitoring the Bank of Ireland. International regulators, like domestic regulators, were also surprised at the fragility of Irish banks, which had similar risk management practices to British and European banks, even though Ireland's lending was apparently more reckless. As a result, there was conformity and consensus in assessments, and reporters did not have a variety of views to reflect. Conor Brady (2010) noted that the dissent that was printed or broadcast came mainly from academic economists and commentators. Newspaper columnists are expected to provide a counter-view, as part of their professional role is to provide an alternative, sometimes contrarian voice on current affairs (Fahy, 2009). But during the boom years, their voices and those of other experts were marginalised. They were, in Carswell's words, 'dismissed and ridiculed as cranks' (Carswell, 2011, 72). This pattern of marginalisation is typical of a country in the grip of what economist J.K. Galbraith (1990) termed financial euphoria. He argued that those who spoke out at a time of collective exhilaration are 'the exception to a very broad and binding rule' where personal interest, public pressure and 'seemingly superior financial opinion' conspire to sustain this euphoric belief.

For example, in 2004 journalist and former banker Michael Murray noted in a column in the *Sunday Business Post* that Anglo Irish Bank was stuck on what he called 'an unenviable and dangerous treadmill' of aggressive loans. Carswell (2011, 58–59) noted that this insight 'proved to be prophetic, but at the time few were worried about the prospect of a slump. The other banks' main concern was to try to keep up with Anglo.' As Carswell (119) noted, a senior official at Anglo Irish Bank often personally chastised bank analysts or financial reporters or commentators who criticised the bank. As one business journalist put it, his peers operated self-censorship in such a climate of opinion:

> For the most part they [journalists] were not critical enough and even those that were in private conversation didn't express those views in their stories. There were some reporters who did criticise policies, but they were in a minority and no matter how vocal they were, there is an argument that no one wanted to hear it.

The economic interest of some commentators also contributed to the process of marginalisation. Writing about why so few mainstream economists came to the defence of Morgan O'Kelly – who is, it must be noted, a specialist in medieval populations – after his *Irish Times* opinion articles were harshly criticised, O'Toole (2009, 125) noted that the vast majority of Irish economists gave 'timid and carefully couched murmurs of unease'. He argued that those economists that dominated media discussion were usually employed by financial institutions and had a strong motivation for their predictions that the economy would not suddenly collapse. Likewise, Shane Ross (2009) described a similar process (in a chapter entitled 'Poodles and Spoofers') whereby economists who worked for banks and brokers helped inflate the property bubble and castigated critics.

Political and financial figures were wary too, of the potential effects that negative media coverage could have on the economy. A study of economic headlines in the *New York Times* (Blood and Phillips, 1997, 107) found that increased numbers of unfavourable economic headlines in the paper dampened consumer sentiment. The study's authors concluded that 'the amount and tone of economic coverage exerted a powerful influence' on the real economy. This may explain why, in 2006, one high-profile developer criticised those whom he referred to as the 'the harbingers of doom and gloom' in the media (McDonald and Sheridan, 2008, 268). It may also provide a conceptual base, at least, for government fears about talking down the economy, a trend articulated most sharply when Taoiseach Bertie Ahern wondered why those predicting the worst for the economy did not 'commit suicide' (RTÉ, 2007).

As recently as 2010 the then minister for finance, Brian Lenihan, called on journalists 'to be aware of the self-fulfilling nature of doomsday scenarios' because media coverage could 'undermine or promote confidence in our economy'. Negative reports at home were, Lenihan declared, 'beamed around the world and can influence the decisions of foreign investors and multinationals' (Cullen, 2010). This desire too is evident in the way political figures and economists predicted the property market would have a soft landing – that is, that the market would not suddenly collapse, but would experience a gradual fall that would not be a shock to mortgage holders. Cooper (2009, 303) argued that the idea of a soft landing emerged as a 'rebuff to a number of economists and commentators, such as David McWilliams, George Lee, Alan Ahearne, Morgan Kelly, Richard Curran and Brendan Keenan' who warned of Ireland's weakening competitiveness and property bubble inflation.

Furthermore, the dominant political party during the boom years, Fianna Fáil, engaged in auction politics. At the party's 2007 ard fheis, then Taoiseach Bertie Ahern – amid increasing political pressure over revelations about his personal financial dealings more than a decade earlier – promised free health screenings, pension increases, more teachers and gardaí, as well as €4.2 billion of tax cuts if his party was returned for a third term in power (McGee and O'Brien, 2007). And as Stafford (2011, 345) noted, the government's budgetary policy in the economic boom can be 'summarised in the apocryphal comment by Ahern's one-time finance minister Charlie McCreevy on his budgetary policy: "When I have it, I spend it. When I don't, I don't".' McCreevy's view was representative of a central message of governmental political communication during the boom years that was framed around the advocacy and defence of its liberal economic policies. In another example, McCreevy in a 2005 speech to the financial regulator, after a series of scandals in financial services, said: 'My political philosophy is based on giving people freedom. That includes freedom to make money and to lose it.' He classed himself as one of 'the "unregulated generation" – the generation that has produced some of the best risk takers, problem solvers, and inventors' (cited in O'Toole, 2009, 147). For international audiences, the message communicated was one of Ireland as a model for rapid economic development, a message that resonated 'because the globalised Irish economy had itself become a global brand' (O'Toole, 2009, 8).

In addition to these influences on their reporting, during the boom, financial journalists also faced practical constraints on their daily journalism. For instance, they were, and remain, constrained by stock market regulations concerning the public disclosure of market-sensitive information that affects share prices. Also, strict laws on defamation not only restrict what can be reported, but can be used to deter journalistic investigation. Financial reporters work each day under the threat of legal action from well-funded companies and individuals that could afford extraordinarily expensive litigation. One journalist noted that many legal actions by wealthy individuals or companies are 'executed purely to stifle genuine inquiry'. Commercial information is routinely denied to financial journalists. Public companies must communicate, but private organisations are not legally required to reveal their financial performance. Cooper (2009) noted that during the boom years, there was a trend for businesses towards unlimited liability status, a move that meant owners were liable for losses, but also meant companies avoided public scrutiny of their accounts. This move to private status often occurred before a public company was sold. Furthermore, some of the structural weaknesses of Irish banks were not publicly disclosed. Anglo Irish Bank made a series of bad loans to developers who continued to be optimistic about the future of the property bubble. For instance, the developer Seán Quinn was able to amass a huge equity stake in Anglo – almost 30% funded through speculation – without being legally obligated to disclose it publicly.

News organisations themselves benefited from the increased advertising revenue during the boom. In the course of interviews that I conducted, journalists noted that the reliance of some media outlets on real estate advertising, in particular, contributed to a lack of critical coverage of property. For example, one financial journalist observed: 'much of the mainstream media seems to me to be very conflicted because of their reliance on real estate and recruitment advertising. That doesn't mean reporters consciously avoid writing bad news stories, but it's hard to run against the tide when everyone is getting rich.'

The importance of property advertising to media organisations was illustrated in 2006 when the *Irish Times* paid €50 million for the property website myhome.ie, established in 2001 by estate agents Sherry FitzGerald, the Gunne Group, and Douglas Newman Good. A study of that newspaper's housing and property pages in the months before the 2007 general election found that coverage was biased in its selection of sources, which came predominantly from the mortgage, real estate, building, and banking industries. Moreover, housing and property was reported uncritically in the paper. For example, of the 60 articles included in the study's total sample that described residential properties and the 19 that referred to commercial properties, 'not one (this at the height of the Irish bubble) considered the possibility the properties might have been overvalued.' The paper's news section covered corruption among politicians and property developers. But the study found that no 'articles concerning corruption in property appeared in the property or business sections' and argued that structural problems, such as the overproduction of houses, rising prices of property and land, and the zoning of land, were ignored (Preston and Silke, 2011, 60).

In this context, no consensus emerged in the interviews that I conducted about whether or not the journalists judged their own and their peers' journalism to be sufficiently critical of financial institutions' practices and government policy in the boom years. One journalist stated that he and his colleagues 'constantly questioned the sustainability of the Celtic Tiger economy, but it was not always given the proper foregrounding'. He also noted that there were few 'outside forces suggesting the problem was as big as it later became'. Those engaged in critical news analysis were marginalised according to another journalist: 'The problems that we have seen in Irish financial journalism in recent years have been due largely to its unquestioning support for the elite consensus' he said. 'For instance, during the property boom, journalists shouldn't have been just reporting what the developers said, they should have been asking "Where's the demand for all these houses?" and "How do you propose servicing your debt?"'

As the crisis escalated, marginalised voiced became mainstream. The spate of books on the crisis wrapped the systemic failures in Ireland and internationally inside compelling narratives. Economics was a bestseller and economists became celebrities. Reviewing Cooper's *Who Really Runs Ireland?*, author and commentator Eamon Delaney (2009) argued that these types of book were a welcome counterpoint to the 'simplistic shorthand [that has] emerged whereby the bankers and developers have brought the whole economy down'. And, as recounted by some of the interviewees, financial journalism has also changed. As one journalist put it, 'reporters have become much quicker to question figures presented by either government or companies and to ask whether the information has been independently audited as accurate.' Another noted that coverage has 'became more critical, more investigative and more sceptical'. Journalists, he believed, have developed 'a healthy scepticism' towards the business community. Yet, Irish print news media in the first two years of the economic crisis, from 2008 to 2010, examined the crash not as a complex set of interconnected developments, but as a conflict between the public and private sectors (Cawley, 2011).

Systemic, networked, and curatorial financial journalism

The lack of sustained critical coverage in the boom years and before the economic crash was not due to a single factor or force. It cannot be explained by a simplistic argument that business reporters somehow neglected their assumed role. Instead, a fully developed explanation points to a collection of forces that influenced the production of a dominant type of financial journalism that neglected sustained systemic analysis and marginalised alternative voices. These factors were the specialism's unresolved split conception of its audiences, its reliance on a closed set of agenda-driven routine sources and expert commentators, the nature of routine information gathering, and its marginalisation of dissent. These factors largely encouraged fragmentation of coverage and prevented systemic critique. Sustained and critical Irish financial journalism did not occur until the recession had reached its most devastating phase. After that, journalists adopted a much more critical tone, as the culture-wide importance of financial news was enhanced in post-bailout Ireland.

The unprecedented scale of the crisis indicates that weaknesses in reporting will contain critical lessons for future financial journalism, and for the public understanding of economics. Anthropologist David Graeber (2011, 15) has argued that the crash had the potential, among advanced industrial countries, to begin 'an actual public conversation about the nature of debt, of money, of the financial institutions that have come to hold the fate of nations in their grip.' While he observed that this conversation did not occur, it has the potential to do so within the journalism genres of commentary and analysis, which are becoming increasingly important, even as more and more services are providing up-to-the second financial information. These genres could feature the type of holistic business journalism articulated by *Financial Times* journalist Gillian Tett in the epilogue to her book *Fool's Gold* (2009). This reporting would, according to Tett, make explicit the sometimes hidden connections in the global financial system, connections between the macroeconomic system, the practices of individual banks, the actions of individuals within those banks, and the impacts on the consumers of financial products.

Fool's Gold is an exemplar of the future practice that she advocates. It examines the creation of a form of derivatives by a group within J.P. Morgan that, as it spread through the system, was a catalyst in the crash. The book analyses the bankers, their personalities, the system in which they worked and the global system that took their financial innovation and corrupted it. Tett drew on her own training as a social anthropologist – a background that she says was derided by one banker as too "hippie" – to tie these strands together in a compelling explanatory narrative.

This style of reporting is not restricted to books or long magazine articles. New ways of reporting individual stories can overcome some of the constraints faced by financial journalists. The respected analysts of American journalism Bill Kovach and Tom Rosenstiel (2011, 65–73) propose two types of storytelling that allow for big-picture analysis. 'Sense-making news' adds new information that gives greater meaning to other news and facts while 'New paradigm reporting' establishes new understandings about broader phenomena, understandings that often challenge conventional wisdom. Both story genres aim towards holistic analysis. Moreover, journalists in the digital era must be curators of information. They must be proficient in evaluating multiple perspectives on an issue and be able to highlight for their audiences the most important details and interpretations from a mass of information on a topic. Seeking out and presenting a range of perspectives on a financial or political topic can lead to richer storytelling.

Journalists are no longer the only ones who can tell these stories. The digital space in which much communication now occurs allows for more participatory forms of journalism. An example of a nascent form of what has been called networked journalism was evident in the communications work of the 'Budgetjam project', organised after the bailout of Ireland and before the implementation of austerity measures (Titley, 2013). This network of political and community activists, journalists, and academics produced material that contributed to public debate. Its work aimed to challenge the dominant interpretation, as the network saw it, by policymakers and mainstream journalists that strict austerity measures were needed. The network collated alternative budget calculations, conducted assessments of the social cost of budget measures and provided alternative economic interpretations of financial data to that provided by the IMF. It disseminated this evidence and analysis through social media and into newspaper material and broadcast appearances. It was a form of networked journalism in that audiences were no longer just sources and targets for journalism, but actively produced information that mixed and intersected with mainstream journalism content, providing richer and deeper public affairs journalism.

As Ireland's austerity measures grind on, these forms of journalism can help overcome the myriad factors that blunted critical business coverage in the boom years. These forms have the potential to break the elite–elite communication networks, propose perspectives from alternative sources that can become part of the media agenda, and prevent coverage being corralled into traditional story structures that emphasise conflict and crude binary oppositions. The ultimate aim of this journalism is to explain and interpret the globally interconnected financial processes that impact on the lives of Irish citizens. This accountability-orientated business journalism will focus less on fragmentary coverage and more on the more difficult journalistic task of telling comprehensible narratives that help citizens understand the often obscured nature of the systemic global problems that shape their lives.

References

Blood, D.J. and Phillips, P. (1997) 'Economic headline news on the agenda: new approaches to understanding causes and effects' in McCombs, M., Shaw, D.L. and Weaver, D. (eds), *Communication and democracy: exploring the intellectual frontiers in agenda-setting theory*, Mahwah, NJ: Erlbaum.

Bourke, S. (2008) *Ethical trends and issues in Irish journalism, 1973 to 2008*, Dublin: Dublin City University.

Brady, C. (2010) 'Did the media fail to sound alarm bells before the financial crisis?' in *Irish Times* (6 March).

Carswell, S. (2011) *Anglo Republic: inside the bank that broke Ireland*, Dublin: Penguin Ireland.

Cawley A. (2011) 'Sharing the pain or shouldering the burden: news-media framing of the public sector and the private sector in Ireland during the economic crisis, 2008–2010' in *Journalism Studies*, 13(4): 600–615.

Cooper, M. (2009) *Who really runs Ireland? The story of the elite who led Ireland from bust to boom … and back again*, Dublin: Penguin Ireland.

Cullen, P. (2010) 'Lenihan critical of doomsday media coverage' in *Irish Times* (25 September).

Davis, A. (2000) 'Public relations, business news and reproduction of corporate elite power' in *Journalism*, 1(3): 282–304.

Delaney, E. (2009) 'Not quite the last word' in *Irish Times* (26 September).

Fahy, D. (2009) 'The Irish punditocracy as contrarian voice: opinion coverage of the workplace smoking ban' in *Irish Communications Review*, 11: 50–62.

Fahy, D., O'Brien, M. and Poti, V. (2010) 'From boom to bust: a post-Celtic Tiger analysis of the norms, values and roles of Irish financial journalists' in *Irish Communications Review*, 12: 5–20.

Galbraith, J.K. (1990) cited in Tambini, D. (2010) 'What are financial journalists for? Ethics and responsibility in a time of crisis and change' in *Journalism Studies*, 11(2): 158–74.

Graeber, D. (2011) *Debt: the first 5,000 years*, New York: Melville House.

Grant, J. and Murray Brown, J. (2010) 'ISE chiefs say Irish opacity must be stopped' in *Financial Times* (30 January).

Hester, J.B. and Gibson, R. (2003) 'The economy and second-level agenda setting: a time-series analysis of economic news and public opinion about the economy' in *Journalism & Mass Communication Quarterly*, 80(1): 73–90.

Kovach, B. and Rosenstiel, T. (2011) *Blur: how to know what's true in the age of information overload*, New York: Bloomsbury.

Lavery, B. and O'Brien, T. (2005) 'For insurance regulators, the trail leads to Dublin' in *The New York Times* (2 April).

Lee, G. (2002) 'Economic and financial journalism as a public service' in Kiberd, D. (ed.), *Media in Ireland: issues in broadcasting*, Dublin: Open Air.

Leonard, N. (2006) 'The invention of financial journalism' in Whittaker, A. (ed.), *Bright brilliant days: Douglas Gageby and the Irish Times*, Dublin: A. & A. Farmar.

Madden, C. (2007) 'Entrepreneurs face burden of compliance' in *Irish Times* (22 June).

Manning, P. (2013) 'Financial journalism, news sources and the banking crisis' in *Journalism*, 14(2): 173–89.

Marron, M. (2010) 'The scorecard on reporting of the global financial crisis' in *Journalism Studies*, 11(2): 270–83.

McDonald, F. and Sheridan, K. (2008) *The builders: how a small group of property developers fuelled the building boom and transformed Ireland*, Dublin: Penguin.

McGee, H. and O'Brien, P. (2007) 'Poll setback forces Ahern into auction politics u-turn' in *Irish Examiner* (26 March).

McWilliams, D. (2009) *Follow the money: the tale of the merchant of Ennis*, Dublin: Gill & Macmillan.

Nyberg, P. (2011) *Misjudging risk: causes of the systemic banking crisis in Ireland*, report of the commission of investigation into the banking sector in Ireland, Dublin: The Stationery Office, available at <http://www.banking-inquiry.gov.ie/>

O'Dwyer, M. (2005) 'The evolving role of public relations in Ireland' in *European Journal of Marketing*, 39(7/8): 809–20.

O'Toole, F. (2009) *Ship of fools: how stupidity and corruption sank the Celtic Tiger*, London: Faber and Faber.

Preston, P. and Silke, H. (2011) 'Market "realities": de-coding neoliberal ideology and media discourses' in *Australian Journal of Communication*, 38(3): 47–64.

Ross, S. (2009) *The bankers: how the banks brought Ireland to its knees*, Dublin: Penguin Ireland.

RTÉ (2007) 'Ahern apologises for suicide remark', rte.ie (4 July).

Stafford, P. (2011) 'The 2011 general election in Ireland: the political impact of the Irish recession' in *Representation*, 43(3): 343–56.

Starkman, D. (2012) 'A narrowed gaze: how the business press forgot the rest of us' in *Columbia Journalism Review*, January/February: 24–30.

Tett, G. (2009) *Fool's Gold: how the bold dream of a small tribe at J.P. Morgan was corrupted by Wall Street greed and unleashed a catastrophe*, New York: Free Press.

Titley, G. (2013) 'Budgetjam! A communications intervention in the political–economic crisis in Ireland' in *Journalism*, 14(2) 292–306.

PART THREE

Political Communication
and the Public

A private affair?
Lobbying and transparency
in modern Ireland

Gary Murphy

Across the modern democratic world, lobbying governments and policy-makers is considered integral to the process of policy formulation. The work carried out by interest groups is a central and legitimate part of the policy process within all liberal democratic systems. Although the term lobbying has often had negative connotations, the work of lobbyists is essential when policy is being formulated. Lobbyists are an accepted element within society, providing the necessary input and feedback into the political system, thereby helping to develop the policy outputs that drive political, social, cultural, and economic aspects of people's daily lives. Ireland is no different in this regard than any other democratic society.

Lobbying in Ireland and the questions of private influence, access, and expectation have been prominent in public policy debates given the catastrophic collapse of the Irish economy since late 2008 and the role played by lobbyists in contemporary Irish politics. The dramatic fall of the so-called Celtic Tiger and the ensuing misery faced by the Irish people has brought the shadowy world of lobbying to the fore of Irish public consciousness. As unemployment and emigration dramatically increased and negative equity and house repossessions became common it quickly emerged that Ireland's economic miracle of the 2000s was built on rather shaky foundations. But these were foundations that had been built under the urgings of lobbyists. In September 2008 the government decided to bail out the private banks, placing an enormous debt burden on the population, as well as ultimately bringing the IMF to Ireland's shore. Lobbyists were again a crucial part of this decision, one that has had enormous consequences for every citizen of the Irish state.

In that context this chapter explores the relationship between lobbying and private interests in Ireland and assesses whether lobbying as a form of political communication has resulted in a politics dominated by a small elite that has access to the avenues and levers of power within the Irish body politic.

Definition and process

There has long been a vigorous academic debate as to the exact meaning and definition of a lobbyist. Classifying lobbying or interest groups, and explaining what exactly lobbying is, have proved immensely difficult. Two eminent scholars in the field (Baumgartner and Leech, 1998, 34) have pointed out that the word lobbying has seldom been used the same way twice by those studying the topic and they themselves define lobbying as simply 'an effort to influence the policy process'. For Nownes (2006, 5) lobbying is an effort designed to affect what the government does, while Hunter et al. (1991, 490) argue that a common definition of a lobbyist is someone who attempts to affect legislative action. As Beyers et al. (2008, 1107) point out, interest group activity provides a means of influencing governments between elections as interest groups are largely focused on 'influencing policy outcomes, trying to force issues onto, or up the political agenda, and framing the underlying dimensions that define policy issues'. However, it is not simply governments that interest groups lobby to affect decision making: they may also pursue their aims and exercise their influence on policy through public or private channels, both directly and indirectly.

Beyond access to policymakers and others who may influence decision making, the other key element to take into account regarding interest group behaviour is the expectation that such groups have for the lobbying they engage in. Gaining access to decision makers is one thing; the expectation that a group has, once it has been received inside the inner sanctum of power, is quite another in representative democracies where power lies with governments. That said, interest groups often have significant input into how public policy is directed in a representative democratic state. Such groups may include, but are not necessarily limited to, those with economic interests (such as businesses and corporations), professional interests (such as trade unions or professional societies), and civil society interests (such as environmental groups). They may directly, or indirectly, through consultants they have hired, seek to have public policy outputs reflect their own preferences and beliefs.

In essence, lobbying can take two forms: in-house, and through hired, professional lobbyists. In-house lobbying refers to the practice whereby the lobbyist is an employee of the organisation engaged in the lobbying. Paid lobbying takes the form of professional lobbyists who perform that function for an organisation for a fee. Influencing political decisions may take place by various means, including direct communications with government officials, presentation of draft reports to such officials wherein specific details of policy itself are suggested, and even simple telephone conversations with government personnel (Chari et al., 2010, 3–4).

In Ireland the growth of lobbying has been facilitated by a concomitant growth in those providing professional lobbying services. The list of lobbyists, or public affairs consultants as they like to be known in Ireland, now includes former government press secretaries, former officials of all the major political parties, some ex-TDs, and a host of former journalists. While these lobbyists originally catered primarily for foreign interests wishing to operate in Ireland, they are now involved in much more mainstream lobbying. Politicians argued that in the past, private companies made donations to political parties not for particular purposes but for the access to government that such donations provided. It would appear that companies and others are paying lobbyists for the same purpose, though now on a more formal footing. In general lobbyists claim that what they are doing is providing advice and access to the decision-making process for business people who are ignorant of the public policy process and need a specialist to introduce them to the complex workings of government. Most lobbyists now working in Ireland have long experience of how the political and adminis-trative systems work and claim that the people they represent, in practically all cases large business interests, have no idea of how government works.

Lobbyists speak of trying to convince their clients that there is rarely if ever any point in talking to the relevant government minister and that it is more important to talk to the senior civil servant who is handling the specific file. This is where their role is questionable in a parliamentary democracy. While all lobbyists claim that the lobbying system is above board, there are no guidelines governing the interaction between lobbyists and civil servants, who are, after all, servants of the state and are supposed to offer advice impartially without recourse to any interest group pressure. In April 2013 the Irish government finally moved towards establishing a lobbying regulatory framework by publishing a draft regulation of lobbyists bill that would cover such interactions between lobbyists and representatives of the state.

In any case, advice from the civil service can be ignored by the minister – as was shown at the beef tribunal in the early 1990s. This tribunal, investigating allegations of malpractice in the beef industry, found that Albert Reynolds, as minister for industry and commerce, was legally entitled to make all the decisions he had made in relation to export credit insurance of Irish beef firms operating across the globe and had done so in good faith. Reynolds, however, through the whole period under investigation by the tribunal, had systematically overruled the advice of his senior civil servants in relation to such export credit insurance (O'Toole, 1995, 79–85). The tribunal could find no link between such decisions and the relationship between highly powerful beef industry figures and either politicians or political parties in general. What the tribunal did find was that one such beef figure, Larry Goodman, profited from advance business information that he had acquired because he was on the 'inside political track'. Goodman, the tribunal found, 'had reasonably ready access to members of the government [...] for the purpose of discussing his plans for the development of his companies and his exports. It is clear that he had similar access to previous governments' (Collins and Ó Raghallaigh, 1995, 706).

The closeness of relations between senior members of various governments and the business community would seem to cast doubt on the view of the majority of lobbyists that dealing with the civil servant, not the minister, is what counts. One Irish lobbyist is of the opinion that it is the ear of the minister that is key. He maintains that politicians are swamped with paperwork and that the case has to be made to them in a personal way: 'Our job is to get our client into a position to make their case but at the end of the day the decisions are made by the politicians themselves' (Murphy, 1999, 287). While lobbyists deny that it matters who is in power, many major companies are now covering their options by having different lobbyists handle approaches to different political parties: this is now quite easy as there are so many former officials and government press secretaries involved in the lobbying business.

Such developments led the Public Relations Institute of Ireland (PRII), the organisation that promotes the professional practice of public relations in Ireland, in December 2003 to adopt a specific code of professional practice for public affairs and lobbying. For the PRII, professional public affairs practice and lobbying are proper, legitimate, and important activities that ensure an open two-way communication process between national and local government, including the Oireachtas and the citizen. It also believes that the existence of a defined code for the practice of public affairs and lobbying serves to enhance the integrity of the democratic process. Yet public relations lobbyists are not obliged to make it publicly known whose interests they are representing under this code of conduct.

The code does require PR professionals to tell the subjects of their lobbying exactly who they are representing. For the PRII, 'public affairs practice' is taken to mean 'all activity associated with representing the interests of a client or employer in relation to any matter of public policy', including the provision of information and 'professional advice' and the 'making of representations, or the advocacy of a point of view, to any persons or institutions' (PRII, 2003). Thus, lobbyists themselves clearly recognise that 'lobbying involves more than simply direct contact with policymakers, and that it does encompass information gathering and dissemination' (McGrath, 2011, 131). The PRII is also active in professionalising the lobbying and public relations industries and offers professional qualifications for entrants into the profession and for experienced practitioners.

Interest groups and lobbyists pursue their goals through a number of different channels. These include public and private pressure on government, individual politicians and other interest groups and the use of the mass media. Yet despite all the other avenues open to groups it is still the Oireachtas – most particularly the Dáil and its members – that remains the prime focus, principally because parliament is the centre for information, access, and publicity for such groups. TDs have access to insider information, can generate publicity, particularly given the televising of Dáil proceedings, and are in a position to put pressure on governments and individual ministers by tabling parliamentary questions.

Two levels of lobbying of parliament are apparent in Ireland. One seeks to influence national policy, the other local or constituency issues. While members of parliament are lobbied by the full range of interest groups, they are most sensitive to representations that have a constituency resonance, because these concern a local issue, or a national issue with a local dimension, or are simply so emotive that they can affect the electoral preferences of a significant number of voters. In this context it is important to note that Ireland operates a proportional representation system of government whereby members of the same party compete against each other as well as other parties in national and local elections.

Saving the banks: a peculiar case of Irish lobbying

Interest group activity in Ireland spans numerous strands and was identified on one level with the process of social partnership, whereby sectional groups, such as trade unions, employers, and farmers' interests, had central roles in the economy from 1987 to 2009. The collapse of the economy also led to the end of social partnership. Self-regulating professional groups, such as accountants, doctors, and lawyers, also come under this category of sectional groups, as they represent and articulate the interests of certain sections of society. At a second level, interest group activity spans what we call cause-centred groups that attempt to influence policy outcomes in specific areas. They advocate for a particular outcome and articulate the interests of people who promote a specific cause. Moral issue groups and environmental issue groups are two examples of such causes that have resulted in significant activity in the interest group sphere in modern Ireland. But beyond these two categories a new form of interest group activity has emerged that has involved vigorous lobbying on behalf of business or private interests, in an attempt to influence specific government policy, as distinct from the sectional demands of the wider business community. This was a feature of evidence heard between 1997 and 2010 at the Flood/Mahon and Moriarty tribunals of inquiry into rezoning in County Dublin and payments to politicians respectively.

There has long been a view held by practically all sections of Irish society that the main political parties, but Fianna Fáil in particular, had an especially close relationship with property developers and the construction industry. This was particularly important in relation to local government in Ireland and planning decisions where county councillors charged with deciding on land rezoning were continuously and vigorously lobbied by property developers. Such lobbying was probably best epitomised by the career of Frank Dunlop who, while he started off his role in public life as press secretary in 1978 to the then majority Fianna Fáil government, later set up his own lobbying firm, in the mid-1980s (McGrath, 2009, 257–58). His clients were mostly property developers, and in dramatic evidence to the government-appointed Tribunal of Inquiry on Certain Planning Matters in Dublin (commonly known as the Flood tribunal, and later the Mahon tribunal) in April 2000 he admitted to having paid numerous bribes to county councillors in return for their votes on rezoning land. His evidence over the course of 124 days in the witness box implicated property developers and politicians and he ended up being convicted of corruption and sentenced to two years' imprisonment in 2009 (Murphy, 2006, 96).

In late 2008 the Irish property market crashed spectacularly, causing the virtual failure of the banking industry due to the enormous sums loaned by all the main banks, on little security, and with little oversight by the regulators, to property developers. The result of such lax regulation by the Central Bank and regulatory authorities and colossal lending by the banks to property developers was the collapse in the solvency of the Irish banks, and the government had to step in to bail out these banks on the fateful night of 29 September 2008. Ireland had, since 1987, prided itself on an economic model of low taxation and little regulation in relation to foreign direct investment. The establishment of the Irish Financial Services Sector in the late 1980s was a classic example of this. Private interests with access to politicians were able to persuade such politicians that a light regulatory and low tax regime in relation to financial services and banking was crucial in making Ireland an attractive place for foreign direct investment in those services.

Such business interests have long had the ear of the Irish political class, dating back to the 1960s, when Fianna Fáil, in particular, began to accept large donations – out of which the organisation Taca ('support' in the Irish language) was born. The original idea behind Taca was to bring together 500 large subscribers whose money would be invested for a year and then transferred into the Fianna Fáil election account (Keogh, 1994, 270). With the development of Taca, Fianna Fáil realised that the financial support of the entrepreneurial class could be substantial and would become vital as the business of running a large political organisation became more expensive. Taca, however, soon acquired a reputation for influencing ministerial decisions (Collins and Ó Raghallaigh, 1995, 707). While it was later disbanded its influence over Fianna Fáil remained and was showcased by that party's famous fundraising tent at the annual Galway race festival. This tent was basically a Fianna Fáil fundraising initiative and served as a sort of annual gathering of some of Ireland's richest property developers and construction company owners. The tent was reckoned to have raised €160,000 for the party at its height but was abandoned by Brian Cowen just over two weeks after he became Taoiseach in 2008.

Financial success by such firms saw them make increased demands for even less regulation. This was perhaps best epitomised by the chairman of Anglo Irish Bank, Seán FitzPatrick, who in June 2007 claimed that Ireland's prosperity was being put at risk by what he termed 'corporate McCarthyism' in which excessive regulation was shackling Irish entrepreneurs. This 'move to a heavily regulated economy needs to be challenged vigorously and challenged now' he declared in a speech to business executives (Cooper, 2009, 208). Fifteen months later, when his bank was saved from imminent failure by the government's bailout, it became clear that it was the lack of any regulation at all that was at the heart of its downfall.

On the night of 29 September 2008 Brian Goggin the chief executive of Bank of Ireland and Eugene Sheehy the chief executive of Allied Irish Banks, Ireland's two largest and most important banks, came together at 6.30 p.m. to ring then Taoiseach Brian Cowen requesting an immediate meeting with him and then minister for finance, Brian Lenihan. Although the request was granted by the government, the well-heeled bankers who turned up at the department of finance at 9.30 p.m., with their respective chairmen Richard Burrows and Dermot Gleeson, were made to wait until 11.30 p.m. to have their case heard. In the meantime Cowen, Lenihan, the governor of the Central Bank, the secretaries general of the departments of the Taoiseach and finance, the chief executive of the Financial Services Regulatory Authority, the attorney general and a whole raft of advisors were grappling with a crisis of unprecedented proportions within the history of the Irish state; the very survival of the Irish banking system and with it the prosperity of the Irish state and its people.

The bankers feared the immediate failure of Anglo Irish Bank due to its over-exposure to the property market, and perhaps one more financial institution, probably Irish Permanent Building Society. If that were allowed to happen, they argued, contagion in the banking system could sweep away their institutions as well and in turn bring the solvency of the Irish state into question. Shares in Anglo Irish Bank had fallen by almost 50% that day alone and threatened to depreciate much more the following day, leading to what would be the inevitable failure of that bank and the high likelihood of a domino effect on all other Irish banks. The bankers told the politicians in no uncertain terms that the government had to act or the entire Irish banking system could fail (Cooper, 2009).

The cabal of politicians, civil servants, and advisors that met on that September night took the view that doing nothing was not an option. The experience of the fall of Lehman Brothers, the enormous Wall Street investment bank, just two weeks earlier in the United States demonstrated the huge risk with the 'leaving the market to decide' approach. In that context the group led by Cowen concluded that some form of state underwriting of the banking system was necessary. When told by the bankers that Ireland's two largest banks were at risk there was some scepticism in government circles. Allied Irish Banks in particular had previously received state aid. In 1986, during a serious recession, it sought government help to the tune of £100 million after its purchase of the Insurance Corporation of Ireland went disastrously wrong. The scale of that particular rescue was later viewed as overly generous to the bank, yet here it was again seeking government assistance.

Not wanting an Irish bank to fail, a staple view of both the Irish government and the European Central Bank, or be taken into public ownership, the decision was taken to guarantee the deposits, loans, obligations, and liabilities of the six Irish banks, a total sum, it later turned out, of €440 billion – more than twice the country's gross national product. This was one of the options presented to the government by the giant financial consultancy firm Merrill Lynch earlier that night, wherein it also warned that the market would 'be aware that Ireland could not afford to cover the full amount if required' (Lyons and Carey, 2011, 181–82). The ultimate result of the near-collapse of the Irish banking sector was the acceptance in November in 2010 by the Fianna Fáil-led government of an €85 billion rescue package from the EU and the IMF. The economic mayhem in Ireland caused by the recklessness of bankers and property developers, along with the evidence heard at the Flood/Mahon tribunal, has brought the role of lobbyists in these industries, amongst others, to public prominence.

Lobbying, money, and private influence

If the bank guarantee scheme tells us anything about how Ireland is governed it is surely that those interests that control significant sums of capital are listened to far more closely than other groups in Irish society. There is ample evidence that those groups with money can be a corrosive influence on the body politic. While investigating the evasion of the DIRT tax in 1999, the Oireachtas public accounts committee sub-committee found that there was a particularly close and inappropriate relationship between banking interests and government: 'The evidence suggests that the State and its Agencies were perhaps too mindful of the concerns of the banks, and too attentive to their pleas and lobbying' (Oireachtas, 1999, 5). The banking crisis of late 2008 and the decision to guarantee the banks would seem to copper-fasten the view that those with more money can wield more influence. While one could well argue that the whole banking infrastructure, and thus monetary survival of the state, was at risk during this period, the crisis is still instructive as an example of lobbying influence.

The question of access to decision making is crucial to interest group politics and in Ireland was bound up with financial donations to both individual politicians as well as to political parties. It is clear that Fianna Fáil and Fine Gael have received substantial donations from business interests over a long number of years. In its second interim report of September 2002 the Flood tribunal found that the former minister for foreign affairs, for justice, and for communications, Ray Burke, had received 'corrupt payments' from a succession of builders (Tribunal, 2002, 34). It also found that Burke, during his time as minister for communications in the late 1980s, had made decisions that were not in the public interest after receiving payments from a private radio station's main backer, Oliver Barry (Tribunal, 2002, 65). Burke was eventually imprisoned for six months in 2005 for failing to make tax returns on over £100,000 that he had received in payments over a ten-year period between 1982 and 1991. The link between business contributions to political parties, and by extension to the political process, and favourable treatment for such business interests had been proven to Justice Flood's satisfaction. In recognition that corporate donations, if nothing else, gave the public the impression that undue influence could be linked to private donations, Fine Gael, under the ill-fated leadership of Michael Noonan, went as far as banning corporate donations in 2001. Once Enda Kenny became Fine Gael leader, after the 2002 election, he promptly overturned this decision.

Yet throughout the duration of the Flood/Mahon and Moriarty tribunals only one politician admitted that a link between corporate donations and political decision making existed in modern Ireland. Former Fianna Fáil leader and Taoiseach Bertie Ahern regularly voiced his view that those who financially supported Fianna Fáil, and all political parties for that matter, did so out of a sense of altruism and loyalty to the state, maintaining that the 'vast majority of donations to Fianna Fáil are not made in expectation of either favours or special access'. However, when asked by the Flood tribunal why land developers gave money to councillors, Fianna Fáil local councillor and senator Don Lydon stated: 'I believe that they hoped to influence (them). That's my firm belief. They did it then, they did it before, they do it now' (Murphy, 2006, 94). There can be little doubt that Fianna Fáil had a particularly close relationship with property developers and the construction industry. This dates back to the early 1980s when those 'involved in county council politics rapidly realised how their influence could be exploited, and on this fertile ground countless corrupt relationships began to flourish' (Foster, 2007, 87).

The question of financial donations and influence is particularly important considering the difficulties, personally and professionally, that Bertie Ahern faced once the *Irish Times* revealed in September 2006 that as minister for finance in 1993 and 1994 he had accepted payments of somewhere between €50,000 and €100,000 from a variety of business people and that the matter was being investigated by the Mahon tribunal. Ahern subsequently went on to win the 2007 general election but resigned as Taoiseach within a year stating that the effects of the tribunal had taken its toll on him, his party, and those closest to him but insisting that he had done nothing wrong. He had endured some agonising days in the witness box at the Mahon tribunal trying to explain apparent discrepancies between his oral accounts to the tribunal of various payments he had received and the evidence from banking records that the tribunal's legal team had uncovered in the course of its investigations. Most of Ahern's answers as to the sources of his money were opaque, not backed up by any documentary evidence and consisted of explanations from the then Taoiseach that were different to his previous enunciations on the matter of his finances. Finally Ahern was reduced to telling the deeply sceptical tribunal judges that he could not remember a number of crucial events central to the controversy. The sheer oddness of Ahern's evidence culminated after he had left political life, when he told the tribunal in June 2008 that he had won a significant amount of money on a horse (Clifford and Coleman, 2009, 360).

Lobbying regulation: the cure to private influence?

Due to concerns with issues surrounding the openness of the policymaking process, an increasing number of countries have recently sought to regulate the activities of lobbyists. As Bertók (2008, 18) argues, 'when public concern is about the integrity of government decision making, measures to ensure transparency and accountability become essential.' Many democracies have attempted to do this by means of freedom-of-information legislation, while others have sought to regulate lobbyists through the decision-making process. In both cases, the focus is on transparency and accountability. There is a large literature on the themes of transparency and accountability in democratic societies and a growing awareness of the global importance of citizens being reassured by transparent politics in their respective polities.

In relation specifically to lobbying, Largerlof and Frisell (2004, 16) contend that lobbying regulation helps promote transparency and is thus justified in order to render government officials more accountable and to promote the activities of lobbyists in a more open and transparent fashion. Moreover, by imposing an obligation on lobbyists to disclose the identity of those on whose behalf they are acting, a government is making laws that take account of the public interest (Graziano, 2001, 99). For Thomas (2004, 287) such rules 'constrain the actions of lobbyists and public officials alike, even if they do not ultimately affect which groups are powerful and which ones are not'. Through contributing to transparency and accountability, lobbying regulations shed light onto policymaking and in so doing should improve the overall nature of the decisions reached by policymakers (Dryzek, 2000; Elster, 1998). The basic rationale behind implementing regulations is that the public should have some insight into, as well as oversight of, the mechanisms that draw lobbyists into the policymaking environment, in order to understand better how they influence policy outputs (Chari et al., 2010, 1–2).

One of the reasons advanced by politicians in Ireland for not engaging in lobbying regulation is the worrying view that one senior politician imparted to the author in a private interview: 'we are a small state and we all know each other.' While Ireland might be a relatively small jurisdiction of roughly four million people, the cliché of 'we all know each other' does not hold up to any rigorous analysis. It would be true to say that elites all know each other, but it is nothing short of wishful thinking on behalf of Irish politicians to think that there is no reason for lobbying regulation because everyone knows what is going on. The evidence of any number of policy decisions made in relation to banking, for instance, from when the Irish state rescued the insurance arm of Allied Irish Banks in 1985 right up to the bank guarantee scheme of September 2008 (decisions taken by different governments comprising all the major political parties), shows that all these decisions were made in secret and after significant lobbying by the banks. These decisions have had catastrophic implications for Irish citizens, as the bank guarantee scheme has proven to be a gigantic millstone around the necks of ordinary Irish people and of the Irish state itself (Murphy et al., 2011, 116).

In 2003 the then minister for justice, equality, and law reform, Michael McDowell, eloquently noted that lobbying regulation would result in a professionalisation of the lobbying industry with the result that 'professional ethical lobbyists' would take the place of 'fly-by-night secretive intermediaries with dubious motives and ethics' (McGrath, 2009, 269). Coming just a year after his party, the Progressive Democrats (PDs), had performed well in the general election and were seen publically as the watchdog element of the Fianna Fáil–Progressive Democrats coalition, McDowell's pronouncement seemed a clear indication that the government was of the view that some sort of lobbying regulation was essential to a well-run society. While low taxation and a weakening of the regulatory system were PD mantras during its years in politics, it seemed that regulating lobbyists constituted recognition that many of the corporate entities that the government was trying to attract to Ireland were used to dealing with a professionalised, regulated lobbying industry, such as exists in the USA.

Yet, in 2007, McDowell, still the minister for justice, equality, and law reform but now Tánaiste as well, told the Dáil 'that it is not intended at this stage to introduce lobbyists' registration legislation' (McGrath, 2009, 265). Why he took this stance is something of a mystery. The revelations of both the Flood and Mahon tribunals showed a vast network of opaque and complex payments by lobbyists to politicians. The view of Bertie Ahern and others that these were payments for no political response now holds little currency in a country where such transfers have been inextricably linked to policy decisions. Given the disservice done to professional lobbyists by the likes of Frank Dunlop, the following questions need to be asked: Why has some specific form of lobbying regulation not taken place in Ireland? Why did Michael McDowell fail to act on his 2003 statement? Why have other politicians equally failed to act on similar promises made to the electorate?

During the years of the tribunals, from 1997 to 2010, Irish political parties actively considered the issue of regulating lobbyists. In 1999 the Labour Party introduced the first of five specific private member's bills on this issue while in opposition. At the 2011 general election it again promised that it would introduce a register of lobbyists once returned to power. During the 2007 general election campaign the Green Party pledged in its election manifesto to establish a register of lobbyists. Once it entered government the pledge appeared on the last page of the 2007 Agreed Programme for Government as 'Consider legislation to regulate lobbyists' (Government, 2007, 87). However, when the programme for government was renewed in late 2009, in light of the changed economic circumstances of the state, this decision appeared to have become more concrete: it was no longer located on the final page of the document and it was stated unequivocally that the government 'will introduce a Register of Lobbyists, including professional, corporate and NGO' (Government, 2009, 33). That government fell, however, without having made any progress whatsoever in introducing a lobbying register.

In March 2010 the then main opposition party, Fine Gael, published a comprehensive political reform plan entitled 'New Politics'. This document called for substantial political and constitutional reform and provided specific details on how lobbying would be regulated under a Fine Gael-led government. Within a year, in the February 2011 general election, Fine Gael and the Labour Party won a crushing victory and formed a coalition government with the largest majority in the history of the state. The new government promised in its programme for government to introduce 'a statutory register of lobbyists, and rules concerning the practice of lobbying' (Government, 2011, 20). Two years on from its election, in April 2013 the government approved the drafting of the Regulation of Lobbying Bill 2013, which aims to 'bring greater openness and transparency on public policy formulation and to provide valuable input to the decision making process. The intention of the bill is to continue to encourage such participation in the decision making process, but to ensure that it is done in a fully open manner' (Government, 2013).

This is clearly a welcome step and the Fine Gael–Labour Party government's commitment to openness in Irish public life is to be commended. However, the question of whether such regulation will be a panacea for the problems of the Irish state needs to be addressed. Is lobbying regulation a form of political communication to the public that the Irish state operates in an open and transparent manner? For instance, would lobbying regulation have prevented the bank guarantee scheme decision being taken? The answer to the latter question is surely no, while the answer to the former question is somewhat more complex although we could probably give a qualified yes.

In an age when disenchantment with public life has been a feature of Irish politics, particularly given the dramatic economic downturn and when tribunals of inquiry and the collapse of the banks have opened up all sorts of questions about the influence of lobbyists in Irish public life, it would seem reasonable that establishing a mandatory register of lobbyists is an essential step for the Irish state to take to ensure that undue influence over public policy and governance cannot take place. Such a register would not have stopped the bank guarantee scheme. But as we still know very little about the events of that murky night, a lobbying regulation scheme, if it had been in existence at the time, would at least mean there would have been more openness and transparency about the decision than there was.

Conclusion

There can be little doubt that private influence has resulted in an unhealthy situation in Ireland where those with access to money and capital appear to have had significant influence over political decision making. Lobbying regulation, as per the government's proposed bill will, if nothing else, put an end to the perception that undue influence is an issue in Irish politics. What is being regulated is behaviour by interests that have the money or clout to have their expectations met by the access they have. Registering lobbyists is not about regulating speech, but about preventing undue influence, including abuse of dominant financial position of some interest groups, private organisations such as the banks, or even private citizens. In essence it is a form of political communication between citizens and the politicians and civil service bureaucracy that runs the Irish state. The key point is that the system should be transparent. This benefits the lobbyists, the legislators and the citizens. Regulation should be something that gives all stakeholders confidence in the system. Public confidence in the process is essential. If private influence is to be removed from the way the state operates then the state's political communication apparatus needs a register of lobbyists to ensure just that. The government's decision in April 2013 to commit to a lobbying regulation bill may just be a sign that Ireland is facing up to both its past and its future.

References

Baumgartner, F.R. and Leech, B.L. (1998) *Basic interests: the importance of groups on politics and in political science*, Princeton, NJ: Princeton University Press.

Bertók, J. (2008) *Lobbyists, governments and public trust: building a legislative framework for enhancing transparency and accountability in lobbying*, Paris: OECD.

Beyers, J., Eising, R. and Maloney, W. (2008) 'Researching interest group politics in Europe and elsewhere: much we study, little we know?' in *West European Politics*, 31(6): 1103–28.

Chari, R., Hogan, J. and Murphy, G. (2010) *Regulating lobbying: a global comparison*, Manchester: Manchester University Press.

Clifford, M. and Coleman, S. (2009) *Bertie Ahern and the Drumcondra mafia*, Dublin: Hachette Books.

Collins, N. and Ó Raghallaigh, C. (1995) 'Political sleaze in the Republic of Ireland' in *Parliamentary Affairs*, 48(4): 697–710.

Cooper, M. (2009) *Who really runs Ireland: the story of the elite who led Ireland from bust to boom and back again*, Dublin: Penguin.

Dryzek, J. (2000) *Democracy and beyond*, Oxford: Oxford University Press.

Elster, J. (1998) *Deliberative democracy*, Cambridge: Cambridge University Press.

Foster, R.F. (2007) *Luck and the Irish: a brief history of change 1970–2000*, London: Allen Lane.

Government (2007). See <http://www.taoiseach.ie/eng/Publications/>

Government (2009). See <http://www.taoiseach.ie/eng/Publications/>

Government (2011). See <http://www.taoiseach.ie/eng/Publications/>

Government (2013). See <http://per.gov.ie/regulation-of-lobbyists/>

Graziano, L. (2001) *Lobbying, pluralism and democracy*, London: Palgrave.

Hunter, K.G., Wilson, L.A. and Brunk, G.G. (1991) 'Societal complexity and interest-group lobbying in the American States' in *The Journal of Politics*, 53(2): 488–503.

Keogh, D. (1994) *Twentieth century Ireland: nation and state*, Dublin: Gill and Macmillan.

Largerlof, J. and Frisell, L. (2004) *Lobbying, information transmission and unequal representation*, Berlin: Social Science Research Centre.

Lyons, T. and Carey, B. (2011) *The FitzPatrick tapes: the rise and fall of one man, one bank and one country*, Dublin: Penguin Ireland.

McGrath C. (2009) 'The lobbyist with "balls of iron and a spine of steel": why Ireland needs lobbying reform' in *Journal of Public Affairs*, 9(4): 256–71.

McGrath, C. (2011) 'Lobbying in Ireland: a reform agenda' in *Journal of Public Affairs*, 11(2): 127–34.

Murphy, G. (1999) 'The role of interest groups in the policy making process' in Coakley, J. and Gallagher, M. (eds), *Politics in the Republic of Ireland* (3rd edn), London, Routledge.

Murphy, G. (2006) 'Payments for no political response? Political corruption and tribunals of inquiry in Ireland, 1991–2003' in Garrard, J. and Newell, J.L. (eds), *Scandals in past and contemporary politics*, Manchester: Manchester University Press.

Murphy, G., Hogan, J. and Chari, R. (2011) 'Lobbying regulation in Ireland: some thoughts from the international evidence' in *Journal of Public Affairs*, 11(2): 111–19.

Nownes, A.J. (2006) *Total lobbying: what lobbyists want (and how they try to get it)*, Cambridge: Cambridge University Press.

Oireachtas (1999) *Committee of public accounts, sub-committee on certain revenue matters, parliamentary inquiry into DIRT: first report*, Dublin: Stationery Office.

O'Toole, F. (1995) *Meanwhile back at the ranch: the politics of Irish beef*, London: Vintage.

PRII (2003) *Code of professional practice for public affairs and lobbying,* Dublin: Public Relations Institute of Ireland.

Thomas, C.S. (2004) 'Lobbying in the United States: an overview for students, scholars and practitioners' in Harris, P. and Fleischer, C.S. (eds), *The handbook of public affairs,* London: Sage.

Tribunal (2002) *The second interim report of the tribunal of inquiry into certain planning matters and payments,* Dublin: Stationery Office.

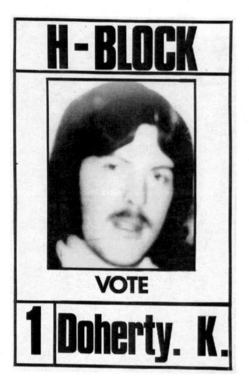

Above In 1981, the 25-year-old IRA prisoner Kieran Doherty was elected to parliament for the constituency of Cavan-Monaghan while on hunger strike in Northern Ireland for political status. Doherty is the shortest-serving Dáil deputy ever, being a TD for just over seven weeks.

Above Mary Robinson's breakthrough in 1990 marked a new era in how presidential candidates campaign.

Below In 1997, Bertie Ahern became the youngest Taoiseach in Irish history and would become the first leader since Eamon de Valera during the 1930s and 1940s to lead his party to three successive general-election victories.

CHAPTER TEN

Equal time for Judas Iscariot?
Broadcast treatment of political contests
in the Republic of Ireland

Colum Kenny

Elections and referenda are hotly contested, and broadcasters sometimes find themselves accused of bias. The Oireachtas has passed laws that are intended to ensure that the radio and television coverage of campaigns is fair and balanced and is in accordance with constitutional rights. Those who feel aggrieved may complain in the first instance to the relevant broadcaster, and subsequently to the Broadcasting Authority of Ireland. The Oireachtas acts on the basis that broadcasting licences are granted by the state. No similar requirements apply to print or online media.

It has been customary for broadcasters to distribute airtime on any relevant programmes to political parties roughly in proportion to their performance at the preceding general election, in order to achieve fairness and balance without having to give every party the same amount of time on air. During elections it has also long been usual for some Irish broadcasters to devote airtime to short 'party political broadcasts'. These are not defined in law and the editorial content of each broadcast is controlled entirely by the party to which it is devoted.

During referenda campaigns, airtime may likewise be devoted to broadcasts controlled by contesting parties and other interest groups. Critics object that the legislative requirement for balance in broadcasting distorts the political landscape during some referenda campaigns if the great majority of elected representatives support change but a small minority of public representatives and others receive a disproportionate amount of airtime to oppose it. When broadcasters themselves believe that a referendum proposal that is favoured by a large majority of politicians is eminently reasonable then they may resent facilitating contrary arguments, and some have been known to compare their dilemma mockingly to that of an editor who is forced to give equal airtime to comparing the respective merits of Jesus and Judas (the latter being the apostle who betrayed Jesus to the Romans for 30 pieces of silver). However, broadcasters are not in fact forced by law to give equal airtime to each side of the referendum argument provided that they can achieve fairness, objectivity, and impartiality in some other way.

This chapter examines the statutory requirements for fairness, objectivity, and impartiality in the broadcast treatment of political contests, including referenda, in the Republic of Ireland. It considers the ways in which legislative provisions have been interpreted by those whose duty it is to prepare related guidelines for broadcasters. It also considers the basis for a number of challenges to the legislation and to interpretations under it, and asks whether the law has an unreasonable impact on media coverage and political communication, not least by ensuring that ostensibly unrepresentative groups have access to the airwaves to an extent that some broadcasters might not otherwise permit.

Legal requirements

The most recent iteration of the relevant legislative requirements is found in the Broadcasting Act 2009. As these provisions are quite simple and so fundamental to a consideration of issues that have arisen, it is worth setting out the relevant subsections before considering some of those issues. Section 39 (1) of the Act states that every broadcaster shall ensure that:

(a) all news broadcast by the broadcaster is reported and presented in an objective and impartial manner and without any expression of the broadcaster's own views;

(b) the broadcast treatment of current affairs, including matters which are either of public controversy or the subject of current public debate, is fair to all interests concerned and that the broadcast matter is presented in an objective and impartial manner and without any expression of his or her own views, except that should it prove impracticable in relation to a single broadcast to apply this paragraph, two or more related broadcasts may be considered as a whole, if the broadcasts are transmitted within a reasonable period of each other.

No broadcaster is obliged by law to transmit party political broadcasts. However, Section 39 (2) of the Act requires that a broadcaster does not, in the allocation of time for such broadcasts, give an unfair preference to any political party. Section 42 (1) of the Act requires that the Broadcasting Authority of Ireland, hereinafter BAI, devise and regularly update a code or codes governing standards and practice ('broadcasting code') to be observed by broadcasters. Similar codes were formerly prepared by the Independent Radio and Television Commission and the Broadcasting Commission of Ireland, which the BAI superseded, as well as by RTÉ.

The code

Immediately prior to the momentous general election of 2011 the BAI issued a document to provide guidance on the rules contained in its current Broadcasting Code on Election Coverage. It noted in its guidelines that:

> Broadcasters play an important role in the democratic process of elections and it is therefore appropriate that they have specific obligations in respect of the approach that they take to the coverage of an election. In this regard, broadcasters should make every effort to ensure fairness, objectivity and impartiality in the approach to coverage of an election, including the approach to the exposure given to candidates, electoral interests and political parties in the various elements of their programming. This includes participation by, and references to, candidates, electoral interests and political parties in all programmes.

> Broadcasters choosing to provide coverage of elections should develop mechanisms that are open, transparent and fair to all interested parties. These mechanisms should be considered and developed at an early stage and information on the approach being adopted should be available to all interested parties in advance.

The guidelines also noted that decisions in respect of editorial content rested with broadcasters; that it was individual broadcasters to decide the most effective way to reflect all the interests involved in an election (on a constituency, regional or national basis); and that 'endorsements of candidates, electoral interests, political parties and/or the policies of any of the aforementioned by broadcasters, including its presenters are not permitted.' It further required that senior staff with overall responsibility for election coverage should become fully familiar with the content of the code and noted that it is inappropriate for election candidates to present programmes during an election campaign. It also obliged senior staff with overall responsibility for election coverage to ensure that a range of views is adequately represented in the questions, comments, and issues raised during programmes that include an element of audience participation. In relation to party political broadcasts the guidelines noted that while there is no obligation on broadcasters to transmit party political broadcasts, if broadcasters chose to do so, they have to do so free of charge (to ensure that the broadcast does not constitute a partisan political advertisement, such advertisements on radio and television being prohibited by Section 41(3) of the 2009 Act). It also stipulated that all such broadcasts should be transmitted at times that are aimed at achieving a similar audience for each of them and that such broadcasts be offered to registered political parties only.

Stopwatch

One way to achieve fairness during elections is by using a stopwatch to measure out airtime, both in respect of political party broadcasts and of news and programmes that deal with campaign issues. Then, should a party complain that it is not being treated fairly, the producer can point to a division of airtime that is proportionate to that party's most recent performance in a general election. While not always applied to the exact second or even minute, this kind of approach to achieving fairness has served both broadcasters and politicians well down the years and there have been few complaints relative to the volume of airtime devoted to politics.

One might have a philosophical discussion about the difference, if any, between the terms 'fairness' and 'impartiality' and 'objectivity', as these have been used but not precisely defined in broadcasting legislation and codes down the years. By now, in practice, the requirements tend to be taken to mean having at least one person represent each principal side of any argument being aired in the news or on current affairs programmes generally – while hearing from all parties in proportionate amounts (but not necessarily on the same programme) in respect of matters that are being contested during an election. The guidelines issued by the BAI specify no particular method of achieving fairness.

Referenda

The coverage of referenda campaigns presents broadcasters with a particular challenge. This is because the Constitution of Ireland can only be changed by a majority of voters in a referendum, regardless of how many political parties desire change. It is the case that only a majority of the Oireachtas may initiate a referendum on a particular proposal. However, a majority of the Oireachtas itself has no power to change the Constitution unless a majority of voters agree.

In this way the Constitution 'belongs' to the public in general and not to the political parties in the way that legislation does. It is possible, and indeed on the basis of precedents can be said to be the case, that the public may disagree with most of their elected politicians on the desirability of a proposed change to the Constitution. For this reason, simply dividing airtime proportionately between parties may distort the debate. Given that voters have at some point previously adopted any and every article in the Constitution that the Oireachtas subsequently proposes to amend or delete, it may be considered fair that the arguments in favour of and against change are given equal time, regardless of how many or how few political parties support each side. Can citizens who have voted for politicians not be trusted to exercise equally good judgement when voting in any referendum? Some people believe that the opinions of the main political parties should be shown preference over all others.

Three key decisions of the Supreme Court have made it abundantly clear that the primacy of the people in respect of the Constitution has direct consequences for the manner in which public monies may be spent, directly or indirectly, in respect of a referendum campaign. The first, the McKenna case of 1995, was instigated by a member of the European Parliament and concerned direct government spending on publicity relating to a referendum question. Gallagher (1999, 82) has written that '[b]efore 1995, the government of the day felt free to use public funds to promote its side of the case exclusively.' The second, the Coughlan case of 2000, was taken by a university lecturer and concerned the content of party political broadcasts in the light of both legislation requiring fairness and the use of public monies. The third case was that taken by McCrystal, in respect of the Children's Rights referendum in 2012. While these decisions are complex, and while it might have been better in terms of public understanding had only a single judgement been delivered in each case, each strongly reinforces the requirement for balance in broadcasting.

In McKenna v An Taoiseach (1995), Patricia McKenna MEP initiated proceedings to stop the government spending public money on a campaign to persuade citizens to vote in a particular way in a referendum relating to Irish divorce laws. She successfully obtained a declaration that the government, in promoting a particular outcome of the referendum, would be acting in breach of the Constitution. The government admitted that it had from time to time spent money from public funds on advertising and promoting a number of referenda campaigns, including some expenditure that was designed to persuade the electors to exercise their right in the manner put forward or suggested by the government. It denied that the government was constitutionally obliged to fund the promulgation of contrary opinions and/or information where groups wished to promulgate such opinions and/ or information. It maintained the right 'in appropriate circumstances and where it seems fit to let its view be known, with the aid of public funds and if necessary in a trenchant and forthright manner'.

In his judgement in the Supreme Court, Chief Justice Liam Hamilton found that

> The role of the People in amending the Constitution cannot be over-emphasised. It is solely their prerogative to amend any provision thereof by way of variation, addition or repeal or to refuse to amend. The decision is theirs and theirs alone. Having regard to the importance of the Constitution as the fundamental law of the State and the crucial role of the people in the adoption and enactment thereof, any amendment thereof must be in accordance with the constitutional process and no interference with that process can be permitted because as stated by Walsh J in Crotty's case, 'it is the people themselves who are the guardians of the Constitution' [...] The use by the Government of public funds to fund a campaign designed to influence the voters in favour of a 'Yes' vote is an interference with the democratic process and the constitutional process for the amendment of the Constitution and infringes the concept of equality which is fundamental to the democratic nature of the State.

Mrs Justice Susan Denham (who was later appointed chief justice) found that

> The Constitution envisages a true democracy: the rule of the people. This case is about the constitutional relationship of the people to their government. The most fundamental method by which the people decide all questions of national policy according to the requirements of the common good is by way of referendum [...] The people alone amend the Constitution. In Byrne v Ireland, [1972] IR 242 the matter was encapsulated by Walsh J who stated at p 262: 'the State is the creation of the People and is to be governed in accordance with the provisions of the Constitution which was enacted by the People and which can be amended by the People only, and [...] the sovereign authority is the People.' In

referenda the people vote on the proposed amendment. Such vote must
be free. The issue is whether the government may spend public monies
to promote a result in a referendum i.e. 'Vote Yes' [...] I am satisfied that
the government are not entitled under the Constitution or law to spend
public funds in this way. To so do would be to infringe upon at least three
constitutional rights: (1) The right of equality; (2) The right to freedom of
expression; and (3) The right to a democratic process in referenda.

Following the McKenna judgment, the Oireachtas passed the Referendum
Act 1998. Under this legislation, the government appointed a Referendum
Commission to supply the public fairly with information, including
arguments from groups on various sides of any referendum campaign. In
1999 Gallagher (82) believed the way in which the commission published
'a simplified version' of the arguments in two referenda that had been held
during 1998 'was widely seen as unsatisfactory' and that in respect of the
important referendum confirming the Good Friday Agreement on Northern
Ireland the commission 'felt itself obliged to publicise some far-fetched
claims simply because someone had made them'. However, few people think
that their own claims are far-fetched or that the circulation of their own
side's arguments is unsatisfactory.

The second important Supreme Court decision in the matter referred
directly to RTÉ. This was Coughlan v Broadcasting Complaints Commission
(2000). This case involved a complaint about RTÉ's use of party political
broadcasts during the divorce referendum of 1995. The complainant accepted
that RTÉ was fair in its general coverage of the campaign in its news and
current affairs programmes that 'represented 98% of the time expended by
RTÉ on the coverage of the Referendum campaign'. In his judgement, Chief
Justice Hamilton noted that

> During the course of the campaign, however, RTÉ transmitted ten political
> party broadcasts aggregating 30 minutes which all favoured a 'yes' vote;
> two uncontested broadcasts from ad hoc campaign groups advocating a
> 'yes' vote aggregating 10 minutes and two uncontested broadcasts from ad
> hoc campaign groups advocating a 'no' vote aggregating 10 minutes [...].

Mrs Justice Denham found that

> Party political broadcasts must be analysed in accordance with the overall
> requirements of the Broadcasting Act [...] Thus, if the political parties
> take different stances on a referendum issue the broadcasting of party
> political broadcasts would present a divided view which would prima

facie be fair even if not mathematically equal. Mathematical equality is not a requirement of constitutional fairness and equality. However, if all the parties are either in favour of or opposed to a referendum then party political broadcasts become prima facie, unfair and unequal and the issue must be approached from the standpoint of the overall obligations imposed by the legislation and the Constitution [...] It might be necessary to decide to hold no party political broadcasts in a referendum campaign.

Mr Justice Ronan Keane, the future chief justice, found that

It is enjoined by the terms of the statutes which created RTÉ to maintain objectivity and impartiality in all matters of public controversy. It would be remarkable if such a body differed from the Oireachtas and the government in enjoying a freedom to interfere with the result of a referendum by allowing political parties and other bodies which supported a particular outcome a considerable advantage in the broadcasting of partisan material over which they had unfettered control, subject only to any relevant laws such as that of defamation. I am satisfied that the High Court judge was correct in holding that the allocation of uncontested broadcasting time in the present case in those circumstances was legally impermissible. I do not overlook the difficulties created for RTÉ by this state of the law. As was emphasised on their behalf, they have no control over the editorial content of party political broadcasts [...] It may be that, having regard to those circumstances, the present state of the law leaves RTÉ in the position that they cannot safely transmit party political broadcasts during the course of referendum campaigns as distinct from other campaigns. Whether the difficulties confronting RTÉ in this area can or should be dealt with by legislation and, if so, how, are not matters for this court.

These are weighty and quite unambiguous judgements, notwithstanding the pragmatic qualification that '[m]athematical equality is not a requirement of constitutional fairness and equality.' The Coughlan judgement irked quite a few members of the political parties, not least because it was interpreted as 'requiring a rigidly equal allocation of campaign coverage by broadcasters between "Yes" and "No" viewpoints' (Carolan and O'Neill, 2010, 95). As subsequent RTÉ and BAI guidelines have indicated, that may be an excessively restrictive interpretation. In 2004 Richard Sinnott (160–77) argued eloquently if not entirely persuasively that the courts might yet uphold a distinction between 'equal funding' and 'equitable funding', where the latter was distributed proportionately to the strength of opinion among elected representatives on a particular referendum question. However, squaring any mathematical inequality with the continuing requirement for fairness and balance remains a challenge for political scientists, politicians, and broadcasters alike.

Under the Referendum Act 2001 the independent Referendum Commission lost the function of putting the arguments for and against any referendum proposal. This Act appeared to be a somewhat resentful response by political parties to the McKenna and Coughlan judgements. From 2001 the Commission's role was confined to explaining the subject matter of referendum proposals, to promoting public awareness of the referendum and to encouraging the electorate to vote at the poll. Many politicians were again annoyed and embarrassed when, on 13 June 2008, the Irish people rejected the proposed amendment to the Irish Constitution that was required to permit ratification of the EU's Lisbon Treaty. Some believed that broadcasters had given undue attention to hitherto unrepresentative groups that opposed change, albeit in accordance with those broadcasters' statutory duties and the constitutional rights of citizens as upheld in the cases considered above.

Parliamentary report

When, in September 2008, the Joint Oireachtas Committee on the Constitution decided to undertake a review of the constitutional framework governing the referendum process, its members' first priority was an examination of the role of the media in the process. Its *Second Report: Articles 46 and 47. Amendment of the Constitution and the Referendum: first interim report* (2009) is both a perspective on the legal context and a record of the opinions of various interested parties. A substantial appendix to the report consists of a useful research paper looking, in particular, at the legal bases and the regulation of referenda campaigns in other EU member states and includes the matters of public funding and transparency of funding as well as the allocation of public and private broadcast air time. Deputies and senators concluded that there might be scope for new legislation to clarify or qualify the existing statutory requirements. They reported that (79)

The practical effect of this decision [Coughlan] – or, perhaps, more accurately, the way that the decision has been applied in practice – is that broadcasters are required to provide an equal platform to the proponents of 'yes' and 'no' during the course of a referendum campaign. If one applies this principle to certain non-contentious referenda, it would mean that broadcasters would be obliged to apply the 'stopwatch' principle and facilitate ad-hoc opponents of the referendum by giving them exactly the same airtime as all the established political parties, even if the level of opposition to the proposal was tiny.

They cited as an example The Sixth Amendment of the Constitution Act 1979 (which dealt with the regularisation of adoption orders and in relation to which a referendum proposal was accepted by more than 98% of voters), and continued, 'There seems to be a widespread sense that the allocation of broadcasting time in this fashion is wholly artificial and unreal.' They recalled that many broadcasters who gave evidence before the Committee testified to the existence of a problem:

> Thus, for example, as has been noted, the Independent Broadcasters of Ireland (IBI) commented that the perceived need for a 50/50 balance in referendum coverage meant that 'broadcasters were "strait jacketed" into dividing time equally in a manner that challenged their professional requirement to deliver balanced content. Real balance in terms of content may require that some groups and some claims require more scrutiny than others.'

The Oireachtas Committee members went on to note that the IBI had added that 'it cannot be in the public interest to give half the airtime automatically to one side in a referendum simply because "they show up on the day", regardless of the merit of their argument, the motivation of their movement or the size of the democratic mandate: to do so amounts to the creation of a "crank's charter".' However, such observations by politicians and broadcasters appear to overlook the Supreme Court's acknowledgement that mathematical equality is not always necessary. The present author referred critically to the IBI contention when invited to give evidence to the committee, as it subsequently reported (59):

> Professor Kenny also commented on the suggestion that the current broadcasting regime was creating a 'crank's charter', by suggesting that if media organisations are free to exclude those they consider to be political cranks in respect of general political matters, then they could conceivably exclude even members of the Committee at some later stage. The abandonment of the 'fairness' doctrine in the United States in favour of commercial and ideological concerns, Professor Kenny opined, had led

to the prevalence of radio 'shock-jocks' and the bias of channels such as Fox News.

In the end, the Oireachtas Committee recommended, among other things, that (80)

> Broadcasters would be entitled to have regard to a range of factors to inform their own judgment about what constitutes fairness of treatment, in the same way as they currently do with ordinary current affairs broadcasts. These factors could include considerations such as the relative strengths and standing of political parties; the standing and views of representatives from various interest groups and the views, expertise and reputation of individual contributors to a programme. The Committee considers that the fact that the referendum is supported or opposed by elected representatives is a relevant consideration in terms of the allocation of broadcasting time during the course of a referendum campaign.

Outside the Dáil, too, the IBI complained loudly about existing guidelines in respect of referenda coverage. Addressing an IBI conference on 3 March 2009, its chairman Willie O'Reilly (then chief executive of Today FM) said that the planned second Lisbon referendum brought the consequences of the Coughlan Judgement back into focus and would require broadcasters in Ireland to think carefully when it came to covering the ensuing debate:

> As an organisation we have already expressed our concerns about the Coughlan Judgement. While the guidelines of the Broadcasting Commission do not stipulate equal airtime, it does require 'equal treatment' and that both sides of the debate be represented in the same programme. There is a huge bias for contrarian opinion. It gives power without responsibility. For broadcasting to be balanced and for arguments to be probed, it is essential that the government and the Broadcasting Commission reflect on the effectiveness of the existing guidelines. It is essential that they do so urgently.

The guidelines that the BCI had issued in April 2008 in respect of coverage of the first Lisbon referendum were in fact adjusted by the BAI in advance of the second referendum that took place on 2 October 2009. Given that the law itself did not change, these adjustments were quite subtle and were a matter of emphasis rather than substance. Although welcomed by the IBI, it is not entirely evident what significant, practical difference, if any, the change in the guidelines has made. The guidelines certainly clarify the fact that the law has never required equal time on every occasion for all political or other parties in dispute. Yet, if broadcasters do not allocate approximately equal time for all political parties, or for the main sides of each argument in a referendum campaign, it is difficult to see how fairness, objectivity, and impartiality can be achieved. The courts may take a dim view of any attempt on the part of broadcasters to interpret the changes as a nod and a wink to producers to stack their programmes in favour of what they consider to be the 'common sense' opinion or in favour of what broadcasting executives consider to be the dominant social and political point of view.

RTÉ guidelines

For its part, RTÉ issues internal guidelines prior to general elections and referenda and these guidelines reflect and elaborate guidance from the BAI. In a preliminary notice to staff prior to the 2011 general election, RTÉ's head of public affairs policy, Peter Feeney, addressed the difficult question of how one might measure balance:

> There is no mathematical formula which guarantees fairness. The achievement of balance and fairness cannot be reduced simply to a stopwatch exercise. The timing of exposure, the context of that exposure, the tone of the journalist, the subject matter and the choice of programme are all as relevant as the amount of time a candidate receives. RTÉ cannot commit to providing candidates with an exact amount of time on air. To do so would lead to non-journalistic decisions as to how much time to allocate and would unnecessarily encumber producers and editors with unwieldy time requirements (RTÉ, 2011).

Having given this broad guidance, Feeney identified the criteria that programme-makers could use in deciding who to invite onto programmes and how much time to allocate to individual candidates:

> Most people running for election are doing so as members of political parties. Therefore the first criterion and the most important is party membership. The allocation of time between and within parties is influenced by the following:
> 1. The percentage of first preference votes won nationally by the political parties in the last equivalent elections.
> 2. The number of candidates being put forward by the political parties.
> 3. Within parties recognition of candidates who are incumbents or who have previously held office.

4. Membership of Seanad Éireann or the European Parliament.
5. Within parties recognition of the fact that parties may be promoting particular candidates.
6. Alliances between parties, taking account of government and opposition, coalitions, common policy platforms, etc.
7. The results of by-elections, European and local elections since the last general election.
8. Opinion polling results over time showing current levels of support for parties.
9. Authoritative commentators' assessments of likely results both nationally and in individual constituencies.
10. Developments which take place during the course of the election campaign.
11. Newsworthiness at any particular time.
12. A minimum amount of attention which may be required to give to candidates from smaller parties to make their participation meaningful.

Feeney noted that candidates who ran as independents or who represented parties that did not have any elected representatives in Dáil Éireann were to be 'treated on a constituency basis rather than nationally'. Previous electoral performance (including local elections) was to be taken into account and Feeney also stressed the 'need to recognise that over 10% of the first preference vote goes to independents and "smaller" parties.' As regards constituency profiles, if an individual constituency were to feature in a report or programme then all declared candidates had to be identified. To monitor the sensitive matter of balance, RTÉ sets up a special steering group during every election. Thus, in 2011 Feeney advised RTÉ staff that all programme-makers involved in any aspect of its election coverage were required to supply details of their coverage to the election monitor, and that all programmes were required to 'take extra care to ensure that we do not disadvantage any party or candidate in the important weeks leading up to polling day'. Feeney also advised that 'political scientists, commentators, etc who appear on programmes may need to have previous relationships to political parties made known to the audience' and that 'programme-makers should ensure that commentators known to hold partisan views or who are very critical of particular parties or politicians are not over-used and are balanced by other commentators who hold different views.'

The matter of balance took on a particularly difficult dimension in 2011 when it became evident that the parties that had formed a government following the previous election were about to be trounced in the general election that was called for 25 February. Even for someone as experienced as Peter Feeney, who had formerly worked as the station's head of current affairs, it was challenging to work out how to be fair when the balance of public opinion was so widely at variance with the relative balance of party representatives in the outgoing Dáil. For this reason, RTÉ brought in some academic expertise to advise it on how to proceed. It also retained the services of a responsible post-doctoral student to work with its manager of audience research on monitoring output. The station evolved a formula that had regard to the results of the previous general election, the percentage of seats held by parties at the dissolution of the Dáil, the percentage of candidates in each party, and the current results of various opinion polls.

RTÉ, which is publicly funded and the dominant source of news and current affairs, clearly went to elaborate lengths to ensure balance, yet its efforts might be undermined at a local level if local non-RTÉ stations to which so many tune do not also make every reasonable effort to be fair. Given that people who are dissatisfied have an independent statutory mechanism for considering their complaints, there is little or no reason to believe that any significant number of people feel that Irish broadcasters are failing in their statutory duties when it comes to the coverage of elections and referenda.

Social media

In 2000, in the Coughlan case, Mrs Justice Denham stated that 'The constitutional principles of equality and fairness applicable to broadcasting [...] will continue to be important as narrow casting is developed, as methods of communication which can be retrieved and viewed individually and repeatedly through electronic communication such as the Internet, is developed.' In 2003 McGonagle (409) observed that to continue divergent regulatory regimes in an environment of convergence 'seems impractical and undesirable, unless justified at the level of principle'. However, given that it is difficult for national regulators to regulate online content, it may be argued that it is desirable to regulate it indirectly insofar as broadcasters rely on online sources. Broadcasters do not work in a vacuum. The arrival of social media also has implications for the practices of broadcasters in that their employees' participation in discussions online or their publication of social media comments from members of the public may influence the audience's perception of the broadcaster itself. For this reason, prior to the general election of February 2011, RTÉ (2011) advised its staff that

> An additional dimension to consider since the last general election is social media such as Twitter. Any person associated with RTÉ must consider that whatever they say on the likes of Twitter enters the public domain and has the potential to damage RTÉ's reputation for fairness and balance. Personal comments may be misinterpreted as 'an RTÉ view'. RTÉ employees should not discuss the election or issues that may become part of any election campaigns on social media. All other programme-makers should take extra care and precautions. This applies to both in-house and independent production companies. [RTÉ later added that] RTÉ staff with newsworthy contributions to make must operate on the basis that RTÉ's own social media sources should be facilitated ahead of any other sources.

It continued, under the heading 'RTÉ publishing social media comments from members of the public', and in words that anticipated the kind of error that it was to make during the presidential election later that same year:

> RTÉ radio and television programmes and rte.ie may include summaries of comments received from members of the public via social media. All such comments must be moderated in advance of publication to ensure that defamation is not an issue. Moderation will also ensure that offensive comments and language are excluded. Comments published should reflect accurately the comments received. In other words there is no requirement to be balanced between the political parties in the publication of comments. What is published should reflect the range of views received and should indicate the relative support for particular views. However as social media may be subject to campaigns trying to influence public opinion great care needs to be exercised to identify planned and organised use of social media. Where there is any suspicion that the opinions being received are being manipulated publication of such views should not take place.

Unfortunately for RTÉ, some of its personnel did not pay enough attention to this advice during the presidential election campaign in October 2011. In a debate between candidates on *The Frontline* television programme on 25 October an allegation in a tweet from a Twitter account erroneously described by the respected programme presenter as that of the official 'Martin McGuinness for President Campaign' was put by the presenter to a leading candidate, Seán Gallagher, in a way that discomforted him.

The originator of the tweet appears to have deliberately set out to mislead its readers about its origin, and its content appears to have been at least partly inaccurate. Gallagher was not subsequently elected president, and the relevance of the tweet to this outcome remains a matter of strong opinion.

The compliance committee of the Broadcasting Authority of Ireland subsequently found 'that the inclusion in a programme of this nature of what amounted to unverified information at the time of the broadcast, from a source that was wrongly accredited by the programme presenter' was unfair and required RTÉ, under Section 48 of the Broadcasting Act 2009, to transmit an apology (BAI, 2011). In covering this story, some journalists searched social media accounts maintained by members of the programme team, thus underlining also the wisdom of RTÉ's advice to its programme-makers about the potential problem of discussing in such fora any matters that might be deemed relevant to a political campaign. A review of the programme published in redacted form by RTÉ in December 2012 concluded that certain social media comments on Twitter by one of its assistant producers had been 'very unwise' (RTÉ, 2012, 21).

The debate continues

Nervousness about trusting people to make decisions about their own state's constitution, when both advocates and opponents of proposals of change are given access to the airwaves in accordance with existing fairness legislation, resurfaced in 2012 during the Fiscal Treaty referendum. This referendum, passed by 60.3% to 39.7%, required people to made a decision on complex matters relating to Ireland's relationship with the European Union in the context of new structures to address the international economic crisis. The government was accused of trying to circumvent the law by running an information campaign that leading columnist Gene Kerrigan (2012) described as being 'self-evidently a YES campaign behind a threadbare disguise, using public funds to party advantage.' However, another leading columnist, who was formerly a candidate for Fianna Fáil, complained that, in referendum campaigns, '[t]he rules on media space mean independents and smaller parties get disproportionate attention' (Whelan, 2012).

Notwithstanding such criticism, the government proceeded to fund its own information campaign at the time of a referendum on the rights of children held on 10 November 2012. It was severely reprimanded by the Supreme Court for doing so, with the court finding that the government had 'acted wrongfully' in publishing an information booklet and website that were 'not fair, equal, impartial or neutral'. Chief Justice Susan Denham, who had been a judge of the courts that had decided both the McKenna and Coughlan cases, now referred to the European Commission for Democracy through Law, better known as 'the Venice Commission', which is the Council of Europe's advisory body on constitutional matters. She noted that the Commission's code of good practice on referenda includes a declaration that

> Equality of opportunity must be guaranteed for the supporters and opponents of the proposal being voted on. This entails a neutral attitude by administrative authorities, in particular with regard to: i. the referendum campaign; ii. coverage by the media, in particular by the publicly owned media; iii. public funding of campaign and its actors; iv. billposting and advertising; v. the right to demonstrate on public thoroughfares.

To some observers this ruling simply confirmed the unreasonableness of the fairness requirement while to others it underlined the importance of fairness (O'Mahony, 2012; Kenny, 2012). What exactly constitutes fairness continues to be controversial but, in the opinion of this author, current legislation serves to protect the political process from abuse, and citizens are well able to decide in the light of both sides of an argument how best to protect the Constitution for which they voted.

References

BAI (2011) Broadcasting Compliance Committee decision in the matter of a complaint made by Cassidy Law Solicitors on behalf of Mr Seán Gallagher against RTÉ, 2011, (Ref. 217/11).

Carolan, E. and O'Neill, A. (2010) *Media law in Ireland*, Dublin: Bloomsbury Professional.

Gallagher, M. (1999) 'The changing constitution' in Coakley, J. and Gallagher, M. (eds), *Politics in the Republic of Ireland*, London: Routledge & PSAI Press.

Joint Committee on the Constitution, Houses of the Oireachtas (2009) *Second Report: Articles 46 and 47. Amendment of the Constitution and the Referendum: first interim report.*

Kenny, C. (2012) 'Coalition was inviting trouble with its biased assumptions' in *Irish Independent* (9 November).

Kerrigan, G. (2012) 'Is this a blatant abuse of funds? Yes' in *Sunday Independent* (29 April).

McGonagle, M. (2003) *Media law*, Dublin: Thomson Round Hall.

O'Mahony, C. (2012) 'Ruling on referendum bias confirms need for change' in *Irish Times* (9 November).

RTÉ (2011) General election guidelines.

RTÉ (2012) Working document of the editorial review of 'The Frontline' presidential debate, redacted version online.

Sinnott R. (2004) 'Financing for referendum campaigns: equal or equitable?' in Garvin, T., Manning, M. and Sinnott, R. (eds), *Dissecting Irish politics*, Dublin: UCD Press.

Whelan, N. (2012) 'Politics distorted during referendum campaigns' in *Irish Times* (19 May).

CHAPTER ELEVEN

'There now follows …': The role of the party political broadcast and the 2007 'peace broadcast'

Kevin Rafter

The 2007 general election in Ireland was notable for the intervention of Tony Blair and Bill Clinton – and former US senator George Mitchell – and their appearance in a political broadcast endorsing incumbent Taoiseach Bertie Ahern. This involvement went beyond what might be described as 'celebrity endorsement' but rather was an attempt to influence Irish voters by strengthening sentiment toward Ahern eight days before the 24 May 2007 poll. The trio of international political figures endorsed Ahern with a focus on his role in the Northern Ireland peace process although they also referenced his leadership in creating the Irish Celtic Tiger economy.

The *New York Times* (Quinn, 2007) described the intervention as 'an unusual gesture of support.' Nevertheless, the decision to call in 'international support' – as the Reuters News Agency (Hoskins, 2007) put it – was part of a carefully planned campaign strategy devised by Ahern's Fianna Fáil party. Seeking a third successive term, after ten years as leader of the major party in coalition governments, Ahern faced an uphill battle to remain in office amid allegations of political impropriety and a resurgent opposition. Positive endorsement from these international figures was an attempt to stress Ahern's 'statesman-like leadership standing' against his more inexperienced challengers. The so-called 'peace broadcast' was a significant departure from the traditional approach to broadcast political advertising in Ireland not just with its external political endorsement but also its overwhelming presidential-style focus in a parliamentary system.

The legislative regime in Ireland prohibits the broadcast of advertisements 'directed towards a political end' (Oireachtas, 2009). The ban on paid political advertising, similar to that in the United Kingdom, applies not just to political parties and election candidates but also to organisations promoting issues considered to be of a political nature. The regulatory arrangements do, however, allow registered political parties access to a system of free but controlled advertisements during election and referendum campaigns.

This system of free political advertising during election and referendum campaigns is known as party election broadcasts in the United Kingdom, but the term party political broadcast (PPB) is more commonly used in Ireland. In a restricted advertising regime these broadcasts remain the main way in which political parties 'communicate in an unmediated fashion with voters' (Negrine, 2011, 390). The broadcasts are widely watched by the electorate, and as a specific form of political communication they have become 'an important role of the ritual of Irish elections' (Collins and Butler, 2008, 43). According to polling data they are considered to be potentially influential in determining voter choice. Research in 2009 showed that 60% of Irish voters agreed with the statement that 'party political broadcasts can influence how people decide to vote' while 21% disagreed (Rafter, 2009, 27).

This chapter places the political advertising regime in Ireland in a wider international context while considering specific local regulations that shape the Irish attitude to political advertising. The development of broadcast political advertising in Ireland is examined by way of providing a backdrop to understanding the stand-out nature of the 'peace broadcast' that aired in 2007. The first section discusses the regulatory rules applied to broadcast political advertising. The development of the system of party political broadcasts is examined in the second section. The 'peace broadcast' is the focus of the third section, which discusses in detail the content, production values, and electoral context in which the broadcast was aired in 2007. The impact of the 'peace broadcast' is assessed in the final section, which considers the future of party political broadcasts in Ireland.

The regulation of political advertising

Political campaigns in the United States are very much media campaigns and political advertising is at the heart of these campaigns (Kaid, 2004). In this environment political advertising is equated with liberal expenditure limits and protected political speech, and as such any attempt to curtail political advertising would be considered a violation of the First Amendment of the US Constitution. However, the American system is very much 'an exceptional case' underpinned by limited regulation (Kaid and Holtz-Bacha,

2006, 10). More common in international experience are countries with a regulated advertising regime alongside countries that prohibit all advertising of a political nature. Countries that allow paid political advertising in a controlled environment frame their regulatory systems to include restrictions on scheduling, regulations on the duration, and limits on the costs that broadcasters can charge parties and candidates. Other countries, including Ireland and the United Kingdom, have dealt with the issue of paid political advertising by imposing an outright ban while operating a limited and regulated system of free advertising specifically for political parties during electoral contests.

The 'blanket ban' on political advertising in Ireland has been reaffirmed in several pieces of broadcasting legislation approved by the Irish parliament over many years and, most recently, in the Broadcasting Act 2009. Section 41 (3) of that Act states that 'a broadcaster shall not broadcast an advertisement which is directed towards a political end or which has any relation to an industrial dispute' (Oireachtas, 2009). While no definition of what is understood as a 'political advertisement' is provided in Irish law, the scope of the ban as reaffirmed in 2009 remains wide reaching and includes all advertising that might contain political content (Rafter, 2009). In the view of the regulator, the Broadcasting Authority of Ireland (BAI), all advertisements of a political nature are 'strictly prohibited' (BAI, 2011, 4). A very narrow construct has been applied to the word 'political' and, in this regard, the prohibition also applies to advertisements for events as well as notices of meetings or events organised by those with an interest in an election or referendum campaign. The regime means, in effect, that in addition to advertising for political parties, any advertisements that are directed towards procuring or opposing changes in legislation, government policies or policies of government authorities have been deemed to be directed towards a political end and have, therefore, been banned.

While none of the main political parties have ever sought to challenge the prohibition on their right to advertise on television and radio, the restrictive nature of the political advertising regime has led to ongoing controversy with other groups covered by the ban. Specific difficulties have arisen with organisations including book publishers, charities, and trade unions when they have sought to promote issues considered to be of a political nature. Such advertisements would, if approved for broadcast, have promoted issues such as a book written by an active politician, a music concert to raise funds and increase awareness of the war in Iraq, and a campaign to encourage the Irish government to fully implement an international resolution on gender equality. In one of these cases, radio advertisements for a memoir written by Sinn Féin leader Gerry Adams were banned in 2003. The decision of the BAI was based on the fact that the book was written by a serving politician who was giving his views on events in which he and his party continued to be involved and which was still the subject of political debate. The book's publisher argued that 'banning a straightforward ad for the memoir is nonsense' as the book was a personal memoir of Adams' involvement in the peace process in Northern Ireland (Rafter, 2009, 15). Radio advertisements for other books written by Adams had also been banned – in 1987 and 1992 – but on those occasions under the Section 31 broadcasting ban that applied to members of Sinn Féin, among other groups (Corcoran and O'Brien, 2005).

In more recent times, there have been growing arguments that these types of decisions relating to political advertising by non-political parties might not withstand a legal challenge in light of judgments by the European Court of Human Rights (Jones, 2004). Nevertheless, during parliamentary consideration of the 2009 legislation there was no serious discussion about the merits, or otherwise, of amending the current regime although, in a brief reference to the longstanding prohibition, then communications minister Eamon Ryan made the case for retaining the status quo:

> we should not open up political advertising as it would be almost impossible for an authority to judge the political aspect of such advertisement and to make calls in terms of whether it is accurate, inaccurate, acceptable or unacceptable. It is a difficult and grey area. (Ryan, 2009)

The broadcasting system in Ireland has been dominated by a state-owned station, RTÉ, which operated a national radio service from 1926 and oversaw the introduction of a national television channel that first broadcast on New Year's Eve 1961. This monopoly system remained in place until 1989 when licenses for privately owned radio and television services were first issued. Coverage of politics on the state controlled radio service was, in its initial decades, limited, passive, and reactive to events and announcements (Savage, 2011; Rafter, 2010). Until the 1950s there were no political discussion programmes, while the first unscripted political discussion programme was only broadcast in 1951. In the same year a weekly commentary on parliamentary proceedings was introduced.

The nature of political reportage underwent its first significant development with the arrival of an Irish television service in late 1961. The new domestic channel gave politics an increased sense of importance and, with their frequent television appearances, politicians were held to account by the media in a way not experienced previously. Reporting was less deferential and the perspective of journalists was increasingly called upon as analysis and comment were given greater prominence alongside news reporting of political developments. In this regard, the Irish situation was similar to the British experience with political broadcasting (Negrine, 2011, 392).

The role of RTÉ as a state-owned public broadcaster had been developed with the BBC model in mind although unlike its British counterpart, which was solely funded from the public purse, the Irish station's funding model was a mixture of public licence fee and advertising. Paid political advertising was banned on British television and the Irish authorities adopted a similar approach. The legislative restrictions, which banned paid political advertising on radio and television, meant unmediated political communi-cation between the political parties and the public was only possible through a new system of party political broadcasts.

Party political broadcasts

Party political broadcasts (PPB) have been a staple of Irish elections since the 1965 general election. Records indicate that the first PPB was transmitted on 8 February 1965 and featured incumbent Taoiseach Seán Lemass sitting in an armchair as he addressed watching voters. In the broadcast Lemass, the leader of Fianna Fáil, talked about recent economic progress including increased job creation and rising living standards. With cutaway images of half-demolished inner city slums followed by newly constructed housing estates, Lemass asked for a new mandate 'to ensure that progress is maintained and that the people who know how to run the country keep the wheel in their hands' (Irish Film Archive, 1965).

In a study of British party election broadcasts in the 1950s, Negrine concluded that by avoiding innovation and relying on 'tried and tested formats' the parties were displaying a degree of uncertainty not just with the television medium but also with the merits of free political broadcasts at election times (Negrine, 2011, 395). The Lemass broadcast was undoubtedly influenced by the initial British experience, although while parties in the UK went on to display a greater willingness to experiment, their Irish counterparts have only rarely strayed from the format of having senior party figures taking to camera combined with cutaway images of representatives of key voter groups including the elderly, families, and workers. The visuals are usually combined with music and are, on occasion, complemented by graphics. There were, of course, some exceptions: two smaller parties, the

Progressive Democrats and Democratic Left, made use of comedy sketches, but these broadcasts were exceptional departures from the norm.

The dominant style of Irish PPBs is captured in the archive listings for one such broadcast from February 1982: 'Campaign song over opening montage of [leader] being greeted by members of the public on the election trail. [Leader] speaks to camera [...] There are shots of children in class, a young couple, a student, factories, a farmer and some old age pensioners' (Irish Film Archive, 1982). In one respect, however, the Irish advertisements display a discernible American influence – personalisation. So while the Irish broadcasts are allocated in national parliamentary elections to qualifying political parties, they tend to be exclusively dominated by leading politicians and, particularly, party leaders. This latter fact can be taken as a sign that personalisation and presidentialisation comfortably co-exist with Ireland's parliamentary system of government.

Production values in Irish PPBs have increased significantly in more recent elections so that the political parties now produce 'slick and polished three-minute advertisements' (Collins and Butler, 2008, 43). Similarly, UK broadcasts 'have become increasingly sophisticated and some have entered election folklore' (Pattie and Johnston, 2002, 334). Scammell and Langer however, observed that British election broadcasts, while informative, are 'remarkably unpopular'. They concluded that 'it might do political parties a power of good to be more entertaining, more emotionally intelligent' (2006, 764). The evidence from Ireland over the past half-century suggests that there has been an even stronger conservatism at play combined with an unwillingness to approach these broadcasts as television advertisements that directly engage viewers. Respondents to a 2009 study on political advertising in Ireland were presented with a series of adjectives to describe party political broadcasts including boring, informative, misleading, and biased. One quarter (25%) opted for 'boring' as the best way to describe party political broadcasts, while 20% said these advertising spots were 'informative'. One in ten (10%) believed that the material in the broadcasts was false and misleading. Other assessments included interesting/helpful/useful (12%), persuasive (4%), and biased (4%) (Rafter, 2009).

The PPB allocation criteria are determined following negotiations between the broadcasters and the political parties. Free broadcast time is allocated to all qualifying parties at national, European, and presidential elections. The outcome is generally governed by reference to the results of previous equivalent elections and the number of candidates nominated by the parties in the election under consideration. So, for example, at the 1997 general election any registered party – with a coherent set of policies and which nominated a minimum of seven candidates – was guaranteed at least one slot of between one minute and one minute 45 seconds. The system meant that for the two largest parties the allocation led to Fianna Fáil (which received 40% support in the previous contest in 1992) being allocated six PPB slots totalling 20 minutes of airtime while Fine Gael (which received 25% support in 1992) had four slots totalling 12½ minutes of airtime. The costs of recording and producing the broadcasts are borne by the parties themselves. The broadcasts are transmitted in peak-time slots in the schedules of national television and radio stations. In the case of the two national television services now operating in Ireland the PPBs are generally shown following their evening news programmes.

The broadcasts are intended to encourage public participation in the voting process and also to provide voters with information to support their voting decisions. In the United Kingdom it has been argued that 'the principle that political parties should be able freely to publicise their platforms and policies to voters, and that voters should be able to receive such information, remains compelling' (Electoral Commission, 2003, 5). Scammell and Langer have argued that as television is now the predominant means of political communication in regimes where paid spots are prohibited, the PPB is the 'single most important direct address to voters' (2006, 764). Given the ban on paid political advertising, the system of free election broadcasts is the only direct access that political parties in Ireland, and the UK, have to the broadcast media. There is no external commentary; no journalist providing commentary or interviewer influencing the agenda.

The public's response in Ireland is different to that presented in the UK where their arrival on television screens is 'commonly greeted by mass channel-hopping' (Scammell and Langer, 2006, 765). It has been noted that a minority of the electorate watch the British broadcasts (Pattie and Johnston, 2002, 354). While there is mixed evidence about effectiveness, sizable audiences in Ireland watch these broadcasts – the 16 television broadcasts during the 2007 general election had an average viewership of 500,000 people. In a 2009 study, respondents were asked if they could recall any party political broadcasts from the 2007 election campaign (Rafter, 2009; 2011). Almost six in 10 of all adults (58%) could recall party political broadcasts from 2007 while 39% had no recall. People over 35 years were more likely to recall the party political broadcasts: 70% in the 35–44 age category; 75% in the 45–54 age category; and 68% in the 65+ age category, against 40% of those aged between 18 and 24 years.

Despite the wide variation in opinions on the value of party political broadcasts, the survey evidence pointed to strong public support for the current system. Respondents were asked for their view on the statement, 'regardless of whether I watch or hear them myself, I think it is important that party political broadcasts are shown.' Almost six in ten (57%) agreed that it was important that party political broadcasts were shown, regardless of whether or not they personally watched the broadcasts. Some 41% strongly agreed with this viewpoint while 16% agreed. Only 24% of respondents were in disagreement with this position. Two-thirds of those in the 45+ age category agreed that it was important that party political broadcasts were transmitted, regardless of whether or not they saw or heard them.

The 'peace broadcast'

Voters in Ireland went to the polls on 24 May 2007 following an electoral contest to decide if outgoing Taoiseach Bertie Ahern would win a third successive term. Ahern had already enjoyed a decade in office having led his centre-right Fianna Fáil party in the two previous contests in 1997 and 2002. Following each of those elections he had formed coalition administrations involving the smaller Progressive Democrats party and a handful of like-minded independent TDs. The pillars of Ahern's tenure in power were the peace process in Northern Ireland and the strength of the Irish economy. During most of the 1997 to 2007 period the Irish economy grew significantly, and the term 'Celtic Tiger' entered public discourse to describe the transformation in the wellbeing of a nation defined for much of the twentieth century by economic underperformance.

Ahern was centrally involved in the attempts to secure a peace agreement in Northern Ireland. In a sense his 'place in history' was secured following the cessation of the Provisional Irish Republican Army's campaign of violence and the establishment of a power-sharing deal between the different factions in the conflict region. But Ahern's longevity in office combined with questions about his personal finances, and a more spirited and united opposition than five years previously, created 'a fierce head-to-head confrontation between two opposing teams which looked for most of the campaign to be evenly matched' (Gallagher and Marsh, 2008, xi).

The campaign strategy devised by Ahern's Fianna Fáil election advisors revolved around a number of set-piece non-election events that were to highlight his role in the Northern Ireland peace process and to stress his leadership seniority over his less experienced opposition challengers. Two events in particular dominated news media coverage during the election campaign. First, the restoration of the devolved power-sharing government in Northern Ireland on 8 May 2007 pushed general election coverage from the main pages of the newspapers and the main headlines on broadcast stations. Nevertheless, as the incumbent head of the government, Ahern's response to the development was widely covered by the media. Second, Ahern addressed both houses of the British parliament on 15 May 2007. The British government, led by Ahern's fellow peace process participant, Tony Blair, had issued the invitation to address the joint parliamentary gathering. The timing of the event again cleared the news schedules of election coverage although Ahern remained central to the news agenda of the day in question. The two events received saturation media coverage and it has been argued that the positive imagery presented Ahern with 'a platform to exploit his role in the peace process' (Brandenburg and Zalinski, 2008, 176).

With the set-piece events already in the election diary, Fianna Fáil strategists had, in fact, one further opportunity to emphasise their leader's experience and standing compared to his less experienced challenger for the role of Taoiseach. The 'peace broadcast' was first aired on 16 May 2007. The four-minute video had been recorded a month previously and was produced to capitalise on Ahern's role in the Northern Ireland peace process. Clinton, Blair, and Mitchell had agreed to be interviewed for what they knew would be a promotional broadcast – a PPB – to be aired as part of Ahern's re-election strategy. Ahern had developed good working and personal relations with all three politicians, particularly with Clinton and Blair. In his memoir, Clinton refers to Ahern as his 'partner for peace' (Clinton, 2004, 688). Blair and Ahern had first worked together in the mid-1990s when they were both opposition leaders, and according to Blair, 'we got on immediately like the proverbial house on fire' (Blair, 2010, 159).

The film opens with archive footage from April 1998 when Ahern and Blair delivered a joint media conference at the successful conclusion of marathon negotiations that led to the signing of the Belfast (Good Friday) Agreement. The deal had been stuck following talks involving the Irish and British governments and representatives of the leading political parties in Northern Ireland. During the talks, the Clinton White House adminis-tration had also played a vital role in cajoling the participants to make the necessary concessions to secure a final agreement. In this footage, as Blair looks on, Ahern speaks of the day in question being about a 'new beginning' that promises a 'bright future [...] when a line can be drawn under the bloody past' (Fianna Fáil, 2007).

The 25-second sound bite that opens the broadcast is in fact the only time Ahern's voice is heard in the full PBB. Blair is the first of the three international politicians to speak with a short clip from his recorded interview: 'It's right to say we would never have had the peace process in Northern Ireland without Bertie Ahern.' Following this sound clip the screen goes to black and the word 'Peace' appears. The remaining three minutes and 20 seconds of the broadcast is given over to clips from the interviews with Clinton, Blair, and Mitchell. The three international politicians are glowingly positive about Ahern's leadership ability, his negotiating skills, and his central role in securing the peace deal in Northern Ireland.

> Mitchell: Bertie Ahern made several crucial decisions that led to the Good Friday Agreement. One of them was to come to Stormont along with Prime Minister Blair in the closing days where they took charge of the negotiations. They didn't just supervise them – they conducted them word-by-word, sentence-by-sentence – a high wire act in which one mistake would have resulted in disaster.

> Clinton: There is no question in my mind that while the lion's share of the credit belongs to the parties themselves, who got tired of fighting and wanted a peaceful future, that if it hadn't been for Bertie Ahern and for Tony Blair we would never have had the Good Friday Agreement.

> Blair: Without his leadership and his determination and his strength, and his doggedness in just keeping the thing going and on track, we would never have come this far and certainly I could not have wished for a better partner in peace than Bertie Ahern.

The initial interview material with the three political figures is heard alongside more archive footage from the 1998 peace talks in Belfast. Viewers see the leaders from the two communities in Northern Ireland including Gerry Adams of Sinn Féin and David Trimble of the Ulster Unionist Party. Interestingly, despite the PPB's 'peace' theme Blair and Clinton proceed to offer an assessment of Ahern – and effectively an endorsement – that goes beyond the Irish politician's involvement in the Northern Ireland peace process.

Blair specifically credits Ahern with Ireland's economic prosperity. In this section of the broadcast the archive footage moves away from images of Northern Ireland to show Ahern attending a summit of European Union heads of government – French President Jacques Chirac is prominent in the footage – as well as shaking hands outside the White House with President Clinton.

> Blair: The fact that the Republic of Ireland is such a dynamic and enterprising place and the contribution of Bertie Ahern, both in his previous incarnation as the minister for finance, but then as the Taoiseach, that is a contribution that is immeasurable.

> Clinton: The sheer economic progress in the Irish Republic and in Northern Ireland alone ought to be enough to show people that the path of peace is the best path.

Viewing the 'peace broadcast' offers support for Kaid's contention about the difficulty in distinguishing between issues and images in campaign messages: 'Traditionally, issues have been viewed as statements of candidate positions on policy issues or preferences on issues or problems of public concern, whereas images have been viewed as a concentration on candidate qualities or characteristics' (Kaid, 2004, 162).

The contributions of Clinton, Blair and Mitchell offer a blending of image and issue information. This blending is clearly evident when the broadcast switches gear once more in its final twenty-five seconds to include footage of the Rev. Ian Paisley. As leader of the hard-line Democratic Unionist Party, Paisley had withdrawn from the Belfast Agreement talks and had actively campaigned against the deal. But as part of subsequent efforts to secure a power-sharing government in Northern Ireland, Paisley had modified his stance.

On 8 May 2007 Paisley had been elected first minister of Northern Ireland in a devolved administration involving other parties including Sinn Féin. The footage used in the broadcast was from earlier in 2007 with Paisley arriving at Farmleigh House in Dublin. He is seen getting out of his car and being met by Ahern. The broadcast then switches back briefly to the Clinton interview, and the former US president says:

> He [Ahern] never lost his energy, he never lost his determination, he never lost his vision. He never lost his sense of humour. He just kept going until this last agreement here which may well bring an end to everything.

As Clinton speaks his final words – 'may well bring an end to everything' – the broadcast returns to the footage of Ahern and Paisley. As Clinton finishes speaking the footage is deliberately slowed to emphasise the handshake between Paisley and Ahern. The footage, and the editing tools used, were clearly about stressing for the watching voters not just the success of the peace process in Northern Ireland, and not just Ahern's role in that achievement, but also his status as a peacemaker and as a conciliator.

Discussion

Voter feedback in Ireland shows strong attachment to PPBs as a means of communicating party positions and seeking electoral support despite a lack of satisfaction with the broadcasts themselves. With possible legal and nascent technological challenges to the practicality of the longstanding broadcast ban there may well be room for regulatory initiative to modernise this method of political communication. In this context, a more relaxed regulatory regime may prompt greater party innovation. In this chapter we have examined one recent innovative broadcast, produced within the confines of the current rules, that was a clear departure from all previous election broadcasts over the last half century. Indeed, the four-minute PPB has been described as 'an unusual film' (Collins and Butler, 2008, 43) while Ahern himself judged it 'a powerful broadcast' (RTÉ, 2007).

Ahern's election advisors in his Fianna Fáil party recognised the uniqueness of the broadcast – they considered it a news story in itself capable of generating coverage outside the specific confines of its own transmission. As part of creating a 'buzz' around the PPB, the film was screened for political journalists after the party's daily morning election press conference (RTÉ, 2007). The strategy where the advert is a legitimate news story in its own right had long been in place elsewhere (Scammell, 1995, 228) but given the lack of excitement with PPBs in Ireland they generally received little, if any, news coverage. Screening the 'peace broadcast' for journalists was successful as it placed the broadcast into the day's election news cycle for radio and television news programmes.

Irish PPBs have traditionally been leader-centred, but, given Ireland's parliamentary political system, even when dominated by the party leader these broadcasts frequently include visuals and interview clips with other senior party personnel. The 'peace broadcast' is, however, exclusively candidate-dominated with no mention of Ahern's party, his role as party leader or even his party colleagues. A stranger with no local knowledge watching the broadcast would most likely speculate that Ireland was ruled by a presidential system of government. In this regard, there is little doubt that the creators of this PPB were moving into the territory of 'intense personalisation' evident in more recent election broadcasts in the United Kingdom (Hodess et al., 2000, 64).

The broadcast firmly fits into the acclaim category of adverts identified by Benoit (1999) with the three international politicians making positive claims about the election candidate. Viewers are treated to a potent combination of issue information and image content (Kaid, 2004, 162). While issue-based in terms of stressing Ahern's record, the broadcast is devoid of any statement on Ahern's position on policy issues. No direct reference is made to the election campaign – the compliment to Ahern for his involvement in Ireland's economic success is the only reference to an election issue. The interview material from the three political figures concentrates on delivering positive assessments of the qualities and characteristics of the candidate. The accompanying images are selected to deliver focus on those same qualities and characteristics.

The broadcast is undoubtedly issue-based with strong emotional appeal particularly by reminding voters of the goodwill, and relief, generated by the Belfast Agreement. The generation of emotional responses in political advertisements has been identified as important in several American studies (Kaid, 2004, 166). By reminding voters about Ahern's association with the Northern Ireland peace process, the broadcast obviously sets out to capitalise on the positive emotional sentiment towards the peace process and to enhance public evaluation of Ahern in the election campaign. Political advertisements for incumbents tend to be defined by images that stress their experience and achievements in office. This is clearly the case with the 'peace broadcast'.

The broadcast was unprecedented not just in the departure from the tried and tested PPB formats produced by most Irish political parties over many elections. The intervention of three recognisable international political figures in an Irish national election, and their willingness to endorse one of the participants, was highly unusual. There was no ambiguity about the involvement of the three politicians. A spokeswoman for Ahern stated that '[t]hey were all asked to participate. They knew they were participating in a party political broadcast.' The interviews with the three politicians had in fact been recorded a month previously in April 2007 and they had been shown the final version of the four-minute broadcast: 'They cleared it before it went ahead. All three approved [the interviews], and they saw the version. They were all cleared personally' (de Bréadún, 2007).

The main opposition parties were placed in a difficult position. The peace process in Northern Ireland had been a tremendous success. It was difficult to attack the PPB without being criticised for undermining the peace process. Moreover, all three international politicians were not just highly recognisable with the Irish public but they were also widely admired and liked. Blair and Clinton had enjoyed positive receptions on their visits to the Irish Republic. There was considerable respect for the investment made by Mitchell while he was chairman of the talks process that culminated in the Belfast Agreement. Against this background – and having had to publicly congratulate Ahern for his Westminster speech the previous day at which the main opposition leader Enda Kenny of Fine Gael was an invited guest – the opposition parties offered limited public criticism of the intervention of the three external figures.

If anything Fine Gael and the Labour Party sought to play down the intervention of the three politicians. The Labour Party leader, Eamon Gilmore, couched his reaction in terms of 'the end of an era' with Clinton retired and Blair about to depart office: 'I don't think they [voters] are going to be greatly influenced by valedictory comments of other political leaders who have left office or are going out of office.' The underlying hope in the reaction was obviously that Ahern might also shortly be joining Clinton and Blair in retirement. Ahern's main challenger for the role of Taoiseach, Enda Kenny, expressed similar sentiments: 'They're all gone or they're on the way out', while adding that Fianna Fáil was entitled to use any figureheads or personalities it wanted in its broadcasts (de Bréadún, 2007).

Given its position as a small nation, and the strong historical relationship with its two English-speaking neighbours, the UK on one side and the USA on the other, it is not surprising that Irish politicians would look to these countries for inspiration. Imitation and adoption of successful campaign techniques have been features of the professionalisation of electoral campaigning in Ireland. Establishing an association with popular American and British leaders is a long-established tactic. In the first PPB back in 1965 with another Fianna Fáil Taoiseach – Seán Lemass – those involved saw fit to include static photographs of John F. Kennedy and Harold Wilson. Moreover, the visits of US presidents, for example Kennedy, Reagan, and Clinton, seeking to stress their Irish roots to enhance their Irish-American vote back home have also been used by their local political hosts to generate positive domestic sentiment.

Irish leaders have also sought to capitalise on their political links with European figures, and in this regard prior to the 2007 general election a 'goodwill' letter from German Chancellor Angela Merkel was read out at the Fine Gael national conference. Merkel's CDU party and Fine Gael are both members of the European People's Party alliance. With a touch of irony one of Ahern's Fianna Fáil colleagues attacked the letter noting that '[t]he Irish people have a very deep-rooted sense of not being told what to do by foreign powers.' He also claimed that the main opposition party had demonstrated 'a massive inferiority complex' by seeking and receiving endorsements from people in other countries (de Bréadún, 2007). But exploiting established cross-national political links in a party political setting is very different from the direct electoral intervention and explicit candidate endorsement offered by Clinton, Blair, and Mitchell. In a similar vein, the 1965 attempt to create 'positivity by association', by using photographic images, was very different from the direct public endorsement offered by Kennedy's and Wilson's successors.

In summary, this analysis of the 'peace broadcast' in the 2007 Irish general election shows a willingness to make party political broadcasts part of the campaign and to innovate with a long-established format. This specific broadcast advertisement shows that personalisation has become central to election strategies in Ireland. Moreover, the role of 'celebrity' political endorsements, even in what was a strongly issue-focused broadcast, may be worthy of further research to determine wider relevance and to identify possible trends over time in other countries. From a regulatory viewpoint, the 'peace broadcast' may point to the type of innovation in political information provision that could become increasingly a feature of election campaigns with considered and imaginative relaxation of the current restrictive regulatory regime for broadcast political advertising in Ireland.

References

Benoit, W. *Seeing spots: a functional analysis of presidential television advertisements, 1956–1996*, Westport: Praeger.

Blair, T. (2010) *A Journey*, London: Hutchinson.

Brandenburg, H. and Zalinski, Z. (2008) 'The media and the campaign' in Marsh, M. and Gallagher, M. (eds), *How Ireland voted 2007*, London: Palgrave.

Broadcasting Authority of Ireland (2011) *Broadcasting code on referenda and election coverage*, Dublin: BAI.

Clinton, B. (2004) *My Life*, London: Hutchinson.

Collins, N. and Butler, P. (2008) 'Campaign strategies and political marketing' in Marsh, M. and Gallagher, M. (eds), *How Ireland voted 2007*, London: Palgrave.

Corcoran, M.P. & O'Brien, M. (eds) *Political communication and the democratic state: the Irish broadcasting ban*, (Dublin, 2005).

de Bréadún, D. (2007) 'Parties dismiss Blair, Clinton praise for Ahern' in *Irish Times* (17 May).

Electoral Commission (2003), *Party political broadcasting – report and recommendations*, London: Electoral Commission.

Fianna Fáil (2007) Peace broadcast, copy in possession of author.

Gallagher, M. and Marsh, M. (eds), (2008) *How Ireland voted 2007*, London: Palgrave.

Hodess, R., Tedesco, J. and Kaid, L. (2000) 'British party election broadcasts: a comparison of 1992 and 1997' in *Harvard International Journal of Press/ Politics*, 5(4): 55–70.

Hoskins, P. (2007) 'Blair, Clinton enter fray of tense Irish election', Reuters (17 May).

Irish Film Archive (1965) *Let Lemass lead on*, Ref. AE750.

Irish Film Archive (1982) Fianna Fáil party political broadcast, Ref. AE776.

Jones, C.A. (2004) 'Regulating political advertising in the EU and USA: a human rights perspective' in *Journal of Public Affairs*, 4(3): 244–55.

Kaid, L. (2004) 'Political advertising' in Kaid, L. (ed.) *Handbook of political communication research*, New York: Lawrence Erlbaum.

Kaid, L. and Holtz-Bacha, C. (eds) (2006) *The Sage handbook of political advertising*, London: Sage.

Negrine, R. (2011) 'British election broadcasts in the 1950s' in *Media History*, 17(4): 389–403.

Oireachtas (2009) Broadcasting Act 2009.

Pattie, C.J. and Johnston, R.J. (2002) 'Assessing the television campaign: the impact of party election broadcasts on voters' opinions in the 1997 British general election' in *Political Communication*, 19(3): 333–58.

Quinn, E. (2007) 'Ireland votes on whether to give the prime minister a third term' in *New York Times* (25 May).

Rafter, K (2009) *Political advertising: the regulatory position and the public view*, Dublin: Broadcasting Authority of Ireland.

Rafter, K. (2010) 'Reporting the Oireachtas: Irish political and parliamentary journalism since 1922' in Manning, M. and MacCarthaigh, M. (eds), *The Houses of the Oireachtas: Parliament in Ireland*, Dublin: Institute of Public Administration.

Rafter, K. (2011) 'Hear no evil – see no evil: political advertising in Ireland' in *Journal of Public Affairs*, 11(2): 93–99.

RTÉ News (2007) 'Election: Clinton, Blair, in FF party broadcast' (16 May).

Ryan, E. (2009) Speech of minister for communications, Dáil debate, 4 June.

Savage, R. (2010) *A loss of innocence? Television and Irish society 1960–72*, Manchester: Manchester University Press.

Scammell, M. (1995) *Designer politics, how elections are won*, Basingstoke: Macmillan Press.

Scammell, M. and Langer, A. (2006) 'Political advertising: why is it so boring?' in *Media Culture & Society*, 28(5): 763–84.

CHAPTER TWELVE

Social media
and political communication

Martin Molony

The election of Barack Obama in 2008 was widely regarded as being an internet election victory. Greengard (2009, 16) described Obama as 'the first internet president' and there was widespread agreement amongst political commentators and digital media experts as to 'how politicians and the public interact [would] never be the same.' In the days following Obama's election, the *New York Times* reflected on the repetition of history in the effective use of a new medium: 'One of the many ways that the election of Barack Obama as president has echoed that of John F. Kennedy is his use of a new medium that will forever change politics. For Mr Kennedy, it was television. For Mr Obama, it is the internet' (Miller, 2008). Commentators, such as *Huffington Post* founder and editor-in-chief Arianna Huffington (2008) went further and believed that the Obama win was entirely due to his use of the Web: 'Were it not for the Internet, Barack Obama would not be president. Were it not for the Internet, Barack Obama would not have been the nominee.'

But was Obama's win entirely down to successful use of the internet? Why did he win when, just four years earlier, Howard Dean had failed having used the same approach? One might assume that Barack Obama perfected Dean's trial use of internet technologies but it is also reasonable to suggest that such electronic communication had come of age and that the electorate was sufficiently comfortable with the technologies to engage with their preferred candidate. The Web had intrinsically changed between the presidential elections of 2004 and 2008 with the growth of Web 2.0 technologies, specifically the advent of social media. The revolution promised by Web 2.0 was based on participation and interactivity rather than the publication/broadcast or one-way communication flow that had defined the Web up to then.

Whatever can be said about the medium itself, there can be little doubt that Obama's candidacy was particularly suited to the use of an interactive, two-way communication facility provided by Web 2.0 in general and by social media in particular. As a community organiser, Obama understood the potential of crowdsourcing – and not just for financial support, but for idea generation and policy support also. For Obama, social media communication became an online version of both a sense of community for participants and in its use in organising and galvanising his supporters into action.

Hoping to emulate Obama's success, political candidates across the globe scrambled to adopt social media to their advantage. The UK's 2010 general election was predicted to be the 'internet election' but was dominated by the first televised leaders' debates, with television providing the principal innovation of the campaign. It seemed that the internet and social media were more important in influencing how traditional media operated, rather than in influencing the outcome of the election itself. British print and broadcast media were able to harness the immediacy of social media responses to an event, often resulting in the social media response itself becoming the focus of the news coverage. For candidates, the most effective use of social media was in managing their campaign workers and in providing them with the most effective information for offline campaigning. Although the parties attempted to imitate Obama's perceived success with social media – such as the Conservative Party's creation of an e-campaign system, 'MyCon', it became clear that whatever US social media success there had been, it could not be directly mapped onto the UK political landscape.

But what about Ireland? This chapter considers the growing impact of social media for political communication in Ireland. It examines the extent to which the use of social media has been adopted as a tool of political communication, the extent to which its use has been effective in election strategies, and whether the employment of social media in such instances genuinely represents a significant change in political communication or whether social media is actually far closer to traditional methods of political communication than first appears.

General election 2007

Prior to Obama's 2008 victory, Irish political candidates had not adopted Web-based technologies to any great extent. The Irish general election of 2007 offered the first opportunity for a significant role for use of the internet by candidates and the media, the latter of which experimented with some exclusive Web events and use of the Web to provide breaking news coverage. Citizen journalists provided an alternative media perspective with a number of bloggers providing some useful and popular online commentary on sites such as irishelection.com and politics.ie. Although there was some use of YouTube for party political programmes, with the Green Party using the site to premiere its party political broadcast, generally the Web was not embraced with any great fervour by most candidates. A study of 'cyber-campaigning' in the 2007 campaign (Sudulich and Wall, 2009, 459) found that only a third of candidates set up personal websites. This is surprising, given that a sole reliance on party-based web resources would only provide the same exposure as their party running mate(s). Although the use of electronic campaigning resources was significantly greater than in previous elections, clearly the 2007 general election candidates did not regard the use of the Web as a vital campaigning tool.

This reluctance in taking web-based campaigning seriously may be explained by the traditional campaigning style of Irish elections. Personal contact with as many individual voters as possible is expected by both candidates and the electorate. A reported 69% of voters had spoken with their chosen candidate during the 2002 election campaign (Marsh et al., 2008, 256) while 60% of Irish voters reported that contact was made with their household, either by candidates or their representatives during the 2007 campaign (Sudulich and Wall, 2009, 458). The potential of the new media was described as offering a public sphere, a new 'town square' that, with its emphasis on user-generated content, 'might grow to offer truly alternative, citizen-oriented election coverage' (Brandenburg, 2007, 184). However, in considering the effectiveness of media spending in this election, research has indicated that traditional printed posters and leaflets still produced the most significant return on investment (Sudulich and Wall, 2011).

European election 2009

The European Parliament elections of June 2009 offered a more US presidential-style opportunity for the use of social media in Irish politics. With an electorate of between 778,502 and 861,727 voters in each of the four constituencies, the potential for personal voter contact was obviously limited and offered an Obama-style opportunity for the use of Web-based technologies. In the run-up to the 2009 election, a survey of all sitting European parliamentarians indicated a high use of personal websites (75%) by the incumbent MEPs. On the social media front, just 21% of MEPs had a Twitter account with 62% either never having heard of Twitter or having no plans to use it. Similarly, 24% of the MEPs described themselves as using a blog extensively while 57% believed that TV was either a very effective or effective way to communicate with voters compared with 45% for print and 33% for online communication (Fleishman-Hillard, 2009).

An analysis of the use of social media within the EU constituency of Dublin (O'Connor, 2009) showed that six of the ten candidates had blogs, but that none of these generated sufficient traffic to register on the social media measurement site technorati.com, indicating very low levels of traffic to these blogs. The same study noted that only 30% of the Dublin candidates had a presence on YouTube and that the activity levels, in terms of the number of videos, subscribers, and views were all particularly low. O'Connor also found that while nine of the ten candidates had a Facebook presence, the levels of support (friends) and levels of activity (posts) varied greatly. Successful Socialist Party candidate Joe Higgins led both criteria with 575 friends and 102 posts, while the unsuccessful Libertas candidate, Caroline Simmons, had just 84 friends and did not post to her Facebook page at all. There was no subsequent correlation between the levels of Facebook friends and the first-preference vote achieved by each candidate.

Regardless of the extent to which Fine Gael's use of social media in the 2009 EU election might have contributed to its success in winning over 29% of the vote and four of the 12 Irish seats, Feargal Purcell, the party's deputy director of communications, was not convinced of the potency of social media: 'The evidence is that the electorate still gets its hard political information from TV and print' (O'Connor, 2009, 77). This supports the view that it is not social media, per se, that offers a magic bullet, but that it is the application of social media to engage with the electorate that provides dividends at the ballot box. Other commentators recognised that while the technology might allow for engagement between the electorate and candidates, provision of the technology does not necessarily mean that this happens. The *Irish Times* political correspondent and political blogger, Harry McGee, was unequivocal about suggestions of such engagement during the 2009 election campaign: 'Two-way conversations have not opened up online in the Irish political parties and their supporters' (O'Connor, 2009, 76).

Twitter's impact

Although only three years old in 2009, the micro-blogging service Twitter had enjoyed huge growth in the 18 months before the 2009 European election. Twitter featured on the front page of *Time* magazine on the day of the election in Ireland, with a cover story proclaiming that 'Twitter will change the way we live' (Johnson, 2009). Statistics for the service showed a 1,460% rise in its worldwide audience over the previous 12 months, with it having attracted 44.5 million unique visitors to its website during June 2009 alone (Schonfeld, 2009). Only six of the ten Dublin EU candidates had Twitter profiles during the campaign, with incumbent Fianna Fáil MEP Eoin Ryan and Green Party challenger Deirdre de Burca topping the poll of followers with 628 and 612 followers respectively, and with Joe Higgins not far behind with 526 followers. The remaining three candidates had attracted only a fraction of this interest on Twitter (O'Connor, 2009).

Despite this level of engagement with Twitter, it was not until early 2010 that its potential impact on the Irish political scene became apparent when it played a part in the resignation of a minister in the then Fianna Fáil–Green Party coalition government. It was Green Party chairman, Senator Dan Boyle's prolific use of the medium that prompted calls from some of his parliamentary colleagues for him to stop his 'irresponsible' tweeting about political issues (Minihan, 2010). Boyle's use of Twitter certainly identified the potential of the medium, particularly capitalising on its semi-official nature. One could not have imagined many of Boyle's views expressed via Twitter, which were presented as being shared by his party, being published as a party press release in the usual manner. Twitter seemed to provide a means to whisper an aside, but to the general populace. Somehow, publishing a statement within 140 characters seemed to provide a degree of latitude not otherwise permitted – or expected.

The informality of the medium allowed Boyle to fan the flames of a given controversy or to rekindle an affair that might otherwise have run its course. Indeed, it was one of Boyle's missives that gave Willie O'Dea the honour of being the first politician to be tweeted out of office, when the latter had to step down as minister for defence in February 2010. O'Dea had survived a vote of no confidence in the Dáil, following a revelation that he had sworn an inaccurate affidavit in defence of a defamation action against him. He was forced to revise the affidavit when a recorded interview was made public. Just as O'Dea's position appeared to be safe, Boyle tweeted: 'As regards Minister O'Dea I don't have confidence in him. His situation is compromised. Probably a few chapters in this story yet.' As speculation on the minister's future was rekindled, O'Dea was forced to resign a little over 24 hours later.

In addition to being the catalyst for controversy, Twitter also came into its own for the extent to which it enabled coverage of political controversy.

In May 2010 the *Sunday Independent* published an article detailing €81,015 claimed in expenses by Fianna Fáil Senator Ivor Callely. Subsequent news stories revealed that Callely had claimed travel expenses from a home in Co. Cork, some 370 kilometres from the Dáil – and his other home in Dublin's suburb of Clontarf, in his former Dáil constituency of Dublin North Central, and in which house day-to-day appearances suggested he still lived. The unfolding story caught the imagination of social media participants. An analysis of social media commentary over the following two months showed that some 5,000 tweets, or other social media comments, were made on the topic, while three days after the publication of the initial article there were 584 mentions of the senator during a 24-hour period (O'Leary, 2010a). Most of this social media traffic was driven by messages on Twitter.

What is interesting about the social media coverage of the Callely affair was the extent to which those discussing it, based on their number of social media connections, were deemed to have a high 'measure of influence' – a measure calculated by a series of algorithms that takes into account multiple aspects of the individual author's online profile, including but not limited to the number of followers they have on Twitter, the number of friends on Facebook, and the number of posts on a message board such as boards.ie or politics.ie. The measure of influence of those talking about Ivor Callely ranged on a scale from 0 to 10 with 27% of the comments made by people with a measure of influence of 5 or higher, while 17% of the comments were made by people with an influence measure of 9 or 10 (O'Leary, 2010a). This level of influence illustrates the extent to which Twitter, in particular, can impact on other forms of social media and on the agenda of traditional media.

For other tweets, it is often only when traditional media, particularly print media, republish the messages, complete with interpretation and context, that the tweets acquire potency. The release of some tweets places a perspective and / or opinion in the public domain that was previously known, or assumed, by media sources. The publication of these via Twitter provides carte blanche to correspondents to build a story around the tweet, thereby generating far more media coverage than might be expected from 140 characters. The media coverage of Dan Boyle's Twitter traffic may have prompted fellow Cork South-Central TD, Simon Coveney, to attempt to garner similar public attention. Although this did not seem to come naturally to the Fine Gael deputy, he struck gold when he tweeted a comment on a particularly poor performance by then Taoiseach Brian Cowen in the now infamous *Morning Ireland* radio interview of September 2010. Although

Coveney's tweet was not the first to comment on Cowen's performance, his wording – 'God, what an uninspiring interview by Taoiseach this morning. He sounded half way between drunk and hungover and totally disinterested …' – offered the media an opportunity to push the story into new territory, in particular the then Taoiseach's drinking habits.

Coveney's tweet prompted international media coverage, with some 457 articles published in the 24 hours following the tweet, appearing in publications in 26 countries, including the USA, UK, India, and China (O'Leary, 2010b). The wording of Coveney's tweet demonstrates the 'aside type commentary' that is afforded by Twitter. It is difficult to imagine that such a remark would have been issued in a press release – or even during an interview with a journalist. Although the deputy did not accuse Cowen of being either drunk or hungover, the suggestion that he sounded like this legitimised the media questions that were put to an unsuspecting Cowen later that morning. While there had been previous comment in media circles about his drinking habits, it had been regarded as inappropriate or off-limits to broach the subject. Whatever the wisdom of Cowen going on live radio while sounding hoarse, his response to the social media coverage demonstrated a serious lack of awareness by Fianna Fáil in monitoring social media traffic and in failing to gauge properly the potential fallout.

Of course, the informality of Twitter has not always worked to the advantage of the tweeting party. Some of Dan Boyle's messages may have crossed the line from time to time. In particular, his 2011 comment on the arrest of the managing director of the IMF, Dominique Strauss-Kahn, on allegations of sexual assault in an upmarket New York hotel – 'Strauss-Kahn sexual assault allegations are of course of the utmost seriousness, but paying $3,000 for a hotel room isn't all that far behind' – resulted in a backlash. While such a remark might have passed without too many ripples – or even unnoticed – had it been made as part of an informal conversation or speech, Twitter, despite appearing to be a transitory medium, does appear in 'writing' and, as with traditional media, the written word remains 'on the record'. Boyle soon back-pedalled on his association of a humorous remark with an accusation of a sexual crime: 'In the words of Hilary Clinton, I miscommunicated – and badly, it seems.'

General election 2011

The 2011 general election saw a significant increase in the use of internet tools and social media, placing the medium alongside traditional media. Two social media platforms in particular, were, by this time, being engaged with by a critical mass of the Irish electorate and were adopted by candidates in a meaningful way. Facebook reported some two million Irish accounts, while just under 200,000 Irish people had Twitter accounts. Accordingly, the 2011 election candidates focused their social media efforts principally on these two services: 79% of the 566 candidates had a Facebook account, while 57% had Twitter accounts (McMahon, 2011).

The main political parties sought the advice and expertise of international social media consultants, some of whom had been associated with Barack Obama's success just three years previously. Each party website was integrated with social media, with links to their presence on Facebook, Twitter, Flickr, and YouTube. In addition, the websites invited visitors to keep up-to-date through email subscriptions – and, of course, invitations to join the campaign.

The most dramatic use of the Web in the 2011 campaign was Fine Gael's conversion of their existing website to a three-page site, featuring a video of an informal Enda Kenny inviting the public to comment on what was wrong with the country. The site also featured pages on 'How we can improve the country' and 'How can we win your support?' Although the site generated a lot of media commentary and appeared to engage the public in offering their opinions, it attracted the most attention when it was was hacked within a week. The site was transformed several times during the campaign, with the party claiming 400,000 hits (Wall and Sudulich, 2011, 96). The party also created a 'digital task force' of 30 full-time volunteers to drive their digital strategy, which included the creation of an 'e-canvasser' tool similar to that adopted by Obama in 2008, allowing the party to organise and manage their supporters.

The Labour Party also adapted its website in an innovative manner with constituency-specific video messages featuring Eamon Gilmore, links for which could be emailed to others by those visiting the site. This represented an interesting application of the technology to provide targeted material, but which was driven by user interaction. The party broke new ground with the provision of an iPhone 'app' that allowed users to follow the party leader's public appearances via an interactive map and view images of party hustings. Party political use of Twitter before and during the 2011 election campaign demonstrated some strategic thinking in how to maximise its impact, rather than just attempting to blindly build a large group of 'followers'. Attempts made to develop a distinct relationship with Twitter followers include Fianna Fáil's announcement, first on Twitter, of the results of its leadership contest shortly before the campaign. Other parties released sections of policy documents first to social media followers before releasing them more generally.

Such attempts at a strategic use of Twitter took place against a background of Twitter-based controversies that had managed to capture the public – and media – imagination in the 18 months prior to the election. While Twitter was a significant element of the 2011 campaign, it was generally more gainfully employed by the observers, rather than by the participants, including media organisations, political commentators, and interested members of the electorate. Voters with a particularly well-informed view on a given topic could now contribute to online public debate alongside the political candidates – often getting a head start on the debate as Twitter discussions grew organically while candidates were embroiled in television or radio debates on the topic. The use of Twitter hashtags such as #ge11 (general election 2011), #rtedeb (RTÉ leaders' debate), and #tv3ld (TV3 leaders' debate) provided online banners under which people gathered to follow and contribute to ongoing discussions. The level of engagement in political conversation using social media could be seen in the levels of Twitter traffic around these hashtags: 63,000 tweets were sent using the #ge11 hashtag during the final four days of the campaign, while a further 22,000 were sent on the first day of the count (Healy, 2011).

What was particularly interesting in the use of hashtags was the extent to which discussions grew using media hashtags such as #vinb (TV3's *Vincent Browne Show*), #lastword (*Last Word* radio show), #sixone (RTÉ's *Six-One News*), #twip (RTÉ's *The Week in Politics*) and #rtept (RTÉ's *Prime Time*). The widespread adoption of these hashtags meant that Twitter conversations and debates evolved around particular media programmes, often in parallel with the actual broadcast and sometimes in response to topics prompted by the producers. This parallel media experience, referred to as social viewing/ listening, was to become a challenge and opportunity for broadcasters. They could no longer expect to hold the exclusive attention of their audiences – but the flip side was the opportunity to feature centrally in the parallel social media conversation.

For party-based candidates, headquarters provided advice, training, and support. There were attempts by most of the main parties at a 'one size fits all' approach to the adoption of social media by candidates. However, as with any skillset, there was a great variance in the expertise and experience across the range of candidates. The extent of the lower end of the spectrum of social media experience was evident in the story of one incumbent politician asking for his social media communications to be restricted to voters in his constituency. The irony of a 'social' media being used by an organisation to emulate the expressions of individuals was not lost on social media commentator Suzy Byrne (2011), who was unequivocal in her view of the use of social media accounts on a party-wide scale: 'Candidates who hand over control of their personal accounts to someone else are silly, parties who take control of their candidates accounts give the impression of a) having no faith in their candidates or b) having no clue or c) complete paranoia of message control.'

For independent candidates, social media could provide the proverbial level playing-field, particularly if the candidate was prepared to really engage with voters. The 2011 election attracted 235 candidates outside the main five parties, with some 189 of these being free of any party affiliations (Wall and Sudulich, 2011). This was the greatest number of independent candidates in any Dáil election and provided an opportunity for the electorate to move away from traditional party politics. One such independent was 23-year-old student candidate, Dylan Haskins, who seemed to understand social media best practice: 'I'm taking questions from constituents and answering them on my website. It's a conversation, not a speech. It's a way of communicating with people' (Devlin, 2011). While candidate Haskins never made it to Deputy Haskins, successful independent candidates did ensure that they were sufficiently covered on the social media front. For example, Luke 'Ming' Flanagan had over 3,000 Twitter followers during the campaign, together with some 1,700 Facebook 'likes', while Michael Lowry boasted over 5,000 Facebook friends.

There were mixed opinions on the extent to which such electronic campaigning translated into votes. Positive correlations were found between a candidate's popularity on Facebook or Twitter and the number of first preference votes they received (McMahon, 2011). However, this is just as likely to be an indication of the stronger candidates having adequately covered themselves on these social media platforms, rather than their election success having been due to their social media activities. Correlations can be made between the levels of internet activity by Fine Gael and the party's gradually increasing support throughout the campaign, mapped by the various campaign polls. Much was made of the party's e-canvasser tool, based on Obama's 2008 approach, and Fine Gael's temporary substitution of its party website and its use of Twitter. However, Fine Gael was also the largest opposition party to a government whose unpopularity was unprecedented, with a significant proportion of the electorate favouring anybody but Fianna Fáil.

Despite buying in the best advice on the subject, most candidates still failed to understand the 'social' part of social media. Many still considered this new form of communication as just another channel through which they should 'broadcast' their message to the electorate. The other misunderstanding that most candidates had was about the personal nature of social media. Given that it is an individual who subscribes, or follows, a particular social media account, it is most effective when the tone is that of an individual conversation, rather than an en masse 'my constituents' approach. The growth in the use of mobile devices to access social media services has increased this expectation of a personalised experience. Experiencing social media in this way suggests a personal relationship and, ironically, a level of privacy in the manner in which one communicates. It is not that social media participants expect the development of a unique relationship with each and every follower or subscriber, but that the attitude and tone of communication would be more closely related to a personal conversation rather than to a town hall meeting.

Creating, developing and maintaining social media communication in such a personal manner is time consuming. It also requires the ability to be comfortable with the conversational tone required. Most importantly, if it is to work well, it requires genuine engagement that can only work with two-way communication. In some respects, this is one of the hallmarks of Irish politics, i.e. that such a high number of voters have traditionally met and spoken to their preferred candidates. However, with some notable exceptions, the 2011 election campaign did not allow this traditional personal contact to transfer to social media conversations. Mirroring the perceived role of social media in the previous year's UK election, political commentator Kevin Rafter, echoing the views of many commentators, was unambiguous about the overstated expectation of social media: 'Social media got plenty of attention, but in terms of political communication the 2011 election was all about television, and, in particular, about the televised leaders' debates' (Farrell et al., 2011).

Again, one must ask if the interactivity provided by social media is needed in a society where relatively easy access to personal contact with existing and aspiring deputies already exists. Conversely, as social media grows in everyday use, perhaps it will provide the means by which the electorate can continue to enjoy personal contact with their preferred candidates, but by electronic means. As to the impact of social media use on a candidate's potential for success in the 2011 general election, correlations have been made that suggest successful candidates had a higher social media profile (McMahon, 2011; Curran and Singh, 2011). However, one has to question the cause and effect for such correlations. Was the use of social media a determining factor in their electoral success or did the better-placed/better-resourced candidates ensure that they had an effective social media strategy? It is difficult to prove the former, while the latter could be assumed of all forms of political communication.

Presidential election 2011

If the social media revolution was to have the anticipated impact on Irish politics, then the Irish presidential election of 2011 would offer an opportunity to see this in action. Effectively, the entire state represented a single constituency for each candidate. Presidential elections are also, by definition, more personality-focused than other Irish elections. Given these factors, social media should provide a means to connect directly with potential voters and to represent the personal voice of the candidate to electors and to the media. Little did anyone know at the outset that a single tweet would ultimately tilt the balance to determine the outcome. With seven candidates, the 2011 election was to provide the greatest ever range of choice in an Irish presidential election. The inclusion of four independent candidates also diluted the influence of party allegiances in determining the outcome. These factors should have increased the potential for social media to influence the ebb and flow of electoral support during the campaign – whatever the extent to which it might influence, or determine, the outcome.

In his analysis of the adoption of social media throughout the campaign, Ciarán McMahon of candidate.ie, pointed to the 'upward only' general trend of social media followers, in that social media users rarely 'unfollow' or unlike accounts. Although McMahon was to revise that contention slightly as the campaign unfolded, the observation is a valid one and must be borne in mind when attempting to make any link between social media support and electoral support – each voter has only one vote, but can like as many candidates as takes their fancy. Despite that health warning, the five-week analysis of the social media 'support' for each candidate reflects the cut and thrust of the campaign as the ultimate real contenders became apparent. By the final week of the campaign, social media figures reflected the opinion poll results of a two-horse race between Seán Gallagher and Michael D. Higgins. While there was certainly a correlation between social media support and electoral support, it is likely that the social media support was reflecting the wider electoral support, rather than the former determining the latter (see candidate.ie, blog entries at pages 1364, 1393, 1405, 1415, and 1430).

It was widely accepted throughout the campaign that Seán Gallagher was the candidate that was most effectively harnessing the potential of social media (Browne, 2011). As an independent candidate, the numbers of followers he garnered on Facebook and Twitter were impressive. Despite this, Gallagher was at one with each of the other candidates in using social media as a 'broadcast' medium, to 'push' their communications to voters. None of the presidential hopefuls adopted any aspect of social media in an interactive manner, either by inviting followers to influence the campaign or, indeed, in putting a question to their followers via social media. Whatever advantage the party-based candidates might have had in accessing other resources, very little attempt was made to harness the network of social media accounts of fellow party politicians. When one considers the number of friends and followers connected with each individual account, it is quite surprising that party strategists did not capitalise on this social media potential.

Despite the social media shortcomings of the 2011 presidential election campaign, it will be remembered for the impact of social media on the outcome, or rather, the impact of one tweet in the dying days of the campaign. As the candidates gathered in an RTÉ studio for a final campaign debate hosted by *The Frontline* current affairs programme, Seán Gallagher enjoyed a substantial lead in the polls that appeared to be growing as polling day approached. This lead was to be swept aside within 24 hours following the airing of a bogus tweet promising the appearance, at a press conference, of a witness to Gallagher's collection of funds for Fianna Fáil. This announcement seemed to wrong-foot Gallagher completely and his inability to provide a solid response was reflected in the negative reaction of the studio audience. The swing against him was reflected in final opinion polls published in the following days before a media-blackout took effect.

Conclusion

'Tweet-gate', as the Gallagher affair came to be known, represented something of a watershed in the relationship between media (old and new) and politics. Many have attributed Gallagher's fall at the final hurdle to the use or abuse of social media; others have blamed sloppy journalism in the failure of *The Frontline* team not to validate the source or content of the tweet. Others disregard the manner, or means, of the communication and point to the revelation of close ties between Gallagher and Fianna Fáil that had not previously been publicised. It is in this latter explanation that the truth about the potential of social media for Irish politics is to be found. In itself, social media will not radically change Irish political life. However, as a means to an end it does present important opportunities for new modes of genuinely two-way political communication. Regretfully, the most beneficial use of social media – that of real engagement with the electorate – is likely to be ignored in favour of its potential to damage opposing candidates' campaigns or to abuse politicians in relation to policy. The tragic suicide of Fine Gael TD, Shane MacEntee in December 2012 following persistent and anonymous abusive comments that were directed towards him on social media websites was a stark reminder of the potency of such technologies and the multitude of purposes to which they can be put.

References

Brandenburg, H. (2007) 'The media and the campaign' in Gallagher, M. and Marsh, M. (eds), *How Ireland voted 2007*, London: Palgrave.

Browne, M. (2011) 'Social media has been used to build up support, in addition to traditional campaigning. How have the candidates fared?' in *Irish Examiner* (25 October).

Byrne, S. (2011) 'Pravda in Mount Street'. See <http://www.mamanpoulet.com/pravda-in-mount-street/>

Curran, T. and Singh, R. (2011) 'E-democracy as the future face of democracy: a case study of the 2011 Irish elections' in *European View*, 10(1): 25–31.

Devlin, M. (2011) 'Eager to prove he's not just a pretty Facebook campaign' in *Irish Independent* (25 February).

Farrell, S., Meehan, C., Murphy, G. and Rafter, K. (2011) 'Assessing the Irish general election of 2011: a roundtable' in *New Hibernia Review*, 15(3): 36–53.

Fleishman-Hillard (2009) 'European Parliament digital survey'. See <http://www.epdigitaltrends.eu/s2009/home>

Greengard, S. (2009) 'The first internet president' in *Communications of the ACM*, 52(2): 16–18.

Healy, B. (2011) 'Defeat by Tweet' in McCarthy, D. (ed.), *Election 2011 and the 31st Dáil*, Dublin: RTÉ.

Huffington, A. (2008) *Web 2.0 Summit: The Web and Politics*, Los Angeles. See <http://www.youtube.com/watch?v=CBeePcCOBQM>

Johnson, S. (2009) 'How Twitter will change the way we live' in *Time* (5 June). See <http://individual.utoronto.ca/kreemy/proposal/04.pdf>

Marsh, M., Sinnott, R., Garry, J. and Kennedy, F. (2008) *The Irish voter: the nature of electoral competition in the Republic of Ireland*, Manchester: Manchester University Press.

McMahon, C. (2011) 'Social media usage by candidates in the 2011 ROI general election', paper presented at the Political Studies Association of Ireland Annual Conference, Dublin. See also <http://candidate.ie>

Miller, C. (2008) 'How Obama's internet campaign changed politics' in *The New York Times* (7 November).

Minihan, M. (2010) 'Boyle told to stop "irresponsible tweets"' in *Irish Times* (20 May).

O'Connor, P. (2009) 'The use of social media as a political communications tool: a case study of the 2009 Dublin constituency European Parliament elections', unpublished MA dissertation, DCU.

O'Leary, S. (2010a) 'Ivor Callely: how social media responded to the expenses scandal', Dublin: O'Leary Analytics. See <http://olearyanalytics.com/>

O'Leary, S. (2010b) 'The Brian Cowen interview: the global media response', Dublin: O'Leary Analytics. See <http://olearyanalytics.com/>

Schonfeld, E. (2009) 'Twitter reaches 44.5 million people worldwide in June'. See <http://techcrunch.com/2009/08/03/twitter-reaches-445-million-people-worldwide-in-june-comscore/>

Sudulich, M.L. and Wall, M. (2009) 'Keeping up with the Murphys? Candidate cyber-campaigning in the 2007 Irish general election' in *Parliamentary Affairs* 62(3): 456–75.

Sudulich, M.L. and Wall, M. (2011) 'How do candidates spend their money? Objects of campaign spending and the effectiveness of diversification' in *Electoral Studies* 30(1): 91–101.

Wall, M. and Sudulich, M.L. (2011) 'Internet explorers: the online campaign' in Gallagher, M. and Marsh, M. (eds), *How Ireland voted 2011*, London: Palgrave.

Seán Gallagher
FOR AN INDEPENDENT PRESIDENT

Let's put **our strengths** to work

www.seangallagher.com

Sinn Féin
PUTTING IRELAND FIRST - EU 2014

VÓTÁIL LYNN
1 BOYLAN

Above Seán Gallagher's Icarus-like performance during the 2011 presidential election highlighted the dangers of peaking too early in opinion polls and of media failure to verify allegations circulating in social networks such as Twitter.

Above right Elections to the European Parliament present a particular challenge as candidates have large populations and territories to canvas.

Right During the October 2013 referendum, supporters of the abolition of Ireland's upper house of parliament emphasised that only a small percentage of the electorate could vote for seats in the Seanad.

SEANAD ELECTORATE
DUBLIN 4: 3,491
DUBLIN 10: 126

Make your first Seanad vote **THE LAST** YES

Poster issued by Socialist Party campaign co-ordinator **PAUL MURPHY** MEP SOCIALIST PARTY

CHAPTER THIRTEEN

Mediating elections in Ireland: evidence from the 2011 general election

Eoin O'Malley, Roddy Flynn,
Iain McMenamin, Kevin Rafter

Information is a crucial ingredient in election campaigns. When voters form or change opinions they are widely thought to do so on the basis of information, attention to the information, predispositions, and the interaction of these factors (Zaller, 1992). And voters usually receive most political information, or at least receive it most intensely, during the course of an election campaign. So campaigns should lead to voters reinforcing or changing opinions, which in turn may lead to changes in the vote choice, and this should happen primarily through the media. However, such general arguments may have a limited application to Ireland; politicians may be able to influence voters' decisions unmediated by news outlets because of the small size of constituencies. A majority of Irish voters are likely to receive direct contact from parties (55% according to the Irish National Election Study (INES), 2011), most often in the form of door-to-door canvassing. Furthermore, decisions might be made before the campaign starts; in 2002 and 2007, 71% and 69% of respondents, respectively, reported that they had made their decision as to which party to give their first preference vote to before the campaign officially started (authors' analysis of INES 2002 and 2007).

It has been said of Irish general election campaigns that they constitute 40 or so local campaigns rather than one national campaign (Marsh, 2009, 183). Each constituency might hold a separate campaign where the outcome depends on the nature of the local campaign and the impact of local media – something that is surprisingly strong despite the small size of the country. Certainly local issues and grass-roots campaigning are clearly thought to be important by candidates; a fairly typical quote from a candidate in 2007 was 'I believe that my focus on micro-issues was paramount in my campaign['s success]' (Flanagan, 2008, 70). Furthermore the electoral system, the single transferable vote (STV), asks voters to rank-order candidates, within and across parties. It pits candidates from the same party against each other for support. Most TDs who lose their seats at elections do so to their party colleagues rather than competitors from other parties (the 2011 election was a rare exception, see Gallagher and Marsh, 2011). Marsh (2000, 489) argues that the electoral system essentially promotes candidate-centred campaigns but also provides incentives for alliances between candidates.

Indeed there may be good reasons why candidates might be particularly important in Ireland. The country was famously described as one where politics had no social bases (Whyte, 1974). This might give the impression that there are limited national campaigns, or at least that they have limited impact. In fact if we look at trends in party support, they tend to fluctuate quite evenly across the country; when a party increases its support it does so across the country and when a party suffers, this too is national. So while a good candidate or good local campaign can attenuate a national downward trend or accentuate an upward trend, good candidates rarely buck a national trend.

So we see that party is important in the voting decision of the Irish electorate. Indeed there is strong evidence that the socio-psychological or Michigan model, wherein people held a strong attachment to certain political parties, was important (Carty, 1983). The extent to which long-term party loyalties still influence vote choice is debatable, and Ireland certainly appears to have undergone a period of partisan de-alignment (Marsh, 2006). This de-alignment should mean that voters' preferences are now 'softer' and more likely to be influenced by the short campaign of an election. Certainly Ireland experienced a highly volatile election in February 2011, historically among the most volatile in western Europe (Mair, 2011).

Though many have contact with candidates at election time, Irish voters still rely heavily on newspapers, radio and television for information on election campaigns. Over 80% of people watch television news at least five days a week (INES, 2011). It may be that people are also making their voting decision later on in the campaign as has happened in the USA (Nir and Druckman, 2008), though just 30% of respondents claim to have seriously thought about voting for another party in 2011 (INES, 2011). We might be seeing a more influential media in Ireland in the twentieth-first century, but the traditional media are also being challenged by new social media, which allow parties and advocacy groups to deliver messages to and, with web 2.0, interact with voters, unmediated by the traditional news outlets.

So, the issue of media influence on Irish elections is very much an open question. This chapter sets out the main arguments about election campaigns and media coverage in the literature, looking at how the media might have an impact. It then looks at specific literature on Irish campaigns. Finally, it summarises the most up-to-date empirical research on this topic.

Research on elections and media effects

Although many assume that campaigns and the media coverage of election campaigns are important, there is very little evidence to suggest that either is. Early empirical research found little evidence for such theories (Berelson et al., 1954). It was assumed that because social factors such as class, religion or ethnicity influenced the vote, campaigns at most would activate political predispositions (Lazarsfeld et al., 1968). This view has since been modified such that campaigns help 'enlighten' voters, who essentially go to the party one might expect given their economic and other circumstances (Gelman and King, 1993).

There is still little systematic evidence to suggest direct media effects in campaigns (though see Zaller, 1996). Explanations for the absence of media effects tend to centre on the avoidance of cognitive dissonance – the psychological discomfort of holding two contradictory cognitions (opinions, beliefs, values). In order to avoid this feeling people are selective in the news to which they expose themselves, perceive, and retain (Frey, 1986). So if we think of the UK, *Guardian* readers tend to be left-wing. *Guardian* readers also tend to vote for the Labour party. So are you a Labour Party supporter because you read the *Guardian*? Left-wing people probably choose to read the *Guardian* because they are left-wing, not left-wing because they read the *Guardian*. This is what social scientists call endogeneity – whereby one's choice of newspaper and ideology are linked, or not independent (endogenous). Media bias, then, should not be important as voters actively seek out or avoid the bias to suit their needs.

That is not to say that media are thought to have no impact. It has famously been argued that the press 'may not be successful at telling people what to think, but it is stunningly successful in telling its readers what to think about' (Cohen, 1963, 13). This is encapsulated in the notion that media play an agenda-setting role, and can determine what issues the public regard as important (Funkhouser, 1973; Dearing and Rogers, 1996). Another level of agenda setting is priming, wherein voters are 'primed' by the media-set agenda to evaluate parties or candidates on certain criteria. So if the campaign focuses primarily on the economy, we expect that the party that is seen as strong on the economy will be evaluated more highly by voters than if they were primed to evaluate parties on the basis of honesty or integrity.

Of course, it is not clear that news coverage is determined by media alone. Events such as an economic crisis or war can hardly be avoided by the media. Even in more normal times the media follow a news agenda set by parties, though the media may also attempt to raise important issues the parties may prefer were left unaired. Election news can be described as a 'joint product of an interactive process involving political communicators and media professionals' (Semetko et al., 1991, 3).

But even if the media are not free to set the agenda, they can choose how they cover stories. Framing relates to how an event or phenomenon is portrayed and the resulting perception of the event or phenomenon by people. The work of Kahneman and Tversky (1984) suggests that small changes in question wording can yield very different – yet predictable – results in terms of how individuals understand an event. This is because the different wording can re-orientate an issue for people. So if an Orange March in Northern Ireland is introduced in a frame emphasising cultural rights and multiculturalism, support for allowing the march might be far higher than if it were framed as a community relations issue.

In media research, frames are thought to 'select, organise, and emphasise certain aspects of reality, to the exclusion of others' (de Vreese et al., 2003, 108). In political coverage we can think of elections being framed in terms of 'themes' – highlighting larger issues and trends – or 'episodes', where media focus on individuals and their stories (Iyengar, 1991). In electoral research we can distinguish between media coverage where media choose to frame the election as a contest ('horserace' framing) or where the media choose to focus on the issues and policies (Strömbäck and van Aelst, 2010). Cappella and Jamieson (1997) specify game-framed coverage – coverage that frames political debate as a game played between politicians and not one in which important policy issues are debated – as problematic. They argue that media focus on the 'game' of politics to the detriment of policy issues is at the root of voter cynicism and disengagement, a position supported by other observers (Fallows, 1997; Downie Jr. and Kaiser, 2002; Patterson, 1994). So it is not just information effects, but the more subtle effects of how that information is put to people that matters.

If we are confident that information has an impact on attitudes, it can only do so when people have an awareness of and engagement with the information (Zaller, 1992). If people do not see or cannot understand the message it will not have an impact. How much information one has stored or is willing to gather is related to the strength of people's opinions (Krosnick and Petty, 1995). An important finding in social psychology is that those with strong views tend to be open just to those views with which they agree (Taber and Lodge, 2006). Others have found that, in certain circumstances, those with strong views will harden them when confronted with counterarguments (Spears et al., 1990). But we also observe research in which information has a greater effect on people with more knowledge (Krosnick and Brannon, 1993). It may be that political sophisticates have more elaborate storage structures with which to remember new information, which can then have larger effects over time. Or greater knowledge can be activated by new information, which cannot happen among those less familiar with an issue (Berent and Krosnick, 1995).

Research on campaigning and media in Ireland

So what do we know about election campaigns in Ireland? Research on campaigning in Ireland is limited, mainly because of the small number of academics working on Irish electoral politics. Even less work is available on media coverage of campaigns. However, since 2002 there has been an Irish National Election Study that provides systematic data with which to study campaigns and campaign effects. These data are cross-sectional, with a very limited panel element (panel studies follow the same people over time and make it easier to make causal connections between events). They also take place after the election, making campaign effects even more difficult to observe. What they can tell us, however, is how voters claim to have received campaign messages. There is virtually no systematic research on the individual campaigns themselves. While the *How Ireland Voted* series of books published after each election since 1987 describes each party's campaign strategy, they can only speculate on the impact of the campaigns on voter behaviour (see for instance, Farrell, 1993). Since 2002 there has been some systematic analysis of media coverage of the campaigns (Brandenburg, 2005) but there has been no real attempt to link the media coverage with voters' decisions.

There has been much academic debate in Ireland as to whether the electorate vote for candidates or parties. This is a particularly tricky question as parties obviously choose candidates to maximise the party's vote, but candidates also choose to join certain parties and not others. This may be done on the basis of which party is most likely to get one elected. We also see that Ireland is relatively unusual in the number of non-party candidates who stand and get elected (Weeks, 2009). Asking voters to reveal what factors influenced their vote reveals that personal attributes of the candidate or their geographic location is the primary motivation (69% of voters). Party or policy reasons are cited by just 28% of voters as the main reasons for their first preference vote (Marsh, 2007, 509). However these results might be due to respondents being asked to think about the specific candidate. If we look at actual voter behaviour, 45% of voters in 2002 voted a 'straight-ticket', i.e. for one party only. We can see that in different circumstances, different criteria become important, so in the 'crisis' election in 2011, personality became less important. The proposed Taoiseach and the set of ministers were important criteria for 35% of voters in choosing how to vote in 2007. This dropped to 20% in 2011. Meanwhile the criterion of 'policies set out by the parties' increased from 25% to 43% over the two elections (Marsh and Cunningham, 2011, 185).

The debate over whether voters choose candidates or parties matters because it affects how we think about campaigning, and about media coverage of these campaigns. It makes some sense that the local campaign will be important; Irish constituencies are small as defined by population numbers. Candidates elected in 2011 received on average just 8,332 first preference votes. Most of the more systematic analyses on campaigning have focused on the extent and impact of grass-roots or local campaigns (Marsh, 2004; Marsh et al., 2008). Marsh (2004, 249) reports that in the 2002 campaign over 75% of the electorate had some personal contact with at least one party while 55% had personal contact with at least one candidate. In addition, 83% of voters had looked at campaign posters and almost 70% read election leaflets. These figures were remarkably stable in 2011. Using multivariate analyses, Marsh found a clear association between local campaign contact and voting choice. Of course the relationship could be an artefact of the party strategy – some parties only canvass some areas. Other data tell a similar story. A candidate survey confirms that candidates see themselves as essentially local figures, and their campaigns reflect that, as they emphasise their own merits rather than the party label (Marsh and Cunningham, 2011). This also shows that candidates spend very little time on national campaign events.

As important as local campaigning is, it is built on a party's national campaign. One of the highlights of a local campaign is when a party leader visits the constituency, thus ensuring significant local coverage for the candidate. It is much more difficult to estimate the impact of national campaigns, because there are far fewer cases to deal with. But parties' head offices put significant resources into 'modern and post-modern campaigning: developing manifestos, daily press briefings and policy launches, leaders' tours of the country, party websites and online social networking' (Farrell, 2004).

Research on what is sometimes referred to as 'post-modern' campaigning or cyber-campaigning tends to focus on candidate data, because that is what is most easily available. Cyber campaigning might not be expected to matter much given that we cannot be certain that websites and social media activity are seen by the relevant audience, the constituency voters. Sudulich and Wall (2011) found that having a personal website impacted positively on a candidate's vote share, an effect maintained even when including controls for campaign expenses and front-runner status. Unsurprisingly they found that the impact was much stronger in those constituencies with above median internet penetration. More recent research shows that access to internet news in 2011 was causally linked with political uncertainty; that is, those who searched for news on the internet became less certain of whom to vote for (Sudulich et al., 2013).

Again because of the availability of data, some interesting work tests the link between campaign spending and candidate vote share. Spending limits are imposed on candidates and these vary according to the size of the constituency, but the maximum allowed during the 'short campaign' in 2011 – the three to five weeks between the dissolution of parliament and the election – was €45,200 per candidate. Parties can be allocated a part of this allowance to spend on the national campaign. Reported campaign spending from 2011 shows spending on candidates locally was greater than spending on the national campaign by a ratio of 3.7:1 (Sipo, 2011). The total amount spent in 2011 was €9.3m (about €4.20 per vote). Within this restricted campaign environment Benoit and Marsh (2010) show that the effect of extra spending matters in a variety of contexts: between all candidates, between candidates from the same party, and between incumbents and challengers. As we might expect, they found the effect of marginal spend was much greater among challengers than incumbents. Sudulich and Wall (2011) look at disaggregated spending returns for the 2007 election to show that posters (average €5,726 per candidate) and advertising (€3,341) are the areas of highest candidate expenditure. Their analysis shows a weak positive relationship between spending and electoral performance. In 2011 the national parties' spending was dominated by advertising, posters and publicity. Very little was spent on campaign workers, who tend to work on a voluntary basis.

Ireland's small size means that opinion polling is comparatively expensive and less common than in the UK. For instance there were just nine national opinion polls conducted during the short election campaign for the Irish general election in 2011. The small size of the polling companies and absence of any internet polling means that fieldwork takes place over days rather than hours. This makes it difficult to observe if certain media events, such as a leaders' debate or a campaign gaffe, had an impact. O'Malley (2012) used the timing of the fieldwork of three opinion polls conducted towards the end of the 2011 presidential election to make the link between the final TV debate and the spectacular fall in support for one of the candidates. He also noted the absence of a relationship between spending in the presidential election and electoral performance. Presidential elections in Ireland take place primarily on the airwaves and not on the ground, and rules on broadcast coverage mean that each candidate must receive broadly equal treatment in terms of time. There was no great need to spend more, and indeed the second-placed candidate in 2011 opted not to spend money on posters.

Media coverage of elections in Ireland

There has been a steady increase in the volume of electoral coverage in Irish media over time (Farrell, 1978; Bowman, 1987) and this is a trend that appears to be continuing. Due to reasonably restrictive rules, broadcast political advertising plays a marginal role in national campaigns: while party political broadcasts are a longstanding feature of elections and are watched by sizable audiences it is not possible to say that on their own they significantly influence voter choice (Rafter, 2011). Elections are thus fought out in the print media, for which parties do not have to pay. Incumbent parties can expect to get a reasonable amount of the coverage. The extent of media bias in Ireland has been investigated by Brandenburg (2005) and Brandenburg and Zalinski (2008). They found that there was significant coverage of the elections and campaigns, though this fell away among tabloids. There appeared to be a significant bias in the attention given to the smaller governing party (the Progressive Democrats). These data did not include the tone of the coverage or link it to voter exposure and decisions.

The media context for the coverage of elections has changed significantly in recent times. The broadcasting market was deregulated during the 1980s and is now a highly competitive mix of public service and commercial operators. However, in both radio and television markets there are regulatory rules governing coverage of elections specifically in terms of balance and fairness. There is no equivalent statutory regime governing election coverage in the Irish newspaper market. The print sector is relatively small and unsubsidised, and Irish newspapers must also compete with localised editions of several leading British newspapers. Commercial pressure in 2011 was probably greater than any other stage in print history. As with newspapers elsewhere, Irish newspapers have lost circulation, falling by 22% between 2007 and 2011. The economic crisis put much greater pressure on newspaper advertising revenues, which fell by 56% in the same period (ABC). In this context it is expected that media outlets are more likely to engage in commercially driven coverage of elections. That is, rather than focus on substantive policy issues they might cover elections as 'horse races' between parties and beauty contests between rival candidates.

If 'horse race' coverage is a problem, it might also be one that is getting steadily worse. One of the main arguments for why the media have moved towards covering politics as a game is due to commercial pressures (Patterson, 2000). Competition between the print and broadcast media might have caused a shift of focus onto campaign events and stories at the expense of substantive policy issues. Writing about the situation in the USA, Iyengar and McGrady (2007, 62) argue that 'no matter what the medium, the public affairs content of the news has been diluted.'

More recent changes, including the advent of free sheets and free access to internet news sources, have resulted in newspapers competing for fewer paying readers. The ever-shortening news cycle might also increase the pressure on news outlets to produce copy, reducing the time available to journalists for making considered judgements on policy issues. It is also easier to cover elections in this way, as there has been an increase in the number of opinion polls, and leadership debates are an increasingly important aspect of election coverage. Recent elections have normally seen a single televised debate between the leaders of the two main parties but in February 2011 the number of debates increased to five, and in one of these five party leaders participated. Furthermore a focus on game coverage may well be a normatively defensible strategy for media outlets and for journalists, as it means they can easily avoid accusations of partisan or ideological bias.

As media can only have an effect if people are exposed to it, it is imperative to examine what people read and what parties they are likely to support. The INES asked respondents what media they use for news gathering or other uses. If most used television for their news gathering, almost 60% of respondents claimed to read newspapers at least five days a week and over 80% claimed to use newspapers regularly for political information. Table 1 shows some differences in party support among the readers of different newspapers, but it is notable, if unsurprising, that we do not see the large differences in support among newspaper readers that we see in other countries where the media and parties are more ideologically distinct. Fine Gael support is higher among broadsheet readers than readers of tabloids, whereas Labour Party support is quite stable across all formats. Sinn Féin is the other party with differentiated support in terms of newspaper readership, with much higher levels of support among tabloid readers. Fianna Fáil voters appear to be most distinctive in how they are less likely to read the *Irish Times* and *Sunday Times*, both of which might be thought to have less nationalist outlooks.

Table 1: Party support among readers of various newspapers, 2011

Percentage vote (actual) and acc. INES		(36.1) 42.8	(19.5) 18.5	(17.5) 14.2	(9.9) 10.4	(12.3) 9.9
Party/newspaper	Readership as % of pop.	Fine Gael	Labour	Fianna Fáil	Sinn Féin	Inds.
Irish Times	18.8	52.5	20.0	10.4	4.5	8.8
Irish Independent	34.2	49.7	16.4	17.7	4.3	9.6
Irish Examiner	10.2	47.7	15.8	15.7	5.9	11.4
Daily Star	11.9	31.0	20.5	12.8	16.0	14.8
Irish Sun	7.1	29.5	20.8	16.1	18.5	8.6
Sunday Independent	14.4	50.5	14.9	20.0	3.8	7.0
Sunday Times	8.0	56.5	18.9	10.7	5.7	5.9
Sunday Bus. Post	3.5	36.3	22.3	22.6	5.0	10.4
Sunday World	10.3	37.2	16.7	14.7	17.7	6.9
Read no newspaper	17.2	38.4	12.8	17.2	16.0	9.8

Source: authors' own analysis of INES data asking respondents which newspapers they regularly use for political information. Compare the figure of party support among the readership of each paper with the party's support on the top row. Percentage vote between the actual result and the INES data differ due to sampling error, response bias, and recall errors.

The 2011 general election was unusual in that it was one where the incumbent was expected to do particularly badly due to the economic crisis. This compares with the 2002 and 2007 elections that took place in the so-called Celtic Tiger era. The economy had undergone a severe contraction from 2008, leading to a number of emergency budgets aimed at reducing the yawning budget deficit. These measures ultimately failed. With a deteriorating fiscal position, combined with the impact of a severe banking crisis, Ireland found it difficult to access funds on international money markets and was forced to enter a funding programme with the European Union, International Monetary Fund, and European Central Bank in late 2010. The government essentially collapsed, remaining in office only to oversee a budget that was passed in early 2011.

Voters clearly identified the economy as important in 2011. When asked to identify the single most important issue or problem, 35.6% mentioned the economic crisis and a further 13.5% mentioned related economic issues, such as unemployment (Lansdowne/RTÉ exit poll, 2011). The 'troika' funding programme arguably restricted the policy options open to any newly formed government; however, there was no evidence of a narrowing of the policy space in 2011 (Suiter and Farrell, 2011) and even between the parties that accepted the inevitability of the lending programme terms there were sharp disagreements about its implementation. As such we might expect 2011 to be different to the preceding elections.

Using content analysis we can track the coverage of these three Irish elections. The content of a random sample of (1,440) newspaper articles from 12 newspapers over the course of the short campaign (2 February to 26 February) was analysed. A similar content analysis of broadcast data from the election campaign was also completed – the first time broadcast and print media were systematically compared. These tell us quite a bit, not just about election coverage by Irish media, but also about the nature of the media in Ireland.

How did these newspapers cover the elections? A common way of distinguishing framing of elections is between substantive policy issues and the election as a horserace or the campaigns themselves. The data can be used to test whether, and why, the 2011 election was framed as a game between competing teams or as a debate of issues and policies and a choice between political parties/ideologies. Though analysis of media coverage of elections before 2002 is limited, there exists some data for the *Irish Times* (Farrell, 1990; 1993) that indicates that 2011 reversed a long-term trend of policy coverage in that newspaper. The decline was significant between 1973 and 1992, and the research shows that the 2002 and 2007 elections continued this decline both for the *Irish Times* and other newspapers. However, in 2011 the election was dominated by coverage of policy discussions. The economy was a major feature of coverage, whereas it received just about 5% of coverage four years earlier. We see in Table 2 that there was a significant reduction in the coverage given to campaigning that could be considered game-framing.

Table 2: Election coverage in 2002, 2007, and 2011, % of total coverage (point change since earlier election)

	2002	2007		2011 (all)		2011
Political System	2.7	0.9	(−1.8)	11.9	(+11)	11.3
Justice	4.0	1.8	(−2.2)	1.3	(−0.5)	1.3
Economy	8.5	5.3	(−3.2)	**19.8**	**(+14.5)**	21.2
Social Welfare	**9.6**	5.6	(−4.0)	5.0	(−0.6)	5.7
Other Policy	7.7	6.7	(−1.0)	7.6	(+0.9)	8.2
Country-specific: Ireland	0.3	1.0	(+0.7)	1.2	(+0.2)	1.1
Campaigning	**37.0**	40.4	(+3.4)	**18.9**	**(−21.5)**	19.1
Polls/Horserace	**16.0**	10.0	(−6.0)	21.6	**(+11.6)**	20.4
Leadership	2.2	5.3	(+3.1)	5.9	(+0.6)	4.3
Political Ethics	4.0	8.4	(+4.4)	2.6	(−5.8)	2.9
Non-political	0.6	0.2	(−0.4)	0.7	(+0.5)	0.5
Election	7.5	**14.4**	**(+6.9)**	3.0	(−11.4)	3.7
Number of articles	1,217	2,095		1,440		976
Number of newspapers (N)	4	5		12		5

Note: The most common types of coverage (biggest changes) are in bold. The final column includes only those newspapers that are directly comparable with the earlier elections. Data for earlier elections are supplied by Heinz Brandenburg, University of Aberdeen.

Table 3 shows the extent to which each newspaper covered the election, and whether this coverage was game or policy-framed. We can see that the difference between the most election-focused paper (*Sunday Business Post*) and the least focused (*News of the World*) is very pronounced. While the *Sunday Business Post* devoted over a third of its articles to the election, just 3% of the *News of the World* articles were electoral in topic. Indeed some of tabloids appear to have quite high levels of policy-framing (see *Irish Sun*), but when this is weighted by election coverage it gives a better sense of what the newspaper's focus was. In the far-right column we can see an intuitively appealing measure of newspaper focus on politics and policy.

Table 3: Irish Newspapers' framing of the 2011 general election weighted by election coverage as proportion of articles in the newspaper

Newspaper	Issue (%)	Game (%)	Election articles as proportion of all articles	Framing weighted by election coverage
Sunday Business Post	0.53	0.44	0.35	0.19
Irish Times	0.54	0.38	0.25	0.15
Irish Mail on Sunday	0.31	0.38	0.25	0.12
Sunday Independent	0.4	0.58	0.27	0.11
Sunday Times	0.53	0.37	0.13	0.08
Irish Examiner	0.49	0.37	0.14	0.08
Irish Daily Mail	0.46	0.48	0.16	0.08
Irish Independent	0.41	0.51	0.17	0.08
Irish Daily Star	0.44	0.49	0.09	0.04
Irish Sun	0.56	0.35	0.04	0.02
Sunday World	0.17	0.83	0.12	0.02
Irish News of the World	0.11	0.56	0.03	0.01

Note: These data include short pieces, editorials, and opinion pieces, as well as articles outside the main newspaper. The last column is the product of rescaled versions of the issue minus game and election articles. Both were scaled to a minimum of 0 and a maximum of 1.

The study of broadcast material also looked at this meta-framing question. The results from the content analysis study show that there were significant differences in election broadcast news coverage in 2011 based on the ownership type of the respective media organisation. In summary, the findings show that there was more policy coverage on public television than on private television; that there was more policy on morning public radio than morning private radio; but interestingly, that there was more policy on evening private radio than evening public radio. As indicated in Table 4, on morning radio the public broadcast programme stressed leadership while its commercial service rival focused on the mechanics of the election. Interestingly, the evening programme on commercial radio displayed a keener interest in policy stories – the economy and justice – against its public alternative which spent more time on campaigning and the mechanics of the election. Overall, the broadcast content analysis from the 2011 general election showed differing editorial approaches were adopted across public and private outlets in the Irish market. Parties, candidates and the voters were presented with a diversity of choice on radio and television although the analysis made no comment on the tone of this content.

Table 4: Public versus private media

Content Analysis Code	Television News: Public v Private	Evening Radio News: Public v Private	Morning Radio News: Public v Private
Political System	−3.73	−0.98	−3.82
Justice	−0.19	−5.69	−0.42
Defence	0.05	0	−0.11
Economy	10.43	−8.72	4.33
Agriculture	0.1	0.03	0.14
Social Welfare	−0.32	1.44	0.52
Education	−0.07	0.49	1.83
Arts/Culture	0.37	−3.85	0.75
Infrastructure/Technology	−0.94	2.07	−1.04
Environment	0.72	−1.79	0.07
Foreign Affairs	1.34	−0.23	2.33
Country-specific: Ireland	−0.15	0.44	−1.3
Campaigning	−13.07	8.32	−3.55
Polls/Horserace	0.13	0.96	−1.39
Leadership	2.77	0.84	5.28
Political Ethics	0.52	−0.43	0.93
Non-political	0	0	0
Election	0.52	6.56	−5.65
Locality-specific issue	1.5	0.55	1.11

Note: These data includes all election news items on *Morning Ireland* and *Drivetime* (RTÉ Radio One), *Breakfast* (Newstalk), *The Last Word* (Today FM), *Six-One News* (RTÉ One television), and *News at 5.30* (TV3). The columns subtract the privately owned outlet's percentage per code from the public station's percentage per code. The positive figures means there was more RTÉ coverage of an area and negative figures mean there was more private sector (either Newstalk, TV3 or Today FM) coverage.

Conclusion

Kaid and Strömbäck (2008) identified a number of factors they consider important in explaining variation in election coverage around the world. These are the political system, the media system, journalistic norms, the style of the campaign, and the nature of voters and media consumers. Many of these factors have changed in Ireland, not least the voters' attachments to parties and the media environment in which elections take place. This chapter has demonstrated that media coverage of Irish elections is not invariable, either across time, medium or outlet. While we still have much to learn about what determines the choices journalists, editors, and proprietors make in election coverage, we have come some way in describing those choices.

We might think that because voters have less partisan attachments, the media and the nature of its electoral coverage should be increasingly important in influencing vote choice. However, new forms of media may decrease the influence of traditional media, as it is now easier to reach potential voters and supporters directly. This is certainly the major change that will take place in election campaigns in the next decades. While we still have yet to see the first true 'internet election' in Ireland, it is surely going to have an increasingly important impact.

References

ABC. Figures calculated from Audit Bureau of Circulation (November 2008); advertising figures are IAPI Adspend/Nielsen Media Research (November 2008).

Benoit, K. and Marsh M. (2010) 'Incumbent and challenger campaign spending effects in proportional electoral systems: the Irish elections of 2002' in *Political Research Quarterly*, 63(1): 159–73.

Berelson, B., Lazarsfeld, P. and McPhee, W. (1954) *Voting: a study of opinion formation in a presidential campaign*, Chicago: University of Chicago Press.

Berent, M. and Krosnick, J. (1995) 'The relation between political attitude importance and knowledge structure' in Lodge, M. and McGraw, K. (eds), *Political judgement: structure and process*, Ann Arbor: University of Michigan Press.

Bowman, J. (1987) 'Media coverage of the Irish elections of 1981–82' in Penniman, H.R. and Farrell, B. (eds), *Ireland at the polls, 1981, 1982 and 1987: a study of four general elections*, Washington, DC: American Enterprise Institute.

Brandenburg, H. (2005) 'Political bias in the Irish media: a quantitative study of the campaign coverage during the 2002 general election' in *Irish Political Studies*, 20(3): 297–322.

Brandenburg, H. and Zalinski, Z. (2008) 'The media and the campaign' in Gallagher, M. and Marsh, M. (eds), *How Ireland voted 2007*, Basingstoke: Palgrave.

Cappella, J. and Hall Jamieson, K. (1997) *Spiral of cynicism: the press and the public good*, New York: Oxford University Press.

Carty, R.K. (1983) *Electoral politics in Ireland: party and parish pump*, Dingle: Brandon.

Cohen, B. (1963) *The press and foreign policy*, Princeton, NJ: Princeton University Press.

de Vreese, C.H., Peter, J. and Semetko, H.A. (2003) 'Framing politics at the launch of the Euro: a cross-national comparative study of frames in the news' in *Political Communication*, 18: 107–22.

Dearing, J.W. and Rogers, E.M. (1996) *Agenda setting*, Thousand Oaks, CA: Sage.

Downie Jr., L. and Kaiser, R.G. (2002) *The news about the news*, New York: Alfred A. Knopf.

Fallows, J. (1997) *Breaking the news: how the media undermine American democracy*, New York: Vintage.

Farrell, B. (1978) 'The mass media and the 1977 campaign' in Penniman, H.R. (ed.), *Ireland at the polls: the Dáil elections of 1977*, Washington, DC: American Enterprise Institute.

Farrell, D. (1990) 'Campaign strategies and media coverage' in Gallagher, M. and Marsh, M. (eds), *How Ireland voted 1989*, Galway: PSAI Press.

Farrell, D. (1993) 'Campaign strategies' in Gallagher, M. and Laver, M. (eds), *How Ireland voted 1992*, Limerick and Dublin: PSAI Press and Folens.

Farrell, D. (2004) 'Before campaigns were "modern": Irish electioneering in times past' in Garvin, T., Manning, M. and Sinnott, R. (eds), *Dissecting Irish politics: essays in honour of Brian Farrell*, Dublin: UCD Press.

Flanagan, T. (2008) 'The view from the campaign trail' in Gallagher, M. and Marsh, M. (eds), *How Ireland voted 2007*, Basingstoke: Palgrave.

Frey, D. (1986) 'Recent research on selective exposure to information' in *Advances in Experimental Social Psychology*, 19: 41–80.

Funkhouser, R.G. (1973) 'The issues of the sixties: an exploratory study in the dynamics of public opinion' in *Public Opinion Quarterly*, 37(1): 62–75.

Gallagher, M. and Marsh, M. (eds) (2011) *How Ireland voted 2011: the full story of Ireland's earthquake election*, Basingstoke: Palgrave.

Gelman, A. and King, G. (1993) 'Why are American presidential election campaign polls so variable when votes are so predictable?' in *British Journal of Political Science*, 23(4): 409–51.

Irish National Election Study (2002). See <http://www.tcd.ie/ines>
Irish National Election Study (2007). See <http://www.tcd.ie/ines>
Irish National Election Study (2011). See <http://www.tcd.ie/ines>
Iyengar, S. (1991) *Is anyone responsible? How television frames political issues*, Chicago: University Press.
Iyengar, S. and McGrady, J. (2007) *Media politics: a citizen's guide*, New York: W.W. Norton & Co.
Kahneman, D. and Tversky, A. (1984) 'Choices, values, and frames' in *American Psychologist*, 39: 341–50.
Kaid, L.L. and Strömbäck, J. (2008) 'Election news coverage around the world: a comparative perspective' in Kaid, L.L. and Strömbäck, J. (eds), *The handbook of election news coverage around the world*, New York: Routledge.
Krosnick, J.A. and Brannon, L.A. (1993) 'The impact of the Gulf War on the ingredients of presidential evaluations: multidimensional effects of political involvement' in *American Political Science Review*, 87(4): 963–75.
Krosnick, J.A. and Petty, R.E. (1995) 'Attitude strength: an overview' in Petty, R.E. and Krosnick, J.A. (eds), *Attitude strength: antecedents and consequences*, Hillsdale, NJ: Lawrence Erlbaum.
Lansdown/RTÉ exit poll (2011). See <http://www.rte.ie/news/election2011/election2011-exit-poll.pdf>
Lazarsfeld, P., Berelson, B. and Gaudet, H. (1968) *The people's choice: how the voter makes up his mind in a presidential campaign*, New York: Columbia University Press.
Mair, P. (2011) 'The election in context' in Gallagher, M. and Marsh, M. (eds), *How Ireland voted 2011: the full story of Ireland's earthquake election*, Basingstoke: Palgrave.
Marsh, M. (2000) 'Candidate centred but party wrapped: campaigning in Ireland under STV' in Bowler, S. and Grofman, B. (eds), *Elections in Australia, Ireland and Malta under the single transferable vote*, Ann Arbor: Michigan University Press.
Marsh, M. (2004) 'None of that post-modern stuff around here: grassroots campaigning in the 2002 Irish general election' in *British Elections & Parties Review*, 14: 245–67.
Marsh, M. (2006) 'Party identification in Ireland: an insecure anchor for a floating party system' in *Electoral Studies*, 25(3): 489–508.
Marsh, M. (2007) 'Candidates or parties? Objects of electoral choice in Ireland' in *Party Politics*, 13: 500–527.
Marsh, M. (2009) 'Voting behaviour' in Coakley, J. and Gallagher, M. (eds), *Politics in the Republic of Ireland*, Abingdon: Routledge.
Marsh, M. and Cunningham, K. (2011) 'A positive choice, or anyone but Fianna

Fáil?' in Gallagher, M. and Marsh, M. (eds), *How Ireland voted 2011: the full story of Ireland's earthquake election*, Basingstoke: Palgrave.

Marsh, M., Sinnott, R., Garry, J. and Kennedy, F. (2008) *The Irish voter: the nature of electoral competition in the Republic of Ireland*, Manchester: Manchester University Press.

Nir, L. and Druckman, J.N. (2008) 'Campaign mixed-message flows and timing of vote decision' in *International Journal of Public Opinion Research*, 20(3): 326–46.

O'Malley, E. (2012) 'The 2011 Irish presidential election: culture, valence, loyalty or punishment?' in *Irish Political Studies*, 27(4): 635–55.

Patterson, T.E. (1994) *Out of order*, New York: Vintage.

Patterson, T.E. (2000) 'The United States: news in a free-market society' in Gunther, R. and Mughan, A. (eds), *Democracy and the media: a comparative perspective*, New York: Cambridge University Press.

Rafter, K. (2011) 'Hear no evil – see no evil: political advertising in Ireland' in *Journal of Public Affairs*, 11(2): 93–99.

Semetko, H.A., Blumler, J., Gurevitch, M. and Weaver, D.H. (1991) *The formation of campaign agendas: a comparative analysis of party and media roles in recent American and British elections*, Hillsdale, NJ: Lawrence Erlbaum.

Sipo (2011) *Report to ceann comhairle re Dáil general election of 25 February 2011*, Dublin: Sipo. See <http://www.sipo.gov.ie>

Spears, R., Lea, M. and Lee, S. (1990) 'De-individuation and group polarization in computer-mediated communication' in *British Journal of Social Psychology*, 29(2): 121–34.

Strömbäck, J. and van Aelst, P. (2010) 'Exploring some antecedents of the media's framing of election news: a comparison of Swedish and Belgian election news' in *International Journal of Press Politics*, 14(1): 41–59.

Sudulich, M.L. and Wall, M. (2011) 'How do candidates spend their money? Objects of campaign spending and the effectiveness of diversification' in *Electoral Studies*, 30: 91–101.

Sudulich, M.L., Wall, M. and Baccini, L. (2013) 'Wired voters: the effects of internet use on voters' electoral uncertainty', Social Sciences Research Network. See <http://www.ssrn.com>

Suiter, J. and Farrell, D. (2011) 'The parties' manifestos' in Gallagher, M. and Marsh, M. (eds), *How Ireland voted 2011*, Basingstoke: Palgrave.

Taber, C.S. and Lodge, M. (2006) 'Motivated skepticism in the evaluation of political beliefs' in *American Journal of Political Science*, 50(3): 755–69.

Weeks, L. (2009) 'We don't like (to) party: a typology of independents in Irish political life, 1922–2007' in *Irish Political Studies*, 24(1): 1–28.

Whyte, J. (1974) 'Ireland: politics without social bases' in Rose, R. (ed.), *Electoral behavior: a comparative handbook*, New York: The Free Press.

Zaller, J.R. (1992) *The nature and origins of mass opinion*, New York: Cambridge University Press.

Zaller, J.R. (1996) 'The myth of massive media impact revived: new support for a discredited idea' in Mutz, D.C., Sniderman, P.M. and Brody, R.A. (eds), *Political persuasion and attitude change*, Ann Arbor: University of Michigan Press.

Conclusion

In the introduction to this book we set ourselves the task of exploring critically the relationship dynamics that are at the heart of political communication. As we have seen, since the foundation of the state these dynamics have been in perpetual flux and have waxed and waned as political parties have come and gone and as new communication technologies have added to the multiplicity of means by which political communication, in its many different forms and with its many different agenda, can occur. Political communication can, in many ways, be described as an ever-ongoing contest for support that is played out in the media. While what we refer to as 'the media' has changed hugely over the past decade or so, it is clear that, whatever their effect in levelling the playing field, the new technologies have certainly added additional platforms to the age-old competition for support of a party, candidate or idea.

One theme that emerges clearly from the chapters is that whether one defines political communication as persuasion, public discourse, an effort to set the agenda or an attempt to frame an issue in a particular way, and whether one is considering print, broadcast or social media in terms of campaigning techniques, an integral part of the political communication process has always been, and remains, convincing the electorate to choose between aspirants to high office. During the early decades of independence the revolutionary generation of 'politicians by accident' monopolised electoral competition, producing – depending on one's vantage point – a remarkable stability or stagnation.

Negative campaigning has been part and parcel of Irish electoral history from the first days of the state established by the Anglo-Irish Treaty of 1921. The civil war produced a tradition of negative campaigning that endured for decades and was characterised by vitriolic and personalised attacks on political leaders. Fianna Fáil and its republican allies were the chief targets of 'red scares' during the 1920s and early 1930s, though as Fianna Fáil switched from opposition to government it launched its own witch-hunt against putative Bolsheviks in parties such as Labour and Clann na Poblachta. Election campaigns are now substantially less confrontational than during the early decades of the state, in spite of the natural preference of journalists and broadcasters for gladiatorial contests between aspiring politicians.

The progressive retirement of the revolutionary generation stalwarts during the 1960s required prospective candidates to devise more creative ways to secure election. No longer able to fall back on glorious war records, politicians confronted new realities. Progression to high office would be gradual, often via a spell in local government, and this in turn encouraged increased localism in Irish politics. As a result the tone of political messages has become – the recent economic crisis notwithstanding – increasingly moderate compared to the early decades of the state. Moreover, the target of these messages is predominately local. Parties are aware that their support base has become less partisan and, combined with the inevitability of coalition and the rise of the floating voter, messages have to be communicated in a manner and tone that alienates no one bar the irreconcilable.

The volume of elections dictates the means to communicate messages at the disposal of political parties. The holding of two general elections within months of each other in 1927 caused several smaller parties to bow out and benefited those parties either with administrative resources (Cumann na nGaedheal) or a professional fund-raising machine (Fianna Fáil). Three elections within 18 months during 1981–82 forced even the major parties to economise and tailor their campaigns accordingly. Generous state subsidies and a boom in private contributions have made political parties less reliant on traditional methods of fund-raising (e.g. church-gate collections) and has also made it difficult for new parties to emerge. Elections have become more costly and associated tasks (e.g. putting up/taking down posters) are increasingly carried out by paid professionals rather than zealous party supporters.

Presidential elections, which involve competing for office rather than for power, have produced increasingly sophisticated and rigorous campaigns. The elections that brought Mary Robinson, Mary McAleese, and Michael D. Higgins to Áras an Uachtaráin were markedly different from those that preceded them in that they incorporated modern features of electioneering such as opinion polls and TV debates. Indeed, the 2011 contest involved a record number of candidates (seven) and TV debates (eight).

Opinion polls have also made a substantial impact on how politicians conduct their activities and frequently frame election debates. Initially thought to be a form of political astrology, the Fianna Fáil election landslide in 1977, despite media predictions of a comfortable win for the incumbent government, occasioned a rethink. Opinion polls, which had in fact charted the swing to Fianna Fáil, would thereafter be a key part of the political landscape, going so far as to become news stories in themselves, not only reflecting peoples' thinking but sometimes influencing how they think and vote. Peaking too early in the polls forewarns opponents and can lead to enhanced media scrutiny as Fianna Fáil discovered during the 2002 general election campaign, and as did presidential hopeful Seán Gallagher almost a decade later.

A strong attachment to parties, combined with an electoral system that promotes candidate-centred campaigns, have traditionally been twin features of Irish politics. The partisan de-alignment witnessed in recent years has only accentuated the focus on the candidate, culminating in the extraordinarily volatile election of 2011 when less than a quarter of incumbent government deputies retained their seats. While a buoyant economy lifted the political fortunes of the incumbent government during the 2002 and 2007 elections, in 2011 the outcome was not in doubt: only the margin of defeat for the outgoing Fianna Fáil–Green Party coalition kept pundits interested.

Another theme that, unsurprisingly, emerges from these chapters is the centrality of media and media professionals in political communication. What might be referred to as 'old media' – radio, television, and newspapers – remain vitally important to those seeking support, and four out of every five voters watch television news at least five days a week. Fairness and balance are an intrinsic part of the legislative framework that dictates the manner in which radio and television cover political campaigns. The requirement for balance can be considered restrictive in referendum campaigns where there is a clear and overwhelming majority in favour of one side. However, broadcasters are not obliged to give a small unrepresentative minority an equal share of the time but rather are obliged to provide balance. TV election debates have not turned out to be the game-changers that some had forecast and face-to-face contact with the electorate remains an integral part of political communication in Ireland.

The state broadcaster steered clear of political discussion programmes altogether during the early decades following independence. Only in 1951 did Irish radio broadcast the first unscripted political discussion programme, the same year as weekly commentary of parliamentary proceedings was introduced. The exiting of the revolutionary generation coincided with the advent of the establishment of RTÉ as a national TV channel in 1961. A number of firsts followed: the first election campaign afforded TV coverage (1965), the first concession of election defeat on TV (1973), and the first election debate between party leaders (1982). The ascendency of television led directly to the slow demise of other more traditional forms of political communication such as the church-gate address and the monster eve-of-poll rallies held in Dublin city centre.

As political leaders wafted into sitting rooms throughout the country, television provided the feeling of intimacy but without the interaction associated with rallies and town-hall gatherings. The direct query of the ordinary voter or the jab of the heckler was replaced by the polite probing of the TV host. In time this gave way to hard questioning as the national broadcaster, bound in law to be objective and impartial in its coverage of news and current affairs, provided a platform for an ever-increasing circle of critical and alternative voices to be heard. As RTÉ pushed the boundaries of political coverage, so too, to varying degrees, did the print media – a process that was not appreciated or understood by many politicians who hankered for the days when newspapers were the only mass medium and they could judge a constituent's political preference by virtue of the newspaper that they purchased.

Television also necessitated further simplification of political messages and marketing of the leader, whose personality was merged with the party brand. Thus, television accentuated the (already deeply ingrained) person-alisation of politics in Ireland, and parliamentary elections have become increasingly presidential in form. Ard fheiseanna have become less about the party faithful who have travelled from far and wide to attend but rather are focused on captivating the mildly distracted viewing public watching at home. Debates are carefully choreographed to maximise the attractiveness of the party brand while alienating as few of the public as possible. The calibre of discussions at party conferences has consequently declined.

As political advertising on radio and television is prohibited by law, party political broadcasts (PPBs), which were first introduced in 1965, offer a unique opportunity for parties to address the electorate on a national basis without mediation or critique. While their influence on voting intentions can be debated, what is not in doubt is that, in stark contrast to the situation in Britain, PPBs attract a large viewing public in Ireland. The 2007 election was noteworthy for introducing a new form of party broadcast, which included political celebrity endorsements of the party leader, in this case Fianna Fáil president Bertie Ahern. While the 'peace broadcast', which contained praise from Tony Blair, Bill Clinton, and George Mitchell and focused on Ahern's role in the peace process, was an imaginative exercise, similar PPBs with high-profile foreign endorsements have not to date been repeated.

Despite the proliferation of new ways of communicating with the electorate via the internet, local media, particularly radio, form the basis of the local political communication process for many politicians. Even though national TV and radio have abetted the presidentialisation of electoral politics, in the era of the 'permanent campaign' the relationship between the TD and the local media in his or her constituency is arguably more vital. While campaigns are essential it is what happens, or is seen to happen, between elections that enables a politician to get elected. A strong constituency profile is required and expected and the local media provide the most effective and accessible means of communicating with the electorate. Publicity in the local media is much easier to secure than its equivalent at national level and much more relevant to winning a seat. Though often used as 'fillers', press releases printed in local newspapers play a part in persuading the electorate that their TD is newsworthy and they are not viewed as nakedly propagandistic as a TD's newsletter.

In terms of those who engage in or facilitate political communication it is clear that politicians and media professionals – be they journalists or media advisors – are bound in a mutually dependent relationship of reciprocity based on two divergent objectives. While it is an exaggeration to state that the job of a politician is to conceal and it is the job of a journalist to reveal – the mutual dependencies go far deeper than that – it is this sentiment that seems to characterise the relationship between journalists and the media advisors of government politicians. Press officers, even those who formerly worked as journalists, find it difficult to understand the behaviour of journalists towards political figures. Conversely, journalists mostly view media advisors and programme managers with thinly disguised distain. While both parties have fairly disparaging views of each other this does not negate the fact that they are very much dependent on one another. The routine nature of their relationship – on the one hand, securing coverage for political figures, and on the other, having something substantial to report on – ensures that even when there is a serious rupture in the relationship, things quickly settle down again into the familiar ritual of mutual reliance based on varying degrees of suspicion and trust. Whatever criticisms may be made of journalists and media advisors in terms of agenda setting or framing, it must be remembered that advisors only advise: it is ultimately up to the politician to accept that advice or not.

Another controversial aspect of the political–media nexus is that of the role of property developers in funding political parties and fuelling a property boom that possibly compromised coverage of that boom by means of boosting the profits of media institutions through inflated property-related advertising revenue. Amid the euphoria of the boom it seems no one shouted 'stop' loudly enough: or if they did they immediately brought upon themselves a chorus of condemnation from developers and politicians who accused them of talking down the economy. This relationship – between developers and political parties – is at the heart of understanding political communication during the years of the Celtic Tiger when lobbyists provided an unfair advantage to members of the socio-economic elite by virtue of their access to decision makers. Public confidence was shaken by successive scandals that suggested that political influence could be systematically bought or acquired through leverage or familiarity, all of which had a corrosive effect on the democratic process. Far from restricting freedom of speech, the regulation of lobbyists is ultimately about establishing a level playing field and inhibiting the abuse of dominant positions of influential interest groups and private citizens. A transparent lobbying system will benefit legislators, citizens and even lobbyists themselves by instilling confidence and clarity into the system.

One final theme emerges from the chapters – that of the advent of social media. Their interactive capacity seemed to herald the arrival of a public sphere in which everyone with access to and ability to use the technology (and that still excludes a significant proportion of the population) could contribute to debates and decision making. While this ideal is still some way off, social media allow parties, candidates, and interest groups to interact with voters directly without the interference or mediation of traditional media. Facebook and Twitter are now part and parcel of the politician's communication toolkit and political parties direct their assistants to maintain party and TD accounts. In terms of political communication, the two networks have proved to have different strengths and uses. Twitter has the immediacy and brevity favoured by mainstream news media and the viewing public. Facebook, on the other hand, is more conducive to detailed press releases and disseminating audio-visual material. Both are used to publicise policies and achievements, counter allegations, and criticise opponents. By blurring the lines between official statement and informal comment, Twitter has allowed politicians to be more candid and cutting.

Initially, smaller and challenging parties embraced social media with greater enthusiasm as it helped compensate for their comparative lack of resources, but this early lead has been steadily eroded by their bigger and/ or more established rivals. One such example is the short-lived United Left Alliance. A combination of assiduous constituency work and an assertive online campaign, with all 20 candidates using Twitter, Facebook, and YouTube to communicate with voters, produced five TDs. But, more than anything else, familiarity had won the day, as the victors of 2011 were established candidates that had been edged out in the previous contest in 2007.

The number of TDs with Twitter accounts more than doubled (38% to 88.55%) during the two years following the February 2011 election. While Facebook users outnumber Twitter users by four to one the number of accounts attached to TDs is fairly even; at the beginning of 2013 individual followers of political party flagship accounts was over 25% greater on Twitter than on Facebook. Thus it would appear that Twitter has emerged as the more political of the two social media networks and therefore of greater influence during forthcoming elections.

There is no direct relationship between the volume of followers and friends on Twitter and Facebook respectively and the number of votes secured on polling day. To follow a candidate or party via social media suggests interest but does not indicate political support, and while one can "like" or "follow" many candidates, a voter can only cast a ballot for one. Moreover, followers are not geographically concentrated and the majority may not even reside in a politician's constituency, which makes them of little value on polling day. Notwithstanding the important potential for new modes of two-way political communication, and despite becoming an integral part of political communication in Ireland, it seems that social media will most likely complement rather than replace traditional means of disseminating political messages.

In conclusion, if, as outlined above, political communication is described as an ever-ongoing contest for support that is played out in the media, it is refreshing to find that come election time – or at least elections held during times of crisis – substance trumps style in that news media treat the election as a serious competition between different policy positions rather than as a personality contest based on the popularity of party leaders. Only time will tell whether, after the severe shock to the system that the economic crash of 2008 represented, political communication returns to auction or personality politics, or at least to the levels witnessed during the Celtic Tiger. In this, the role of memory and history will be crucial for providing a collective context for political decision making. But with less than 25% of students taking history at Leaving Certificate level the shared collective context for making informed political choices is now more fragmented than ever before.

Whether we can rely on the media to provide depth and context is highly debatable. In the realm of 'old media' the outsourcing of the sub-editorial function at one national newspaper group reduced the average age of its subeditors by half and obliterated the institutional memory that is crucial for providing context to political issues. In the realm of 'new media' the ever-increasing array of sites, apps, channels, and platforms presents a multiplicity of avenues for political expression but also present the possibility that such activity is 'narrowcasting' rather than broadcasting. Preaching to the converted, while providing a sense of unity to supporters, does not really translate into building support unless there are very significant resources involved or there is a 'trigger event' that moves the campaign to mainstream media. Similarly, the instantaneous nature of modern reporting within an ever-accelerating news cycle characterised by an emphasis on the latest developments leaves little or no time for depth or context to be provided. What this all means for the future of political communication and whether political communicators – in their many guises – have learned lessons from the events that brought the country from boom to bust remains to be seen.

Index

Abortion 16
Adams, Gerry 188, 194
   Twitter 41
Agenda-setting 16–18
Ahearne, Alan 139
Ahern, Bertie 35, 70, 73, 93, 106
   addresses British parliament 193
   criticises commentators 136
   election promises 139
   election success 30
   Mahon Tribunal 159
   'peace broadcast' 3, 185–86,
      192–96, 241
   peace process 193–94
   political journalists 92
   political donations 158, 161
   popularity 30
   televised election debates 39
Ahern, Dermot 100, 118, 119
Allen, Kieran 65, 66
Allied Irish Banks 156, 157
Althusser, Louis 14
American Enterprise Institute 14
'American Exceptionalism' 16
Americans for Prosperity 14
Andrews, David 89
Anglo Irish Bank 70–71, 73, 129, 137,
   138, 140, 157, 160
Anglo-Irish Treaty 237

Anti-bin tax campaign (2003)
   69
Arab Spring 18
Áras an Uachtaráin 238
Ard Fheis(eanna) 34, 38, 240
Arise and Follow Charlie (song)
   28–29
Aristotle 9, 13
Arms crisis 86–87, 88
Arnold, Bruce 89
Auction politics 139

Bank of Ireland 137, 156
Bank guarantee 103, 115, 149, 160,
   227
   lobbying surrounding 154–57
Barry, Mick 66, 67
Barry, Oliver 158
BBC 119, 189
Béaslaí, Piaras 79
Behan, Brendan 64
Beef Tribunal 152
Belfast Telegraph 80
Blair, Tony 98, 185, 193–96, 198, 199,
   241
Blaney, Neil 33, 86
Blogs 13, 20, 21, 40, 67
Bloomberg 133
Blueshirts 82

boards.ie 206
Boland, Gerry 82
Boland, Kevin 37, 86
Boulianne, Shelley 18, 19
Boyd-Barrett, Richard 64, 65, 66, 70,
    71, 73
Boyle, Dan 205–07
Brady, Conor 129, 137
Brennan, Séamus 27–28, 38
Broadcasting and Wireless
    Telegraphy Act 1988 48, 55
Broadcasting Act 2009 168–69, 187
Broadcasting Authority of Ireland
    167
        election coverage code /
            guidelines 169–70, 177–78
        Lenihan story 93
        political advertising 187
presidential election 2011 37, 182
Broadcasting ban (Section 31) 87, 188
Broadcasting Commission of Ireland
    169, 177
Broadcasting Complaints
    Commission 173
Browne, Noel 82–83
Browne, Vincent 88, 89
Bruton, John 30, 39, 106–07
Burke, Ray 93, 106, 158
Burrows, Richard 156
Burton, Joan 70
Bush, George W. 15
Business and Finance 132, 133
Buttimer, William 80
Byrne, Suzy 210

Callely, Ivor 206
Campbell, Alastair 98
Cameron, David 123
candidate.ie 41, 212, 213
Carswell, Simon 129, 130, 136–37, 138
Central Bank 132, 155, 156
Chirac, Jacques 194

China Daily 119
Cicero 9
CIÉ
    bans Fianna Fáil song 28
Civil war 31, 237
Claffey, Una 91
Clann Éireann 30
Clann na Poblachta 31, 238
Clarke, William 80
Clegg, Nick 123
Clinton, Bill 186, 193–96, 198, 199,
    241
Clinton, Hilary 207
Collins, Joan 65, 70
Collins, Michael 79–80
Collins, Steven 91, 92–93
Communism in Ireland 31, 32, 64
Competitive Enterprise Institute 14
Conlon, Eddie 66
Constitution Unit London 123
Cooney, John 90–91
Cooper, Matt 129, 134, 136, 139, 140,
    141
Corish, Brendan 32
Cosgrave Liam 87
    hostility towards opinion polls
        33–34
    image 27, 38–39
Cosgrave, W.T. 80, 81
Costello, Declan 85
Costello, John A. 82
Coughlan, Denis 90
Coughlan judgment 171, 173–75, 177,
    180
Coveney, Simon 119, 206–07
Cowen, Brian
    bank guarantee 115, 118, 156
    decision not to make national
        address on television 17
Galway races 155
    Morning Ireland interview 94,
        119–20, 206–07

relations with journalists 121–22
satirical painting 118–19
Critical Discourse Analysis (CDA)
14, 16
'Critical discourse moments' 16
Cronin, Bart 109
Cronin, Seán 88
Cuba 33
Curran, Hugh 79
Curran, Richard 130, 139
Currie, Austin 36
Cumann na nGaedheal 31, 32, 238
Cusack, Sinéad 71

Dáil Éireann 26, 41, 70
television coverage of 27
Daly, Clare 64–65, 70, 71, 73
Davis, Aeron 17
D'Arcy, Ray 119
de Burca, Deirdre 205
de hÍde, Dubhghlas 35
de Rossa, Proinsias 39
de Valera, Eamon 30, 31, 32
Irish Press 81
press conferences 83
retirement 83
views on television 27
de Valera, Vivion 84, 85
Dean, Howard 20, 201
Delany, Eamon 141
Democratic Left 106, 110, 190
Democratic Unionist Party 195
Denham, Susan 172–73, 173–74, 180,
183
Dennigan, Joe 81–82
Dexys Midnight Runners 67
Dillon, James 27
Dineen, Maeve 118
DIRT scandal 157
Doherty, Seán 89, 91
Dowling, Joe 33
Downing, John 101, 103, 104, 111

Drennan, John 67
Duignan, Seán 34, 36, 87, 102, 105,
107, 109, 110
Duffy, Jim 36
Dukes, Alan 36, 100
Dunlop, Frank 87, 154, 161
Dunne, Ben 93
Dunne, Cathal 28

Easter Rising 1916 26, 79
E-campaigning 20–22
Economist, The 130
Elections
campaigning 221–23
expenditure 30, 68, 70–71, 73
fund raising 68, 238, 242
media coverage of 224–30
media effects
agenda setting 219
direct effects 219
framing 220
priming 219
negative campaigning 31–33,
237–38
'permanent campaign' 3, 45, 241
songs 28–29
spending 223
televised debates 38–40, 238,
239, 240
Elections Ireland
European elections
2009 203–04
general elections
1927 (June) 30, 238
1927 (September) 30, 238
1932 31, 32
1943 31
1944 31
1948 31, 32
1965 25, 27, 189
1969 32–33
1973 27

1977 27, 33–34, 239
1981 30, 39, 238
1982 (February) 30, 39, 238
1982 (November) 29, 30, 39, 238
1987 29
1989 29
1997 30, 39
2002 30, 35, 39, 239
2007 21, 27, 30–31, 39–40, 185, 192–96, 202–03, 240, 243
2011 4, 40–41, 63–74, 162, 207–12, 224–30, 239, 243
local elections
2004 66–67
2009 66
presidential elections 35–37, 238
1990 36
2011 2, 37, 40–41, 181–82, 212–14, 224, 238, 239
electionsireland.org 72
Elections Australia (2007) 20
Elections UK 202
Elections US 20, 65, 201–02, 208
Electoral system 217–18
European Central Bank 157, 227
European Commission for Democracy through Law 183
European Court of Human Rights 188
European Financial Stability Facility (EFSF) 115, 119
European People's Party Alliance 198
Eurovision Song Contest 28
European Union 2, 18, 69, 103, 115, 122, 123, 157, 182, 194, 227
European Union Fiscal Stability Treaty Referendum (see Referenda)
Evening Herald 81

Facebook 20, 21, 50, 66, 67, 69, 204, 208, 210, 213, 242, 243
as an election tool 40–41
Farrell, Brien 39, 86
Feeney, Peter 178–80
Fianna Fáil 30, 31, 34, 35, 36, 54, 56, 57, 63, 64, 73, 115, 226, 238
as a mass peoples' party 27
banking bailout 156–57
campaign songs 28–29
coalition with Green Party 103, 205, 239
coalition with PDs 1989 107, 108–09
coalition with PDs 1997 106, 111
coalition with PDs 2005 99
Galway races 155
Irish Press 81–82
Labour coalition with 116
negative campaigning 32–33
political donations 38, 158
property developers 154, 242
Taca (fundraising) 155
Twitter 40–41
Financial journalism
Celtic Tiger reportage 129–30, 136–42
development of 131–33
sources and constraints of 134–35
Financial Regulator 137, 155, 156
Financial Times 17, 18, 133, 136, 142
Fine Gael 28, 29, 30, 31, 36, 54, 56, 64, 104, 115, 106, 110, 162, 226
general election 2011 40, 41, 68, 69, 72, 73, 162, 208
political donations 158
Twitter 40–41, 69
FitzGerald, Garret 29, 36, 91, 105
opinion polls 33–34
televised election debates 39
FitzGerald, Martin 132, 134

Flanagan, Luke 210
Flickr 208
Foley, John 105, 110
Fox, Ken 118
Fox News 119
Framing 15
Frankfurt School 14
Freeman's Journal 79
Frontline, The (see RTÉ)

GAA 25
Gallagher, Michael 171, 173
Gallagher, Seán 37, 181–82, 212–14, 239
Garda Síochána 89, 93, 119
Geary, Frank 80
Gilmore, Eamon 40, 73, 198, 208
Glennon, Chris 86, 87, 106
Gleeson, Dermot 156
Goggin, Brian 156
Good Friday Agreement 173, 193
Goodman, Larry 152
Gormley, John 40
Government advisors
    appointment of 116, 120, 122
    comparison with Britain 123, 124–25
    and Fianna Fáil 121–22
    and Fine Gael 122–24
    salaries of 122–23
Government Information Bureau 83, 86
Gramsci, Antonio 14
Green Party 57, 63, 64, 103, 120, 161, 203, 205
    Twitter 40–41
Greene, Brian 73
Guardian, The 219

Halappanavar Savita 16
Halligan, Ursula 94

Halls Pictorial Weekly (see RTÉ)
Hamilton, Liam 172, 173
Harney, Mary 39, 102, 106, 108
Harris, Eoghan 36
Haskins, Dylan 210
Haughey, Charles J. 28, 29 93, 108, 109
    Arms crisis 86–87, 88
    attitude to election manifestos 32
    Hot Press interview 90
    Irish Press political obituary 89
    jettisons anti-coalition principle 30
    political correspondents 84, 89–91
    sacking of 86–87
    telephone tapping 91
    televised election debates 39
Healy, John 84
    'Backbencher' 84–85
    criticised in Dáil 86
Healy, Séamus 65
Healy, Tim 80–81
Heffernan, Tony 110
Herbert, Cathy 100, 103
Heritage Foundation, The 14
Hibernia 88, 132
Higgins, Joe 64, 66, 70, 71, 204, 205
Higgins, Michael D. 37, 212–13, 238
Hillery, Patrick 36
Hot Press 90
Hovland, Carl 11
How Ireland Voted 221
Huffington Post 120, 201
Hurler on the Ditch, (see RTÉ)
Hyde, Douglas (See de hÍde, Dubhghlas)

Independent Broadcasters of Ireland 176, 177
Irish Business and Employers' Confederation (IBEC) 8

Independent Network News 99
Independent News and Media 65
Independent Radio & Television
    Commission 169
Independent TDs 41
indymedia.ie 67
inter-party governments 82–83
Insurance Corporation of Ireland 157
International Monetary Fund 2, 69,
    103, 115, 118, 136–37, 143, 157,
    227
IRA 68, 192
Irish Daily Mail 71
Irish Examiner 102
Irish Free State 31
Irish Independent 71, 80, 81, 104, 105,
    106, 118
    1932 election 31
    financial journalism 132–33
    governor-general 80–81
    Michael Lowry story 93
    see also Arnold, Bruce
    see also Glennon, Chris
    see also Noonan, Arthur
irishpoliticians.com 72
irishelection.com 203
Irish language 31, 40, 71, 155
Irish Media Contacts Directory 120,
    122
Irish National Election Study 217–18,
    221, 225
Irish Permanent Building Society 156
Irish Press 100, 104, 110
    foundation 81
    general election 1932 81
    imprisonment of journalist
        81–82
    Haughey political obituary 89
    Lemass resignation 85–86
    Lynch resignation 87–88
    see also Mills, Michael
Irish Statesman 81

Irish Stock Exchange 132
Irish Sun 93, 228
Irish Times 16, 71, 81, 103, 138, 204,
    226, 227
    1977 election 34
    'Backbencher' 84–85
    Bertie Ahern finances 93, 159
    financial journalism 129–30,
        131–33
    government advisors 116
    governor-general 80–81
    Mother and Child saga 82–83
    property advertising 140–41
    rainbow coalition 107
    Treaty debates 79
    see also Kennedy, Geraldine
    see also McInerney, Michael
    see also Walsh, Dick

Johnson, Mandy 111
Johnson, Thomas 80
Journalist-source relationship 51–52
J.P. Morgan 142–43
'Just Society' 85

Kant, Immanuel 9
Keane, Ronan 174
Keenan, Brendan 139
Kelly, Donal 87
Kennedy, Geraldine 89, 90, 91, 107,
    115
Kennedy, John F. 38, 198, 199, 201
Kennedy, Sinéad 66
Kenny, Colum 176–77
Kenny, Enda 30, 40, 41, 73, 115, 198
    political donations 158
    relations with journalists 122–24
    social media 41, 208
Kenny, Gino 67
Kenny, Shane 100, 106–07, 110
Kerrigan, Gene 182
Kerry Babies case 88

Knightly, Michael 79
Koch Brothers 14

Labour Party 33, 36, 40, 54, 63, 64,
    67, 72, 80, 101, 119, 226
    coalition with Fianna Fáil 1992
        109, 116
    coalition with Fine Gael 28, 39
    general election 2011 68, 73, 162
    rainbow coalition 105, 106, 107,
        110
    regulating lobbyists 151, 161–62
    social media 208
    Twitter 40–41, 69
    victim of red scare 31–32, 238
Lasswell, Harold 10
Last Word, The 209
Lazarsfeld, Paul 11
Lawlor, Eamonn 39
Lawlor, Liam 93
Lawlor, Ned (Edward) 79, 80
Lee, George 130, 132, 139
Lehman Brothers 156
Lenin, Vladimir 33
Lennon, Joe 110
Lewin, Kurt 11
Lewis, Hugh 66
Libertas 204
Lindsay, Patrick 84
Localism 26
Long, Susie 72
Lowry, Michael 92, 100, 210
Lemass, Seán
    political broadcast 1965 189, 198
    political correspondents 82–83 ,
        85–86
Lenihan, Brian (snr) 84
Lenihan, Brian (jnr) 100, 136, 139
    Banking crisis 103, 118, 156
    TV3 broadcast 93
Leonard, Nicholas 131
Le Post 120

Lobbying 15, 242
    growth of 151
    legislation 151
    ministerial influence 152
    process 3, 150–51, 153
    regulation of 159–62
Locke, John 9
Loughnane, Bill 88
Lydon, Don 158
Lynch, Jack 28, 33, 87, 105
    arms crisis 86
    concedes defeat on television
        (1973), 27
    GAA record 25
    image 38
    resignation 87–88

McAleese, Mary 36, 238
MacBride, Seán 32
Mac Conghail, Muiris 87
Mac Coille, Cathal 119
Mac Liam, Conor 72
McCreevy, Charlie 139
McCrystal judgment 171
McDaid, Jim 100
McDowell, Michael 40, 160–61
MacEntee, Shane 32, 214
McGee, Harry 204
McGonagle, Marie 180
McInerney, Michael 82, 84, 85, 86
McKenna, Patricia 171
McKenna judgment 171–73, 175
McLaughlin, Dan 130
McMahon, Ciarán 212
McQuaid, John Charles
McWilliams, David 129, 130, 139
Machiavelli, Niccolò 9
'Magic bullet' approach to media
    influence 12
Magill 88
Mahon Tribunal 93, 154, 157, 158,
    159, 161

Malin, Brendan 81
Mara, P.J. 90–91, 99, 106, 108–09
Marsh, Michael 218, 222
Martin, Micheál 40, 73
Media bias 46, 49, 50, 55–60
Merkel, Angela 198
Merrill Lynch 157
Metro Herald 71
Mills, Michael 83, 86, 87
    appointment as pol. corr. 84
    Hurler on the Ditch, 85
    Lemass resignation 85–86
    Lynch resignation 87–88
Mitchell, George 185, 193–96, 198,
    199, 241
Molloy, Bobby 108
Mongey, Iarla 99, 101, 102, 111
Mooney, John 93
Moore, Richard 100, 101, 103
Moriarty Tribunal 154, 158
Morning Ireland (see RTÉ)
Mother and Child saga 82–83
Murdoch, Rupert 98
Murray, John 102, 106, 110
Murray, Michael 138
mycandidate.ie 72
myhome.ie 140

Nally, Derek 36
National Union of Journalists 120
Negative campaigning (See Elections)
'New media techniques' 65
New Labour 98
New Left 13
New York Times 15, 119, 138, 185, 201
News of the World 228
Newstalk 72
Nighthawks 91 (see RTÉ)
Nixon, Richard 38
Noonan, Arthur 83, 85, 86
Noonan, Michael 30, 39, 158
Northern Ireland

    border overflights 87–88
    devolved power sharing 193, 195
    Good Friday Agreement 173,
      193
    legislature 26
    peace process 192–93, 197
    presidency 36
North Korea 33
Northside People 70
Norton, William 31
Nyberg Report 136–37

Obama, Barack 20, 65, 201–02, 208
O'Brien, Conor Cruise, 87
O'Brien, Denis 65
O'Brien, Michael 66, 72, 73
O'Byrnes, Stephen 104, 108–09
O'Dea, Willie 205
O'Donoghue, John [presenter] 86
O'Donoghue, John [politician] 93
O'Gara, 101
O'Grady, Peadar 66
O'Higgins, T.F. 83
O'Kelly, Morgan 130, 138, 139
O'Kelly, Seán T.
O'Malley, Des 29, 108
O'Malley, Donogh 84
O'Reilly, Emily 91
O'Reilly, Anthony 65
O'Reilly, Willie 177
O'Rourke, Mary 100
O'Rourke, Seán 90
O'Toole, Fintan 129, 138
O'Toole, Michael 83
Ó Cadhain, Máirtín 84
Ó Dálaigh, Cearbhall 87
Ó hAnnracháin, Pádraig 83
Ó Moráin, Micheál 33, 86
Ó Neachtain, Eoghan 111
Oireachtas Committee on
    Constitution 175–77
Oireachtas press gallery 80, 115, 121

Opinion polls 33–35, 39, 224, 238, 239

Paisley, Ian 195
Parliamentary Assistants (PAs) 45–60 *passim*
Payments to politicians 154
People Before Profit 63, 64, 66, 67, 68, 69, 70, 72, 73
peoplebeforeprofit.ie 69
Phoenix, The 132
Plato 9, 13
Political advertising / party broadcasts
    effects of 186, 190, 191–92, 196, 224, 240
    legislation / regulation of 186–89
    party political broadcasts 189–92
    peace broadcast 192–96, 241
    reaction to peace broadcast 196–99
    time allocation 190–91
Political journalism
    Free State 79–83
    Haughey controversies 89–91
    impact of television 83–88
    inter-party governments 82–83
    modern news cycle 92–94
    sources 84–85
politico.ie 67
politics.ie 64, 67, 203, 206
Prendergast, Peter 89–90
Prendiville, Cian 66
Presidency 38
Prime Time (see RTÉ)
PR-STV 26, 239
Public Relations Institution of Ireland 120, 152–53
Public Service Management Act 116, 120
Purcell, Feargal 204

Progressive Democrats 91, 99, 120, 161, 190, 224
    coalition with Fianna Fáil 1987 107, 108–09
    coalition with Fianna Fáil 1997 106, 111
    coalition with Fianna Fáil 2002 192
    election campaigns 29, 35
Putnam, Robert 18

Questions and Answers (see RTÉ)
Quinlan, Patrick 86
Quinn, Paddy 79, 84
Quinn, Ruairí 41
Quinn, Seán 140, 155

Rabbitte, Pat 40
Rafter, Kevin 211
Rainbow coalition 105, 106, 107, 110
'Red Scare' (see Elections, negative campaigning)
Referenda
    Children's rights (2012) 171, 182–83
    Divorce (1995) 171, 173
    Fiscal Treaty (2012) 65, 182
    Lisbon (2008) 65, 175
    Lisbon (2009) 65, 177
Referendum Act 1998 173
Referendum Act 2001 175
Referendum Commission 173, 175
Reagan, Ronald 89, 198
Regulation of Lobbyists bill 151, 162
Reid, Liam 103
Reuters, 133, 185
Revolutionary generation 26, 238
Reynolds, Albert 91, 105, 107, 109, 152
Rezoning 154
Rhetorical Analysis 13
Robinson, Mary 36, 238

Ross, Shane 129, 138
Ryan, Eamon 40, 103, 188
Ryan, Eoin 205
Ryan, Jim 82, 83
RTÉ 33, 65, 71, 72, 100, 102, 130, 133, 240
    bans Fianna Fáil song 28
    Coughlan judgment 173–74
    coverage of elections 27
    coverage of parliamentary
        debates 27
    early political coverage 188–89
    financial journalism 132
    Frontline, The 72, 181–82, 213
    general election guidelines 2011
        178–80, 181
    Halls Pictorial Weekly 27
    Hurler on the Ditch 85
    Morning Ireland 93, 119–20
    Nighthawks 91
    presidential election 2011 181–82
    Prime Time 209
    Questions and Answers 36
    Six-One News 64, 209
    Today Tonight 39
rte.ie 181

Shatter, Alan 93
Sheehy, Eugene 156
Shorthall, Róisín 119
siliconrepublic.com 40
Simmons, Caroline 204
Sinn Féin 30, 58, 63, 72, 73, 188, 194, 195, 226
    Facebook 69
    Twitter 40–41
Sinnott, Richard 174
Six One News (see RTÉ)
Smith, Hugh 79
Smyth, Sam 105
Smyllie, Robert 79, 82–83

Socialist Party 63, 64, 66, 67, 68, 69, 70, 73
Socialist, The 71
Social media 3–4, 48, 50, 59, 242, 243
    cyber campaigning 40–42, 223
    European election 2009 203–04
    general election 2011 69, 207–12
    presidential election 2011 212–13
Social Partnership 154
Socialist Workers Party 64
Socialist Worker 71
Soviet Union 12, 33
Spanish-American War (1898) 11
Spin
    coalition tactics 108–11
    dealing with media 3, 102–05
    journalists' engagement with
        99–91
    origins of term 97
    politicians' engagement with
        105–08
    ULA rejection of 68–69, 74
Spring, Dick 39, 110
Stalin, Joseph 33
Standards in Public Office
    Commission 68
Strauss-Kahn, Dominique 207
Sunday Business Post 132, 128, 228
Sunday Independent 36, 93, 103, 206
Sunday Press 90, 93
Sunday Review 84
Sunday Times 226
Sunday Tribune 89, 93, 118
Sutherland, Peter 104
Swedish House Mafia 7

TDs
    press releases 52–55
    routes to office 26
    relationship with local media
        45–60, 241
    salaries 69

Tea Party (US) 14
technorati.com 204
Telephone tapping 89, 91
Tett, Gillian 142–43
The Man They Call Ahern (song) 29
Think Tanks 15, 37–38
Time 205
Times, The 119
Tipperary Unemployed Workers'
    Movement 63
Today FM 99, 119, 177
Today Tonight (see RTÉ)
Tonight with Vincent Browne
    (see TV3)
Treaty debates 79
Tribunals 93, 106
    Beef 152
    Flood 154, 157, 158, 161
    Mahon 93, 154, 157, 159, 161
    Moriarty 154, 158
Trimble, David 194
TG4 40
TV election debates (see Elections)
TV3 70, 94
    Tonight with Vincent Browne 70,
        209
Twitter 13, 21, 50, 66, 67, 69, 204–07,
    208–10, 213, 242, 243
    bogus tweet during 2011
        presidential election 37, 182
    as an election tool 40–41
'Two-step flow' model of
    communication 12

Ulster Unionist Party 194
United Left Alliance 3, 63–74,
    243

Vietnam 18, 33
voteno.ie 66
Voting patterns 222

Wall Street Journal 133
Walsh, Dick 87, 90
Walsh, Joe 85
War of independence 26
Washington Post 15
Waters, John 90, 93
Week in Politics, The 118, 209
Welles, Orson 11
We're On Our Way to Europe (song)
    28
White, Peter 104
Wilkinson, Colm C.T. 28
Wilson, Harold 198, 199
Workers' Party 36, 88

X-case 91

Young Ireland Association 82
Youth vote 28
Your Kind of Country (song) 28
Youtube 7, 20, 40, 66, 67, 204, 208,
    243

Zapatista Movement (Mexico) 19